S0-BIQ-527

WITHDRAWN

Irving Howe and the Critics

Library & Media Ctr.
Carroll Community College
1601 Washington Rd.
Westminster, MD 21157

Irving Howe
and the Critics

Celebrations and Attacks

Edited and with an
introduction by John Rodden

University of Nebraska Press

Lincoln and London

© 2005 by the University of Nebraska Press
All rights reserved
Manufactured in the United States of America
∞
All photographs used by permission of Nicholas Howe,
literary executor of Irving Howe.
Printed by Thomson-Shore, Inc.
Library of Congress Cataloging-in-Publication Data
Irving Howe and the critics : celebrations and attacks /
edited and with an introduction by John Rodden.
p. cm.
Includes bibliographical references and index.
ISBN 0-8032-3933-5 (cl.: alk. paper)
1. Howe, Irving.   2. Criticism—United States—History
—20th century.   3. American literature—History and
criticism—Theory, etc.   4. Politics and literature—
United States—History—20th century.   I. Rodden, John.
PS29.H68178 2005
809—dc22   2004030745

For Lynn,
with deep gratitude

Contents

List of Illustrations, ix

Nicholas Howe, Foreword: Reading Irving Howe, xi

Preface, xix

John Rodden, Introduction: Irving Howe, Triple Thinker, 1

Socialist

1. *Mark Levinson and Brian Morton*, A Man of the Left, 27

2. *Ronald Radosh*, Journey of a Social Democrat, 32

3. *Ian Williams*, An Ex-Maoist Looks at an Ex-Trotskyist: On Howe's *Leon Trotsky*, 37

4. *Samuel Hux*, Our "Uncle Irving": Howe's Conservative Strain, 48

5. *Marshall Berman*, Irving and the New Left: From Fighter to Leader, 57

6. *Alexander Cockburn*, Irving Howe, R.I.P.: A Few Tasteless Words, 62

7. *Joseph Epstein*, The Old People's Socialist League, 64

Critic

8. *Robert Boyers*, Politics and the Critic, 77

9. *Nathan Glick*, The Socialist Who Loved Keats, 96

10. *Nicholas Howe*, A Lover of Stories, 108

11. *Brian Morton*, The Literary Craftsman, 112

12. *Paul Roazen*, How Irving Howe Shaped My Thinking Life, 114

13. *John Rodden*, "My Intellectual Hero": Irving Howe's "Partisan" Orwell, 117

14. *William E. Cain*, Howe on Emerson: The Politics of Literary Criticism, 132

15. *George Scialabba*, Howe Inside My Head, 143

Jew

16. *Morris Dickstein*, World of Our Grandparents, 149

17. *Leonard Kriegel*, Father Figures, 156

18. *Alvin H. Rosenfeld*, Of Yiddish Culture and Secular Jewishness, 163

19. *Edward Alexander*, Standing Guard over Irving Howe's Reputation; Or, Good Causes Attract Bad Advocates, 173

20. *Leon Wieseltier*, Irving, *In Memoriam*, 179

Revaluations

21. *Gerald Sorin*, The Relevance of Irving Howe, 185

22. *Michael Levenson*, A Steady Worker, 190

Morris Dickstein, *Afterword:* Irving Howe: Finding the Right Words, 201

John Rodden, *Appendix:* Wanted by the FBI: No. 727437B a.k.a. Irving Horenstein, 213

Source Acknowledgments, 227

Index, 229

Illustrations

following page 68

1. Irving Howe, City College of New York graduation, 1939
2. Howe in the army, stationed in Alaska, probably 1944
3. With Nina and Nicholas, 1954
4. With Nina and Nicholas, c. 1958–59
5. With Nina, c. 1958–59
6. Howe at Stanford University, c. 1962
7. With his first grandchild, Anna Bukowski, 1993

Foreword

Reading Irving Howe

Nicholas Howe

In critical reviews and essays about my father, Irving Howe, one frequently encounters a certain neat formulation that declares he was a man who wrote about what he lived and knew. He grew up with Yiddish as his first language, so inevitably he edited many volumes of translations from that language and then wrote *World of Our Fathers*; he grew up as a teenage socialist in the Bronx, so inevitably he edited *Dissent* and wrote books on the American Communist Party, Trotsky, and socialism in America; he entered into a world of ideas about literature around *Partisan Review* that was more European than American in taste, so inevitably he wrote about Dostoevsky, Tolstoy, Turgenev, and Stendhal.

For all the truth in these claims, they seem too retrospectively clever, if not indeed too convenient, in reducing the intellectual work of almost fifty years to covert autobiography. Faced with the range and quantity of his life's work, writers have tried to make sense of it all through claims of the inevitable. And there was a great deal of that work. The books alone make a considerable pile when stacked together on a desk, and there was much that he chose never to reprint in a book: reviews, political articles, op-ed pieces, letters to the editor, all of them part of a writer's daily life.

There was one aspect of the writer's life my father did not understand and could be harshly dismissive about. At the mention of "writer's block" he would scoff and say simply that writers were writers because they sat down each day and wrote just as other people went to work each day. That routine was how one learned to write well. Certainly not every piece was for the ages, nor was everything even to be published, and anything (he would always add) could be improved if it were run through another draft and cut by at least 10 percent. But the act of writing, day in and day out, mattered to him in ways that breathing and eating matter to other people. That discipline explains much about his life and not simply his productivity. It explains as well his understanding that among all of the books and articles of any working critic, some written out of a long life of reading and others fired off in response to that morning's headline, most would fade but a few would, with luck, remain vital and survive.

What counted was remaining engaged with politics and literature, sometimes more with one than the other, sometimes fleeing from one to the other, but always thinking about both. As for the question that seems to have most intrigued those who have written about him—what was the relation in his mind between politics and literature?—the best answer can be found in the practice of his life's work. Or, put another way, the answer can only be that the relation was never fixed but continually shifted, depending on a new novel he was reading or the political events of the moment or a rereading of one of his necessary writers, such as Stendhal.

Perhaps because my relation to my father grew more from literature than politics, I want to begin with a different response to his life's work than the one I sketched at the start of this piece. In the last fifteen years of his life we exchanged our writing for each other's criticism and came to trust each other completely as readers. Whatever else went unsaid between us, we could speak with absolute honesty and frankness about each other's prose. We also spoke frequently about ideas we had for new projects, most of which remained in the realm of talk. But those conversations taught me to wonder how it is that anyone comes to a subject and then spends years working on it for a book. Remembering these conversations now raises a question for me, one that offers a more oblique approach to understanding the shape of my father's career. Put simply, why were all three of Irving Howe's books about individual authors devoted to figures who were far more rural or traditional in their subjects and settings than they were urban or modernist? Why Sherwood Anderson, William Faulkner, and Thomas Hardy rather than Edith Wharton, Henry James, and Joseph Conrad? I choose these three counterpossibilities because he was sufficiently engaged with them to have written a strong essay about each. But not a book. Even for a prolific writer of books, it matters that he should have devoted three to the likes of Anderson, Faulkner, and Hardy.

On the face of it the choice was anything but predictable. And to some it could seem regrettable. Reviewing his book on Anderson, published in 1951, Malcolm Cowley argued in no uncertain terms that my father lacked the imagination and experience to understand such an author:

> [Howe] would have done a better job with Goethe or Gandhi. Anderson, the Midwesterner, is simply out of his orbit. Howe is an easterner and

a city dweller, not a townsman. He has a philosophic mind, thinks in terms of concepts (rather than terms of things or feelings), uses a great many abstract words, and is not afraid to make dogmatic judgments. . . . Howe has no sympathy for [Anderson's] method and I doubt that he understands it. He has little feeling for the rhythm of sentences and none for the shape or color of words. He likes clear ideas, solid constructions based on European culture; essentially, he doesn't like uneducated men who grope and fumble for a new sense of life. . . . Howe thinks in terms of concepts. Anderson feels in terms of tangible things. They speak different languages and belong to different nations of the mind.[1]

In suggesting that Howe was not by temperament or background attuned to Anderson's work, Cowley all but pronounces that one must be a towns-man from the Midwest to be so attuned. In ways that Cowley could not have foreseen, and probably would have found alarming, these sentences anticipate a style of criticism associated with identity politics that flourished in American literary study in the late 1980s and '90s. I quote from this old review, however, not to settle old scores on my father's behalf but rather to suggest how even a wonderfully astute literary critic like Cowley—a critic my father admired deeply for his work on Faulkner—could have been so sure at first encounter that Howe was nothing more than what he seemed: a Jewish socialist from New York with European tastes.[2]

No doubt Irving Howe was a Jewish socialist from New York with European tastes, so much so that he came to represent the species of the New York intellectual in the American press, or at least in that part of the press that cared about such matters. One admirer went so far as to call him, after his death, the last of the Russian intellectuals. But how did he get to be a New York intellectual? It was not simply, I think, by having been born a city boy in the Bronx in 1920. That explanation is too limited, precisely because it does not engage with his belief in literature's power to transform the imagination. There was more to him than his background, and the failure of many critics and now his first biographers to see that in him explains, I think, their partial understanding of him and his work.

So let me go back to Anderson, Faulkner, and Hardy. In one of the most personal paragraphs he ever wrote about literature's power to shape the reader beyond the circumstances of background and experience, my father evoked his boyhood encounter with Sherwood Anderson:

> I must have been no more than fifteen or sixteen years old when I first chanced upon *Winesburg, Ohio*. Gripped by these stories and sketches of Sherwood Anderson's small-town "grotesques," I felt that he was open-ing for me new depths of experience, touching upon half-buried truths

which nothing in my young life had prepared me for. A New York City boy who never saw the crops grow or spent time in the small towns that lay sprinkled across America, I found myself overwhelmed by the scenes of wasted life, wasted love—was this the "real" America?—that Anderson sketched in *Winesburg*. In those days only one other book seemed to offer so powerful a revelation, and that was Thomas Hardy's *Jude the Obscure*.[3]

He published these words in 1993, the last year of his life, and they seem to me some of the most revealing he ever wrote because they speak to his beginnings as a reader and thus as a writer. The phrases in this paragraph that immediately engage me speak of "wasted life, wasted love" because they apply directly to both Anderson and Hardy. And in ways that a reader of his book on Faulkner can understand, they apply to that novelist as well.

Rephrasing my earlier characterization of Anderson, Faulkner, and Hardy would make my point clearer. These writers were not so much rural and traditional (as opposed simply to urban and modernist) as they were chroniclers of the passage from some form of traditional life into the crisis of modernity. The rural setting mattered, I believe, for my father in each case because it limned that transition more evocatively than might have been otherwise possible. Or at least the rural setting helped him see that transition more starkly than he might have in novelists of urban life, who would, perhaps paradoxically, have been too familiar in their terrain to allow him that sort of recognition.

There is another element to consider here, and that concerns the fictional characters that struggle with this transition—some making it successfully but many more being wounded or destroyed in the attempt. George Willard, the narrator of *Winesburg*, and Jude Fawley, the central character of Hardy's novel, are both young men striving toward an intellectual life located in an urban center beyond the villages of their boyhood. Both are on the periphery of a larger intellectual and cultural world, one as a reporter and the other as an architect's draftsman; both are removed from manual labor, but neither is fully able to realize his creative yearnings and satisfy his ambitions. As my father wrote, "Jude is Hardy's equivalent of the self-educated worker: the self-educated worker transplanted into the Wessex world."[4] The waste that each evokes is not just of love; it is also a waste of the mind, of gifted people denied entry into a world of intellectual life because of their background.

That Cowley should have said, "Essentially, he doesn't like uneducated men who grope and fumble for a new sense of life," seems in retrospect an almost willful misreading of Irving Howe. He had grown up among men and women who were uneducated or barely self-educated, who groped and fumbled for a new sense of life. Had it not been for the tuition-free City College of New York (CCNY), he might well himself have been such a figure in the Depression years of his youth. His recognition of that kinship was the basis for his socialism and kept him from renouncing it even as it became less an actual politics than the name of his desire. His commitment to socialism was grounded not so much in ideology as it was in experience. He had the right to claim kinship with Jude Fawley just as he also had the obligation to recognize that his own life was better because there were available to him such things as free public colleges in times of economic crisis. That his politics were grounded in a memory of lives thwarted and denied kept him on the Left, unlike those old comrades who were able to trade off one ideology for another as they became neoconservatives.

This struggle for a decent life, one in which human desires could be articulated freely and with some hope that they might be satisfied, was at the heart of his politics. It extended as well to his response to certain novels. Praising Zola's *Germinal*, for example, he said that it "releases one of the central myths of the modern era: the story of how the dumb acquire speech."[5] It also extended, though on a different scale, to the history he wrote in *World of Our Fathers*. That book may not be principally about how the dumb acquire speech, but it certainly is about how uneducated immigrants groped toward a new sense of life. If now, in the early twenty-first century, the story of immigrant Jews who spoke Yiddish and struggled for a new life seems as much a part of the national experience as does the story of native Ohioans who spoke American and struggled to make their way to the city, then at least some of the credit belongs to him.

After my parents divorced in the early 1960s, my father left many of his books behind in our house. I grew up reading novels with his marginalia, his underlinings, his traces. He was not a heavy annotator of books but worked instead by scribbling a key word or two in the margin or, more frequently, by drawing a series of vertical lines and checkmarks (the more lines or checkmarks, the more noteworthy the passage seemed to him). There would occasionally be a question mark beside a historical reference or foreign word, a signal (I take it) that he left for himself to go back and look something up. Books he used for teaching often had their endpapers covered with page numbers, references, and brief comments; these jottings formed his working index, a set of notes that would never be separated from the book. Reading one of those books, often an old hardcover Modern Library volume, I would sometimes be distracted by his pencilings but would usually stop to reread the passage he marked because it was a way to learn from him. Only many years later did I also come to understand that these markings were the signs of his self-education. For he was neither a trained academic with a Ph.D. nor simply a journalist who reviewed new books or wrote about current events. He was something in between, and that meant leaving himself open to attacks and celebrations from all parties in life and after his death.

Those markings he left in books can be read as his version of graduate school. He told me sometimes that he regretted his lack of formal literary training, and he always spoke admiringly of serious scholars, most obviously of the art historian Meyer Schapiro, but he also knew that his place as a writer was defined by a certain distance from both academic and journalistic writing. Or, perhaps it would be truer to say, he wanted as a writer to have the best of each: the learning of the serious scholar without the pedantry, the engagement of the independent journalist without the superficiality. Occupying a place between academic and journalistic writing meant that no one could predict what would interest him next. I suspect that the most revealing way to track his development as a writer would be to scrupulously map the books he reviewed year in and year out and then consider how those reviews influenced books and articles he went on to write years later. Reviewing, he used to joke, was a way of putting shoes on his kids. (And neither I nor my sister, Nina, ever went shoeless.) It was, more seriously, a way of scanning the landscape to learn what was being written and what was being thought. Writing reviews was for him another form of self-education, an equivalent to those marked-up books of his. It was also a way of continuing to grow as a reader, of searching for new writers to read and new things to say.

Like anyone who wrote reviews, my father also read reviews of his own work. He was not the sort of writer who claimed never to read notices of his books; he was too engaged, too polemical, to remain that aloof. Some of these pieces, he would say, he could have written himself—especially those by his political opponents. Sometimes he would add, wickedly, that he could have written them better. Attacks by old comrades who had changed their politics always angered him. These attacks seemed a kind of betrayal in their condescending insistence that he had yet to see the light that they—now ex-socialists creeping toward the Right—had seen. And were so proud to have seen. Reviews of his literary books by academics that complained he was insensitive to the play of language or the pleasures of the text or that accused him of being a naive, untheorized reader could also annoy him, but he had grown accustomed to them over the years. It was his fate, he knew, to be categorized as a political critic, and then it became his fate later in life to be ignored as a political critic when a theoretical and ahistorical Marxism returned as academic fashion. The reviews that pleased him most, beyond those (naturally enough) that agreed with his position or argument, were those that praised his writing as direct and lucid. And when that praise came from someone he admired as a writer, then it was all the more delicious.

Reading his prose—from his first book, *The UAW and Walter Reuther*, to the final essays in *A Critic's Notebook*—one feels an obvious loosening of pressure, a greater pleasure in the resources of the language. This change may have had something to do with his mellowing as a person, but it was also a way of continuing to struggle and even to grope toward a new sense of life. Good prose was not an absolute value in itself, but writing clearly and directly about even the most complex topics spoke to a shared value of openness and respect for the reader. There was a vision of politics in such prose.

The shape of an intellectual's career is always more clearly marked in retrospect than it is in the present precisely because so much of his or her work is devoted to the moment. That is why the adjective *public*, when placed before *intellectual* as a noun, seems so needless. Who has ever heard of a private intellectual? To have been a voice that mattered for forty years and more in a nation's cultural and political life is a rare achievement. Rarer still is to have been such a voice on so many issues that some wondered if "Irving Howe" designated a syndicate rather than an individual. He wasn't. He was just a man who worked hard, wrote a great deal, and never lost his interest in the world around him.

Notes

1. *New York Herald Tribune Book Review*, April 8, 1951, 3.

2. See Howe's acknowledgment to Cowley in the preface to his *William Faulkner: A Critical Study* (New York: Random House, 1951), xii.

3. Irving Howe, introduction to Sherwood Anderson, *Winesburg, Ohio* (New York: Signet, 1993), vii.

4. Irving Howe, *Thomas Hardy* (New York: Macmillan, 1967), 137.

5. Irving Howe, afterword to Emile Zola, *Germinal* (New York: Signet, 1970), 433.

Preface

I

This collection addresses the achievements and legacy of Irving Howe (1920–93), a vocal radical humanist and the most influential American socialist intellectual of his generation. Howe was also a distinguished literary critic who wrote or edited works on Sherwood Anderson, William Faulkner, Thomas Hardy, George Orwell, Yiddish fiction and poetry, and numerous other authors and literary topics; his most important critical study was *Politics and the Novel* (1957). Howe's most successful works of nonfiction were *World of Our Fathers: The Journey of the Eastern European Jews to America and the Life They Found and Made* (1976), which became a national bestseller, and his intellectual autobiography, *A Margin of Hope* (1982).

Although Howe taught in the English departments of Brandeis University, Stanford University, and Hunter College of the City University of New York (CUNY) for four decades, he considered himself not an academic but an intellectual and literary-political critic (which included his editing of *Dissent*, a quarterly devoted to democratic socialism that he cofounded in 1954). He exemplified what has come to be known as the "public intellectual" and made a significant and enduring contribution to American culture and literary studies.

Irving Howe was the most prominent member of the second generation of New York intellectuals, the chiefly Jewish secular group associated with *Partisan Review*, which, in the middle decades of the twentieth century, became the leading literary-intellectual quarterly in the United States. Ultimately I believe it possible that, given his contributions to the revival of Yiddish literature, his founding of *Dissent*, and his rich *oeuvre* of literary and political criticism, Howe will come to be regarded as an even greater figure than the New York intellectuals of the elder generation, such as Lionel Trilling, Sidney Hook, Harold Rosenberg, and Hannah Arendt.

II

The biographical facts make the literary-political accomplishments of Irving Howe all the more impressive. He was born in New York City, the only child of Ukrainian-Jewish immigrants. Yiddish was the language spoken at home. He learned English on the street and in school. He grew up in the Lower East Side and the Bronx, and he graduated from City College of New York (CCNY). Inspired by his grandmother, who had been a teenage activist in Europe, Howe was a committed Trotskyist in high school and an activist pamphleteer for the Shachtmanite sect by the time he entered CCNY. Howe was, by all accounts, a polemical, dogmatic Trotskyist radical in his youth. However, his intellectual integrity enabled him, not long after World War II, to loosen and eventually break free of this ideological straitjacket.

Irving Howe's postwar literary-intellectual career can be demarcated in three broad phases. In the late 1940s and '50s Howe was best known as the editor and sparkplug of *Dissent*; an activist critic and a member of the *Partisan Review* circle; and a contemporary historian, the latter distinction based on his much-admired volumes *The UAW and Walter Reuther* (1949, coauthored with B. J. Widick) and *The American Communist Party: A Critical History* (1957, cowritten with Lewis Coser). In the mid-1950s Howe met the Yiddish poet Eliezer Greenberg. They began to translate Yiddish prose and poetry into English. Eventually they published six collections of stories, essays, and poems, elevating Yiddish writers, such as Isaac Bashevis Singer, to international attention.

With the publication of *A World More Attractive* in 1964, the praise and castigation of Howe's work intensified in both directions, opening up a second phase of his reputation. During the next decade Howe drew kudos from such Establishment figures as Lionel Trilling and hostile notices from New Left and counterculture voices. Howe also became better known as a literary and political essayist, always ready to comment on contemporary cultural trends. And yet, as generational tensions increased with the progress of the Vietnam War and American campus violence, Howe's moderate socialism seemed too threatening to mainstream critics and too tame for New Left tastes. Nonetheless, Howe's works of strictly cultural criticism, such as *Thomas Hardy* (1967), *Decline of the New* (1970), and *The Critical Point* (1973)—which remained largely free of polemical content—were increasingly admired by both academic and nonacademic critics. During these years he also established friendships with numerous European writers, such as Ignazio Silone and Günter Grass, and through his criticism and reviews helped the Hungarian novelist Gyorgy Konrad achieve renown in the English-speaking world.

Howe's social history of the bygone American Jewish life of his childhood, *World of Our Fathers*, which briefly reached number one on the *New York Times* bestseller list and received the 1977 National Book Award for nonfiction, marked the beginning of a third and final stage of his career. From the mid-1970s until his death Howe was praised and pilloried as the leading radical humanist voice of intellectual America and as a pillar of the liberal-Left. Howe came in for especially harsh attacks from the neoconservative movement that formed around *Commentary* and the *New Criterion* in the 1970s and '80s.

Even as these assaults from the Right grew louder, however, Howe became less and less polemical, turning his attention again to historical issues—though now with an intensely personal and often nostalgic tone. His backward-looking reflections included not only *World of Our Fathers* but also a short biographical study of Trotsky, a moving autobiography (*A Margin of Hope*), an elegy for the lost cause of democratic socialism (*Socialism in America*, 1985), and a last essay collection (*Selected Writings, 1950–1990*, 1990)—which also turned out to be his last book published before his untimely death in May 1993 at the age of seventy-two.[1]

III

Along with his heroes George Orwell and Edmund Wilson, Irving Howe represents a dying literary breed. One leitmotif of this volume is that he stands in their tradition and serves as an example of how and why to revive this older model of writer/critic/intellectual.

Howe's reputation as a critic was partly in eclipse during much of the 1980s and 1990s, as university literature departments moved away from broadly accessible cultural criticism and toward theory, multiculturalism, post-structuralism, and professionalism. But the literary situation today seems again poised to reorient itself toward issues of wider public concern beyond the literary academy. With the republication in 2002 of Howe's masterful critical study *Politics and the Novel*, my hope is that the timing is apt for renewed attention to Howe's life and legacy.[2]

Irving Howe and the Critics also appears as *Dissent*, which Howe faithfully edited for four decades, celebrates its fiftieth year of publication in 2004. Woody Allen's joke two decades ago in *Annie Hall*, that the magazine might merge with the neoconservative journal *Commentary* and be renamed *Dysentery*, elicits today no more than a smile from serious readers. Allen's movie has become a period piece, whereas *Dissent* continues to represent the distinctive voice of American social democracy and radical humanism.

§

In the course of writing this book, I have incurred numerous debts, which it is my pleasure to acknowledge. My thanks first go to Nicholas Howe, who spoke with me about his father and who generously contributed both a foreword and photographs to this volume. I am also grateful to numerous acquaintances and professional colleagues of Irving Howe at *Dissent*, several of whom shared insights about his *oeuvre* and alerted me to little-known biographical facts. In addition, I wish to thank a disparate group of colleagues who enriched my understanding of Howe's world and the milieu of the New York intellectuals: Robert Boyers, Nathan Glick, Alfred Kazin, Richard Kostelanetz, Steven Marcus, William Phillips, Norman Podhoretz, and Richard Rorty.

I am especially indebted to several friends and colleagues who read the manuscript, whole or in part, and gave me both detailed criticism and warm encouragement: William Cain, Morris Dickstein, Jonathan Imber, Beth Macom, Neil McLaughlin, Michael Kazin, Mark Krupnick, Michael Levenson, Jim Sleeper, Harvey Teres, Alan Wald, Michael Walzer, and Dennis Wrong.

To Lynn Hayden, who exhibited endless patience and unwavering trust during the months that she furnished this maturing manuscript and its author a home, I dedicate this book.

JGR
Austin, Texas
August 2004

Notes

1. Howe's very last book was the posthumously published *A Critic's Notebook* (1994), edited by his son, Nicholas.

2. *Politics and the Novel* was republished by Ivan R. Dee. Other books by Howe that have been reprinted since his death include *Short Shorts* (reissued by Bantam in 1997) and *Classics of Modern Fiction: Twelve Short Novels* (New York: Harcourt Brace, 2003).

Irving Howe and the Critics

Introduction

Irving Howe, Triple Thinker

John Rodden

Irving Howe and the Critics focuses on Howe's major works and the disputes they generated. Indeed, given the strong dissents across the ideological spectrum from Howe's dissenting radicalism, this book could alternatively have been titled "Irving Howe versus the Critics" (or even—per the title of his 1979 essay collection—"Celebrations and Attacks on Irving Howe").[1] The collection spotlights the engagement of Howe's critics with his life and legacy and pays Irving Howe the respect of challenge and even combativeness—precisely because ideas mattered so much to him.[2] *Serious* was always a word of honor for Irving Howe. To be "serious" was, to his mind, a prerequisite for understanding and judgment. All his work exhibits this "seriousness," manifested above all in a flair for organization and meticulous detail, whether Howe was writing essays,[3] editing a magazine, or teaching a course.[4]

This volume honors Howe's own frank, direct style by taking his work seriously. *Irving Howe and the Critics* features both *Dissent* contributors and those who have dissented from the Dissenters—on the Right as well as the Left. The collection includes, therefore, a few stern assessments of Howe from his less sympathetic critics, testifying both to the range of response—from admiration to hostility—that his work received as well as to his stature on the Left as a prime intellectual target of neoconservative fire. (But also radical fire: in some New Left circles *Dissent* was dismissed as an irrelevant organ, expressing "the joy of sects.")

My own estimate of Howe's achievement is much more positive, if by no means uncritical, as my contributions to this collection make clear.[5] In my view Irving Howe was the last major American public intellectual, certainly the last of the Old Left. Not only was he prolific—he wrote eighteen books, edited twenty-five more, penned dozens of articles and reviews, and edited *Dissent* for forty years—but he was also competent and more often brilliant in virtually every literary endeavor of his mature years. While some readers may find his work on "politics and the novel" to be most valuable, I believe that his contributions to the study of Yiddish literature and Jewish immigrant history are most likely to last.[6] Indeed, as I suggest in the preface, it is quite possible that Howe's work will endure longer than that of the elder generation of New York intellectuals in whose shadow he sometimes found himself.[7]

Of Celebrations and Attacks

Yes, Irving Howe had his admirers—and his detractors.

"Irving made a lot of enemies in his lifetime," recalls Robert Boyers, an intellectual and friend on the Left. Indeed, Howe was fond of the remark of William Dean Howells that anyone could *make* enemies but the real test was to keep them. By that criterion he succeeded well. Though he occasionally reconciled after falling out (with a few writer-intellectuals, such as Lionel Trilling and Ralph Ellison, and a few New Leftists, such as Jack Newfield, Carl Oglesby, and Todd Gitlin), Howe made and kept an impressive number of enemies.

Howe's chief enemies and most severe critics included one-time friends and colleagues in his New York circle who had moved to the Right in the late 1960s and '70s: Hilton Kramer, Norman Podhoretz, Saul Bellow, Midge Decter, and Sidney Hook. But other harsh critics stayed on the political or cultural Left—or moved even further leftward—such as Alexander Cockburn, Philip Rahv, and the majority of those New Left leaders whom Howe excoriated in *Dissent*'s pages. Still other opponents, such as Richard Kostelanetz and Philip Roth, were literary or aesthetic rather than explicitly political adversaries.

For instance, Bellow dismissed Howe as "an old-fashioned lady."[8] Roth parodied him as Milton Appel, a "sententious bastard. . . . A head wasn't enough for Appel; he tore you limb from limb."[9] During the late 1960s, when acrimonious differences over the Vietnam War and the counterculture split American intellectuals into rival camps, the poet Robert Lowell cast Irving Howe in the role of the archetypal "New York intellectual."[10] Lambasting Howe as an elitist radical looking down on humankind, Lowell wrote in his sardonic poem "The New York Intellectual" (1967):

Did Irving really want three hundred words?
. . . .
How often one would choose the poorman's provincial
out of town West Side intellectual
for the great brazen rhetorical serpent
swimming the current with his iron smile![11]

In the early 1970s Philip Nobile mocked Howe as "the Lou Gehrig of the Old Left," "who is always there when you need him with a clutch position paper on the Cold War, Vietnam, Eugene McCarthy, confrontation or sexual politics." Nobile added that Howe often assumed a gatekeeping or policeman's role, "serv[ing] as the Left's chief of protocol, correcting the manners of apocalypticians and calling for coalitions always and everywhere."[12]

To Lowell and Nobile, Howe was a critic-shark who patrolled New York's cultural currents, an American commissar imbued with the joy of sects, an intellectual iron man whose pen never ran dry. Or, as Nobile once remarked of Howe's circle: "They must be New York intellectuals. See how they loathe one another."[13]

Some of Howe's neoconservative critics—such as his first biographer, Edward Alexander—value his literary criticism and his work on Yiddish literature; they confine their ire largely to his political writing.[14] Alexander and other Jewish neoconservative critics have been especially hard on Howe for his positions on Israel. (Howe supported the Israeli Labor Party and Left-oriented organizations associated with the peace camp, such as American Friends for Peace Now.)[15] Neoconservative opponents have also castigated Howe's sectarian articles for the Trotskyist group to which he belonged in the early 1940s, pieces that Howe wrote in his early to mid-twenties and never reprinted—and for which he felt rather apologetic in later years.[16] A few neoconservative critics seem determined to haunt him with them.

But the celebrations—especially outside the neoconservative fold—vastly outnumber the attacks. Already by the mid-1960s, recalls Kenneth Libo, Howe's graduate student at Hunter College and later his research assistant and collaborator on *World of Our Fathers*, Howe "had become a hero of sorts to many liberal-minded academics of my generation." Upon publication of *World of Our Fathers* in 1976, notes one literary historian, Howe "was greeted as a cultural hero" within the American Jewish community.[17] Reviewing *World of Our Fathers* that year, the Catholic priest-sociologist Andrew Greeley exclaimed that "us Irish, we should be so lucky to have an Irving Howe." In 1977 the editors of *Moment* published a poll in which ten prominent American Jews listed the ten "most formative books of the

Judaic world, representing all times, all places." *World of Our Fathers* was the only book on American Jewish history to make any of the lists—alongside the Bible, the Talmud, the Passover Haggadah, and the daily prayer book.[18]

Such praise drove Nathan Zuckerman (a.k.a. Philip Roth) to exclaim about "Milton Appel" in *The Anatomy Lesson*: "When literary Manhattan spoke of Appel, it seemed to Zuckerman that the name Milton was intoned with unusual warmth and respect. He couldn't turn up anyone who had it in for the bastard. He fished and found nothing. In Manhattan. Incredible."[19]

If anything, the celebrations have only intensified since Howe's death. "A kind of moral hero," Mitchell Cohen wrote in *Dissent*, alluding to Howe's essay collection of the mid-1960s, *Steady Work*. Howe was "one of the steadiest minds in modern American life, and one of the most steadying." "The splendid voice of social democracy," eulogized the *New Republic*. "A monument to a range and a depth almost impossible to imagine in one human being, combined with a quiet decency," Robert Kuttner rhapsodized. Leon Wieseltier went, if anything, even further. "A great-souled man," Wieseltier called Howe in the *New York Times Book Review*, "the man who, more than any American intellectual of his generation, by his work and by his example, conferred greatness upon the homeliest of qualities, . . . the quality that mattered most to Orwell and Silone: the quality of decency."[20]

More recently Richard Rorty has lauded "Howe's incredible energy and his exceptional honesty," making him virtually "a warrior-saint" who "came to play the role in many people's lives that Orwell did in his."[21] Libo has hailed Howe for his "tough-minded realism and sustained hopefulness, as he strove . . . to improve the human condition by advancing Enlightenment goals of equality, fraternity, and progress."[22] "*World of Our Fathers* WAS my ethnic revival," recalls Matthew Frye Jacobson. "There is no doubting that Howe was among the spiritual authors of my most deeply held scholarly and civic convictions."[23]

Indeed, the kudos continue to the present. In 2003 Joseph Dorman called Howe "a true intellectual hero of the Left."[24] Even Ronald Radosh—a former adversary within the New Left who had moved far to Howe's right—has pronounced him "undoubtedly one of our country's most eminent intellectuals, a man of passion and intelligence."[25]

Such paeans strike most neoconservatives as deplorable. (Alexander is a notable exception.)[26] "Preparations are apparently under way to make [Howe] into the American Orwell," laments Joseph Epstein, who views Howe's radicalism as evidence of a politically immature and insecure thinker, indeed, of a card-carrying lifetime member of "the Old People's Socialist League." Hilton Kramer pronounces all of Howe's political writings, including his work on politics and the novel and other literary essays written from an explicitly left-oriented perspective, "worthless."[27] Neoconservatives are not alone in refusing to canonize Howe as "St. Irving."[28] In a memorial column on Howe in the *Nation*, Alexander Cockburn derides Howe as "an assiduous foot soldier" in the campaign to "discredit vibrant political currents electrifying America and supporting liberation movements in the Third World," a lapsed radical whose "prime function in the last thirty years of his life was that of policing the Left on behalf of the powers that be."[29]

The Writer as Culture Hero

However much Howe's "enemies" may ridicule comparisons portraying him as "the American Orwell,"[30] one cannot deny that the ongoing controversy about Howe's heritage does indeed resemble the cultural politics of Orwell's reputation.[31] Indeed, with the exception of Noam Chomsky, probably no American socialist thinker in the post–World War II era has provoked more disagreement within the Left and aroused more vitriol on the Right than Irving Howe. And I would argue further that Howe, like Orwell before him, became the "conscience" of his generation and ultimately even of our nation's intelligentsia. As a result the stakes involved in disputes about Howe's legacy are high. For to elevate or denigrate Howe—as has long been similarly the case with Orwell in Britain—is to affirm or assault nothing less than the recent history of the American liberal-Left, the status of the radical dissenting tradition, and the relevance of social democracy or democratic socialism to the American polity.

To understand how Irving Howe has come to occupy such a cultural role—and how he himself understood that role—it is valuable to recall the literary-political legacy that Howe embraced as his own. Or to put it differently: to understand better the relationship between "Irving Howe and the Critics" (or "Irving Howe versus the Critics"), it is helpful to examine a quartet of intellectuals dear to Howe's heart, those who formed the intellectual-moral center of his critical outlook. A leitmotif of this introduction, quite evident in the critical responses already quoted, is the (contested) perception of Howe as a literary-political hero. I believe that Howe aspired to a kind of intellectual heroism—very much like the writers with whom he identified, the figures who came to figure prominently in his imaginative and emotional life.[32] Indeed, Howe's choice of literary-political models furnishes insight into his much-disputed legacy as well as his impressive achievement.

Howe exalted four near-contemporary figures who inspired him from his youth onward: Trotsky, Orwell, Ignazio Silone, and Edmund Wilson.

Frequently Howe's identifications with his subjects are so deep and intense that they amount to self-portraits.

Howe's first great hero of History was Leon Trotsky, the man whose political orientation Howe embraced as a young teen when he entered the Trotskyist youth organization, the Young People's Socialist League. Howe's enduring fascination with Trotsky's leadership skills—and indeed, his high regard for Trotsky the man and writer as a "figure of heroic magnitude"— are well-known.[33] Trotsky's personal example and writings helped draw Howe to and sustain him in the Trotskyist movement. (Howe remained a committed Trotskyist for more than a dozen years, from the age of fourteen to his late twenties.) Even after officially withdrawing from his Trotskyist sect, the Shachtmanites (led by Max Shachtman), in October 1953 at the age of thirty-three, Howe continued to include Trotsky among his culture heroes, his only explicitly political figure (except perhaps for Norman Thomas).[34] Howe's biographical study *Leon Trotsky* (1977) makes clear his youthful veneration of Trotsky: "How intransigent he remained in defeat! To have come even briefly under his influence during the 1930s was to learn a lesson in moral courage, was to learn the satisfaction of standing firm by one's convictions, to realize that life offers far worse things than being in a minority."[35] On the final page of *Leon Trotsky*, Howe concludes: "A good portion of the writings of this extraordinary man is likely to survive and the example of his energy and heroism is likely to grip the imaginations of generations to come. . . . Trotsky embodied the modern historical crisis with an intensity of consciousness and a gift for heroic response which few of his contemporaries could match. . . . Leon Trotsky in his power and his fall is one of the Titans of our century."[36] Indeed, Howe retained a passionate, conflicted, yet lifelong identification with Trotsky for his "moral courage" and ability to stand alone.[37] (Some critics, including former British Maoist Ian Williams in this collection, argue that Howe whitewashed Trotsky and downplayed his moral as well as political crimes.)

Several contributors to this volume draw attention to Howe's esteem for Orwell, whom Howe repeatedly acknowledged as his "intellectual hero." And this time Howe chose well: Orwell's skepticism toward ideology countered the influence of Trotsky's allegiance to Marxist abstraction and the god of System.

Moreover, Howe rightly intuited that he and Orwell shared significant literary affinities, above all a similar kind of rhetorical, inventive (rather than creative or purely literary) imagination. Like Orwell, who was the great twentieth-century master of enduring catchwords and neologisms, Howe carved lapidary formulations in powerfully, and sometimes beautifully, chiseled prose, whereby he too added phrases to the cultural *Zeitgeist*.

(Howe especially admired those passages in which an author wrote "chiseled" or "clenched" prose—a favorite Howe epithet—and Howe's own best writing possesses a rigorous, taut dynamism.) Indeed, one could say that the prose gifts of both writers crossed from the rhetorical to the journalistic. Like Orwell's catchphrases, Howe's coinages were often polemical—and directed at explicitly political targets: "this age of conformity" (his swipe at the intelligentsia's conservative turn in the 1950s); "socialism is the name of our desire" (adapted from Tolstoy's famous assertion about God); "the New York intellectuals" (a phrase that he gave wide currency, if he did not invent it, in characterizing his *Partisan Review* circle); "guerrillas with tenure" (perhaps his sharpest cut at the New Left's guru scholars);[38] "a world more attractive" (a little-known phrase of Trotsky expressing love for art over politics); "confrontation politics" (what Howe characterized as the New Left's negotiating style); and "craft elitism" (how arcane literary theory, exemplified by post-structuralism and postmodernism, exploits jargon to exclude the nonspecialist reader), among other phrases.[39]

Orwell did not hesitate to borrow words and phrases for his own purposes and to reinscribe them—and neither did Howe. This is apparent in the titles of Howe's books, such as his volume of literary criticism *A World More Attractive*, which recalls Trotsky's phrase. But it is also evident in his edited volumes, such as *The Radical Imagination* and *The Radical Papers*, which nod to Trilling's celebrated *The Liberal Imagination* and to the Pentagon Papers, respectively.

Ignazio Silone was, for Howe, a literary-political hero much like Orwell, another writer and radical about whom Howe felt no ambivalence—and perhaps toward whom he felt a closer fraternal proximity, as if Silone were merely a slightly elder intellectual big brother. ("My favorite living writer," Howe once called Silone.[40] It is also notable that Silone is the only member of Howe's pantheon who ever published in *Dissent*.)

In his essay on Silone, originally published in 1956, Howe acknowledges him as an exemplar of the conscientious, responsible, outspoken dissident intellectual who lived on "an intellectual margin."[41] (I believe this phrase served as the germ for the title of Howe's autobiography, *A Margin of Hope*.)[42] Indeed, Howe came to see himself as a kind of Jewish-American Silone: "The man who will not conform," Howe wrote of Silone, "is a dissenter." Howe elaborates in terms that suggest veiled autobiography: "His own attitude toward socialism was to retain the values, even if he could not retain the doctrine. Silone's demand, at once imperious and relaxed, was that others would share with him a belief in the recurrent possibility of goodness."[43]

Howe calls Silone "a luminous example" of "a patient writer, one who has the most acute sense of the difference between what he is and what he wishes."[44] Howe proceeds in terms suggesting that Silone's heroes—and their author himself—represent a level of heroic living that Howe aspires to reach in his moments of utopian yearning:

> The hero of Silone's fiction feels that what is now needed is not programs, even the best Marxist programs, but examples, a pilgrimage of good deeds. Men must be healed. They must be stirred to heroism rather than exhorted and converted. Unwilling to stake anything on the future, he insists that the only way to realize the good life, no matter what the circumstances, is to live it. The duality between the two imperatives, between the necessity for action and the necessity for contemplation, between the urge to power and the urge to purity, is reflected in Silone's own experience as novelist and political leader. In his own practices as an Italian socialist, he is forced to recognize that the vexatious problem of means and ends involves a constant tension between morality and expediency.[45]

Furthermore, Howe agreed with Silone that heroism is "a condition of readiness, a talent for waiting, a gift for stubbornness." Howe admired Silone's resolution and steadfastness despite the fatiguing labor of striving for a more virtuous social order, what Howe calls Silone's "heroism of tiredness." Howe aspired to such a heroism himself.[46] Ultimately he realized that patience, alertness, and waiting had to be his way too, the way of all those who would hold fast to the ideals of socialism. And so Orwell became for Howe a model of "the intellectual hero," Silone "the hero of tiredness."[47]

Edmund Wilson was the only American member of Howe's heroic quartet. Yet young Howe prized Wilson partly for his mastery of the European literary and political traditions. For the aspiring cosmopolitan writer-critic just beginning his career at *Partisan Review*, the American outpost of European culture in the mid-1940s—indeed, the premier cultural magazine of the American intellectual world from the 1930s through the 1950s—Wilson represented European intellectual sophistication on native ground. He stood before Howe as an *engagé* intellectual (like Orwell and Trotsky) who had never succumbed to the coarseness of ideology (unlike Trotsky—and indeed, unlike the youthful Trotskyist Howe). Of course Wilson was also the only member on this high stage of Howe's literary pantheon connected with Howe's intellectual orbit in New York, a fact that obviously rendered him a figure in even closer proximity (physically, if not fraternally or ideologically) to young Howe than Silone. Howe could (and did) get to know Wilson personally.[48] Ultimately he granted Wilson too a measure of heroism—and Wilson's literary stamina, indeed superhuman energy, matched Howe's own. Unlike Silone, Wilson was a hero of tirelessness: "Almost everyone looked up to him. Writers and critics looked up to him, both those for whom he served as a mentor and those ambitious enough to have him as a model. . . . His career took on a heroic shape, the curve of the writer who attains magisterial lucidity in middle age and then in the years of decline struggles ferociously to keep his powers. One doesn't customarily think of writers as heroes; nor are heroes always likeable. But in Wilson's determination to live out the idea of the man of letters, in his glowing eagerness before the literatures of mankind, and in his stubborn insistence on speaking his own mind, there is a trace of the heroic."[49]

These remarks of Howe on Edmund Wilson came to apply to Irving Howe himself. In *A Margin of Hope*, Howe cites Wilson as his chief literary model (along with Orwell).[50] Here again, as with Howe's other literary heroes, one discerns a resemblance to Wilson in Howe's own "magisterial lucidity" and "stubborn insistence on speaking his own mind"—and also a "trace of the heroic."

Irving Howe, Triple Thinker

The animating idea of one of Wilson's critical studies, which Howe much admired, serves as the title for my introduction: "the triple thinker." I mean it to apply here both in the sense of Howe's immersion in and mastery of three worlds—literary, political, and Jewish—and in Wilson's sense. "The artist should be triply (to the nth degree) a thinker," wrote Wilson in *The Triple Thinkers* (1938), which sets forth Wilson's ideal of the writer's relationship to society and reflects his disillusionment with Marxism as a way of reforming society or even adequately describing it.[51]

Wilson's triple thinkers (above all Pushkin, James, Shaw, and Flaubert, from whom Wilson borrowed the phrase) are unwilling to renounce responsibility either to themselves or to their society.[52] They refuse either to dwell in a private garden of self-cultivation or to turn themselves into political hacks or social do-gooders. Instead they seek meaning in the tensions between their inner and outer worlds. These tensions stimulate intellectual leaps—indeed, imaginative triple jumps. The triple jumper of the mind soars dialectically to the triple thought: art functions as an existential guide. (Aestheticism—art for art's sake—is the single thought. Its antithesis, the double thought, arises from the realization that beauty does not exist as a transcendent, eternal abstraction but rather arises from social circumstances. This insight, if it loses dialectical fluidity and ossifies beyond conviction to dogma, becomes the doctrine that art must promote social reform.) The triple thought is the recognition that art is all this and much more—indeed, that the work of art can enlarge our awareness, ennoble our inner lives, and enrich the human condition.

I regard Irving Howe as a Flaubertian—or Wilsonian—"triple thinker." Although Wilson's exemplary thinkers were nineteenth-century literary men par excellence, triple thinking is not associated with a particular epoch, form, genre, or style.[53] It envisions new relationships, connects the real to the ideal, interweaves the social and artistic planes—and generates disturbance.

Irving Howe certainly was a thinker ("to the *n*th degree") who generated a lot of disturbance. And I would argue that he moved far beyond the double thought (and sometimes doublethink) of his youthful Trotskyist dialectics to become a mature "triple thinker," one of our most sophisticated critics, possessed of a rare gift to appreciate art as an existential guide—like his models Orwell, Silone, and Wilson himself.

Indeed, as I have already suggested, Howe's thinking was also "triple" in another sense: he was fluently trilingual in three domains. Howe lived concurrently in three overlapping, interacting worlds—American socialism, humanistic criticism, and Yiddish culture—and he commuted constantly among them. They were his three great loves—and he witnessed all of them grow pale and frail in his own lifetime.[54]

This collection is organized in light of Howe's lifetime of faithful commitment to his "triple" loves—politics, literature, and Jewish culture—which formed the center of Howe's mature thought. Part 1 deals with Howe's politics, especially Howe the activist, the editor of *Dissent*, the radical humanist, and the committed writer. Part 2 addresses Howe the literary and cultural critic, especially Howe the prose stylist and lover of language. Part 3 concerns Howe the Jew, the faithful steward of *Yiddishkeit*, the author of *World of Our Fathers*. A concluding section features revaluations of Howe's achievement and reputation in these three domains. It is followed by Morris Dickstein's afterword, which reflects on both the writer and the man, and by an appendix, which discusses the extensive FBI dossier maintained on Howe in the 1950s.

Of Life and Letters

Not just Howe the socialist, critic, and Jew but also Howe the man emerges in this collection. So: what kind of man was he?

Howe not only popularized the phrase "New York intellectual" in his brilliant 1968 essay of that title; he also came to personify, as both his admirers and adversaries have recognized, some distinctive features of the species.[55] The personal memoirs in this collection address his complex personality and intellectual temperament. Most of Howe's acquaintances speak with affection and gratitude about both his mentoring role in their intellectual lives and his comradely companionship on their political and professional journeys. The friends and colleagues of Irving Howe whom I've interviewed invariably also speak of him as intense, as an indefatigable worker, a man who strove relentlessly toward his goals, a man capable of single-minded effort, a man of strong moral principles who would not rest until the job was done and done right, a man whose opinions and beliefs on any subject were neither held lightly nor separated from his personal relations.

I spoke with Irving Howe on only two occasions: at an Orwell conference in 1983, when I interviewed him, and during his visit in 1986 to the University of Virginia, when he lectured on the American Renaissance from sections of *The American Newness* (1986).[56] He had just retired from the City University of New York, where he had held the chair of Distinguished Professor of English, and was on the verge of receiving a MacArthur Foundation fellowship in 1987.

I noticed Howe's intensity, but I was also impressed by the way his work became more reflective (and autobiographical) with the years. When I shared that perception, Howe's friends described to me his mellowing, his growing capacity to relax, his increasing ability to transcend partisanship. The mature Howe knew there was also a time for frivolity and lightness— and so he learned in later life to open himself to new pleasures, such as the ballet.[57] He didn't let his purposefulness degenerate into anxiety about achieving a goal. As Daniel Bell put it in his memorial to Howe in *Dissent*: "Irving changed not only his opinions but the way he held them."[58]

For me it is not just Howe the critic and intellectual but Howe the man, and the man within the writings, who proves compelling. It is a quality of human presence, and indeed, of presence in the word, especially the modulation and rhythm of his discerning, composed, often poignant literary voice, that stays with me. What inspires me above all is the trajectory of his career, his wherewithal to change—less his political outlook than his personal manner. When I met and corresponded with him during his last decade, he had already begun to exhibit a patient trust in the slow work of dialogue, in the slow work of time—that is, he was applying his convictions about the need for "steady work" not just to his political vision but to his personal values—the true mark of a Wilsonian "triple thinker."

Howe himself recognized all this. "Looking back at my disillusionment with political ideology," he wrote in 1982, "it would be more correct to say that my politics changed because I became, I like to think, more humane, tolerant, and broadminded. If I'm right in using those adjectives, then it became easier for me to acknowledge things that a rigid ideology would deny."[59] As he grew older, he became more flexible, more open to the alternative views and differing gifts of others.

But if Howe mellowed, he did not become lukewarm. He always ran hot on both justice and equality, the polestars of his radical humanism; and he stayed cool—nay, cold—to neoconservative celebrations of capitalism, far-left diatribes against "Amerika," and academic jargon of all kinds. In short: Irving Howe stuck to his convictions. Opposition only served to fortify his dogged determination. He could be abrupt and flinty when confronted with what he regarded as stupidity. Or when he encountered intellectual complacency or smugness, especially if it rested on academic credentials. (He was proud that he had become a chaired professor without ever bothering to get a Ph.D.) He usually found the most effective way of doing things in the least amount of time and could be irritated by people who he felt were wasting time by questioning his method or his rationale. He was unusually sensitive to criticism because he subjected himself to very high intellectual standards that included sharp self-criticism, so that further negative feedback rarely seemed to him necessary. All of which is to say: he relaxed his manner; he never relaxed his standards.[60]

Talking to his friends, I also became more aware of Howe's rare capacity to hold together the big picture with the fine points. He always had a mind for facts, categories, and technical detail that nonetheless did not lose sight of larger questions. And in his later years his rigorous self-discipline seldom deteriorated into grim determination, even though he maintained the impassioned sense of mission that led him to want to improve the world. As Leon Wieseltier observed in his memorial address on Howe: "He saw the end of socialism. He saw literature mauled by second-rate deconstructionists and third-rate socialists of race, class, and gender. And he saw the world of Yiddish disappear. But he never surrendered to nostalgia. He remained almost diabolically engaged with the politics and culture of his time."[61]

Although Howe was astonishingly erudite, he did not disdain the dirty work of politics, the necessary efforts to bring about the reforms he believed in. He was willing to get into the trenches and bring about the changes he advocated. But there were times—such as during the Vietnam War in 1966–67, when he wrote *Thomas Hardy*—when he also sought to go "far from the madding crowd" and immerse himself in literature in a quiet natural setting.[62] He came to enjoy the give-and-take of political involvement less and less in his last two decades, though he remained politically active.[63] Most of all, as his friends confided to me, he improved his ability to talk *to* others rather than *at* others.

Howe became more tolerant; he did not become permissive. He never granted that people could just do whatever they liked. Rather, he developed the talent of the tolerant man to respect differences of opinion, never believing that everything was equal and nothing made a difference. He learned to drop debating points—and in doing so he became far more accepting of others without ever simply becoming indifferent. He remained upright while becoming less self-righteous.

Howe's hunger for social justice could go beyond moral seriousness to almost messianic longing. In *World of Our Fathers* Howe exalts *menshlikhkayt* (humaneness), calling it "that root sense of obligation which the mere fact of being human imposes upon us." It is a "persuasion that human existence is a deeply serious matter for which all of us are finally accountable. . . . We cannot be our fathers, we cannot live like our mothers, but we may look to their experience for images of rectitude and purities of devotion."[64]

Again that "seriousness." But also "rectitude" and "purity": these attributes too were central to both Howe's literary sensibility and his commitment to socialism. A man of principle, he maintained a "purity of devotion" to the ethos of socialism—and referred to himself as a "radical humanist" even after *Dissent* dropped the masthead motto ("a socialist quarterly") explicitly identifying it with socialism in the late 1950s.[65]

The Crumb on His Coat

Nicholas Howe relates that the phrase "It's like the crumb" became an endearing shorthand joke between Howe and his friends to describe a wonderful, gratuitous detail in a work of fiction—which, as detail evolves into story, assumes the form of an anecdote.[66]

Especially at his memorial service and in the memorial issue of *Dissent* (Fall 1993), his family, friends, and colleagues sprinkled delicious *shtiklakh* (morsels) about Irving Howe's foibles and eccentricities. Everyone spoke about "Irving."

These first-person reminiscences, composed of striking details and revealing anecdotes, vividly evoke the man—and make vivid reading for us today. The crumbs abound: Irving at a baseball game reminiscing with beer-guzzling fans about having seen Babe Ruth play in Yankee Stadium, Irving brusquely ending a phone conversation by hanging up the phone before a friend can say good-bye, Irving leading a *Dissent* editorial meeting with a mixture of benevolence and argumentativeness. Some recollections consist of choice *shtiklakh*, while others are less edible or digestible to his friends. Nonetheless: the crumbs on his coat are there.

One crumb often passed around among his friends was the joke that

Irving Howe was the last nineteenth-century Russian writer. Indeed, Howe does seem made in the image of the Russian intellectual of that era: a utopian, an idealist, a radical reformer, an impassioned advocate. Morris Dickstein once called him "a counter-puncher who tended to dissent from the prevailing orthodoxy of the moment, whether left or right, though he himself was certainly a man of the Left. . . . Whatever way the herd was going, he went in the opposite direction." And these attributes were not confined to his political or cultural criticism. They manifested themselves in his prose style. As his son Nicholas observes, Irving Howe had "a utopian faith in the reader."[67]

Unsurprisingly Howe also deeply identified—ever more so as he grew older—with the greatest nineteenth-century Russian writer, utopian, and reformer/revolutionary: Leo Tolstoy.

I have already discussed Howe's four literary-political models from the generation immediately preceding his own. But Howe revered writers from other generations too. One of them was Tolstoy, who also induced him to hold the looking glass up to himself.

Howe's comments on Tolstoy are transparently self-reflexive: "I love the old magician in the way that Chekhov and Gorky loved him—for his relentlessness of mind, his unquestionable desires. Of course he succumbs to moral crankiness, to intemperate demands for temperance, but stubborn and even perverse, he remains faithful to the contradictions of his sensibility."[68]

And there is more: "Tolstoy keeps groping for some stable position between the esthetic and the ethical. He never quite finds it, but he can write as if indeed he had found it." All this mirrors Howe—with his love of the ballet and the polemic, his affinity for literary criticism and politics, his tense balance between poetical sensibility and ideological conviction. As if to supplement Tolstoy's *Confessions* by voicing his own, Howe adds this (self-)criticism of his moral passion: "In a few instances, Tolstoy's ethical imperiousness does overwhelm his esthetic pattern."[69]

Yes, Howe's own vulnerability to self-righteousness and godlike Final Judgment must also be conceded—and they never vanished completely. But Howe largely avoided the fate of another epic Russian author, one of the greatest twentieth-century writers, Alexandr Solzhenitsyn: "What has happened to Solzhenitsyn?" Howe asked in 1989. "The answer is that his zealotry has brought about a hardening of spirit."[70] Solzhenitsyn lacked what Howe often referred to as "moral poise," which he defined as a sense of "ease in a world of excess." Howe himself heeded the example of the Yiddish writers whom he cherished for their wondrous balance amid adversity, above all Sholom Aleichem, the "dominant quality" of whose literary imagination "is his sense of moral poise. I can't resist a few more words on the matter of 'moral poise.' . . . You see how balanced, at once stringent and tender, severe and loving is his sense of life."[71]

Howe also aspired to such "moral poise"—and that is why Aleichem was also a literary (and political) model for him. For Howe could be a stringent and severe man. That was the form that his tender sense of life sometimes assumed, the means whereby he maintained a poised balance amid all the demands of his triple loves. The balance did indeed sometimes have something of the tenseness—the "intemperate temperance"—of the aged Tolstoy. That was the price that his friends—and above all Irving Howe—paid his daimon for his extraordinary intensity, concentration, and passion.

One is reminded that Howe began his career with a study of another intemperately temperate man. In his first book, *The UAW and Walter Reuther* (1949), coauthored with B. J. Widick, the twenty-nine-year-old Howe wrote that Reuther, a left-wing anticommunist labor leader whom young Howe much admired, was "*an unfinished personality*" battling to reconcile the pursuit of power and the call to a nobler vision. Which would be stronger, mused Howe, the drivenness or the dream?[72]

Howe too remained an unfinished personality. But then—who doesn't?

Irving Howe—skeptical dreamer, chastened revolutionary, driven reformer, and antiutopian animated by utopian longings—held these oppositions in coiled (or "clenched"), productive tension to the unfinished finish, still yearning, still striving, still steadily working toward his vision of a better world.[73]

The Ravages of Time

"Should anyone remember?" Howe asks in the closing lines of his posthumously published *A Critic's Notebook* (1994). Ever the devil's advocate challenging his own positions, Howe is speaking here in the voice of a young skeptic who doubts whether his elders' experience holds any lessons pertinent to the present—yet who is also sanguine about the future: "And isn't it wonderful that we have survived all these catastrophes?"

After a pause, the senex Howe—the old man of the Left—replies. His response echoes today as though Howe were speaking from the grave: "Yes, it's wonderful, but our hearts also sink before the ravages of time."[74]

Many who remember Irving Howe also feel regret about the man's death, which reminds us of the inevitable human fate: we all succumb ultimately to the ravages of time.

But the spirit of a true calling does not succumb; it endures. As Howe declares in his landmark essay "This Age of Conformity," published exactly a half century ago, in 1954: "What is most alarming is not that a number of intellectuals have abandoned the posture of iconoclasm of the *Zeitgeist*. Give them a jog and they will again be radical, all too radical. What is most alarming is that the whole idea of intellectual vocation has gradually lost its allure."[75]

It never lost its allure for Irving Howe. He remained a model of the humanist intellectual, and he impresses me as such today. So let Howe himself have the last word: "The most glorious vision of the intellectual life is still that which is called humanist: the idea of a mind committed, yet dispassionate, ready to stand alone, curious, eager, skeptical. The banner of critical independence, ragged and torn though it may be, is still the best we have."[76]

Notes

1. See Irving Howe, *Celebrations and Attacks: Thirty Years of Literary and Cultural Commentary* (New York: Harcourt Brace Jovanovich, 1979).

2. For Howe political disagreement could quickly take on a personal dimension—and become the grounds for breaking off a relationship with a former friend or ally. (Joseph Dorman's documentary film *Arguing the World* [1998] portrays one dimension of this process, in this case Howe's differences with one-time fellow Trotskyist comrades and intellectual colleagues, such as Irving Kristol and Nathan Glazer.) Several contributions in this volume address "critical points" in Howe's career—to borrow the title of one of his best volumes of literary criticism—such as the Eichmann trial, the Vietnam War, and the 1967 Arab-Israeli Six-Day War, each of which served to trigger several of Howe's political as well as personal breaks.

3. The examples are legion, but here is an instance from Howe's distinguished 1986 essay "Writing and the Holocaust": "Some insurgencies become so coarse, as a segment of the 1960s 'counterculture' did, that serious people have no choice but to oppose its anti-intellectualism, its dismissal of the past, its contempt for anything not conforming to the most recent improvisations." See Irving Howe, "Writing and the Holocaust," *New Republic*, October 27, 1986, 29.

4. But Howe liked the give-and-take of dialogue and even controversy. He never resorted to a method or procedure. As an editor and a teacher he was devoted to excellence. He wanted to teach others how to appreciate the very best. He believed in standards and didn't want them compromised. And yet, although he could be extremely critical, he showed great patience with those who admitted error, were somehow disadvantaged, or exerted effort.

5. I would insist that, in a full and balanced assessment of his achievement, the faults of both Howe's prose and his political-intellectual record must be acknowledged:

the rough, serviceable, often pamphleteer-style prose of his Trotskyist journalism; his early postwar silence on the Holocaust; his fierce polemical zeal against the New Left; his wrongheaded yet well-formulated attacks on James Baldwin and Ralph Ellison in the 1960s and on Philip Roth in the 1970s; the rhetorical overkill in his otherwise intelligent critique of Kate Millett's *Sexual Politics*. But all of these "excesses" or "mistakes" must be weighed in light of his capacity to grow and reevaluate his views of Trotskyism, World War II and the Holocaust, the New Left and feminism, and his critical attacks on Baldwin, Ellison, and Roth.

6. Indeed, my own view is that Howe's critical legacy will ultimately have more to do with his revival of *Yiddishkeit*, including the American Yiddish poets, than with the politics of the novel or his valiant attempt to salvage and renew American radicalism. Robert Boyers and others have built on the strand of Howe concerned with the politics of the novel, but there has been no systematic attempt as yet to honor and further develop his contributions to Yiddish literature and culture.

7. The New York "elders" sometimes compared with Howe include Lionel Trilling, Philip Rahv, Sidney Hook, Dwight Macdonald, Harold Rosenberg, and Hannah Arendt. Even after their deaths Howe was often cast in their shadow via unfavorable comparison or criticized as "too polemical" or "too prolific." In the 1980s he attained the status of a monument on the liberal-Left, but his reputation went into eclipse even before his death. (It is significant that, whereas Trilling's obituary appeared on page 1 of the *New York Times*, Howe's notice ran on page 22 of section D.) The appearance of two excellent biographies in the last few years, Edward Alexander's *Irving Howe: Socialist, Critic, Jew* (1998) and Gerald Sorin's *Irving Howe: A Life of Passionate Dissent* (2002), has brought Howe back into the public eye and more than redressed the previous decade of relative neglect.

The peak of Howe's recognition and broad influence occurred in the late 1970s and early '80s, between *World of Our Fathers* (1976) and *A Margin of Hope* (1982)—just as the height of Trilling's fame, in the 1950s, also occurred long before his death. In the wake of the success of *World of Our Fathers*, Howe and Kenneth Libo edited a popular, illustrated volume of history, *How We Lived: A Documentary History of Immigrant Jews in America, 1880–1930*. Really a coffee-table book, it was selected in 1979 as a main choice of the Book-of-the-Month Club. It was also a selection that year of the History Book Club, the Jewish Book Club, and the Jewish Publication Society. By contrast, *Selected Writings* (1990), a collection of his best essays across more than forty years, received only scattered attention, with no efforts to sum up Howe's career. By the mid-1980s the vogue for theoretical academic criticism meant that concerns in the literary-academic world had moved beyond Howe's methodless, "amateur" criticism.

8. Quoted in David Herman, "The Monday Books," *Independent* (London), April 7, 2003, 18.

9. Philip Roth, *The Anatomy Lesson* (New York: Farrar, Straus, and Giroux, 1985), 474.

10. Several of the leading figures associated with *Partisan Review* (*PR*), "the house organ of the American intellectual community" in the early post–World War II era, have also been nominated by various observers as archetypal "New York intellectuals"—among them Trilling, Rahv, Delmore Schwartz, and Mary McCarthy. See, for instance, William Barrett, *The Truants: Adventures among the Intellectuals* (New York: Anchor Press/Doubleday, 1982). (The characterization of *PR* is by Howe's friend the liberal historian Richard Hofstadter, in his *Anti-Intellectualism in American Life* [New York: Vintage, 1963], 394.)

11. Robert Lowell, *Notebook 1967–68*, rev. and exp. ed. (New York: Farrar, Straus, and Giroux, 1969).

12. Philip Nobile, *Intellectual Skywriting: Literary Politics and the New York Review of Books* (New York: Charterhouse, 1974), 135–36.

13. Nobile, *Intellectual Skywriting*, 13.

14. They take, as it were, two thirds of Howe's corpus and approve it: "two cheers for Irving Howe." Or sometimes less: Edward Alexander, in *Irving Howe: Socialist, Critic, Jew*, gives one rousing cheer for Howe's work—or at best one and a half cheers: socialist—no; critic—yes; Jew—yes (*Yiddishkeit*) and no (Israel). Alexander's harshest criticism of Howe's politics concerns his support of the Israeli Left and the peace process—and his castigation of what Howe regarded as Israeli militarism in the guise of national defense. For Alexander, Irving Howe was critic first, then socialist and Jew. Alexander sees Howe as a great critic, a misguided political thinker—who exhibited a misconceived politics that reflected a refusal to grow up—and a false friend to Israel. Alexander, an English professor, especially identifies with Howe the literary critic and strongly endorses the preservative, traditionalist positions of Howe on the literary canon and his hostility to postmodernism and deconstruction. (The Old Left and neoconservatives are closest on positions with regard to culture and literature. They tend to share a respect for the classics and the literary canon—and even for conservative modernist writers such as Pound and Eliot.) In addition to his biography of Howe, see Alexander's *Irving Howe and Secular Jewishness: An Elegy* (Cincinnati: University of Cincinnati, Judaic Studies Program, 1995).

15. Although Howe was an anti-Zionist before the Arab-Israeli Six-Day War in 1967, he developed strong links and friendships in Israel in the 1970s (and even married an Israeli woman). During his last two decades Howe was a strong and articulate, if critical, supporter of Israel.

16. See Alexander, *Irving Howe*, chap. 2.

17. Hasia R. Diner, "Embracing *World of Our Fathers*: The Context of Reception," *American Jewish History* 88, no. 4 (2000): 449. The American Jewish community celebrated *World of Our Fathers* as an act of homage to American Jewish history and as a Semitic version of Alex Haley's *Roots*, another bestseller in the bicentennial

year. Diner recalls that Jewish community centers "staged 'Lower East Side' fairs to accompany his presentations, and the strains of Klezmer music wafted from the social halls at the reception afterwards."

18. Quoted in Diner, "Embracing *World of Our Fathers*," 453.

19. Roth, *The Anatomy Lesson*, 482.

20. Mitchell Cohen, *Dissent* (Fall 1993); *New Republic*, May 12, 1993; Robert Kuttner, *Dissent* (Fall 1993); Leon Wieseltier, "Remembering Irving Howe (1920–93)," *New York Times Book Review*, May 20, 1993, 31.

21. Richard Rorty, *Achieving Our Country* (Cambridge: Harvard University Press, 1998).

22. Kenneth Libo, "My Work on *World of Our Fathers*," *American Jewish History* 88, no. 4 (2000): 439.

23. Matthew Frye Jacobsen, "A Ghetto to Look Back To: *World of Our Fathers*, Ethnic Revival, and the Arc of Multiculturalism," *American Jewish History* 88, no. 4 (2000): 473–74.

24. Joseph Dorman, "World of Our Fathers," *New York Times Book Review*, March 2, 2003, 13.

25. Ronald Radosh, "A Literary Mind, a Political Heart," *Los Angeles Times Book Review*, April 6, 2003, 10.

26. "One of the most original, principled, and independent minds of twentieth century America," wrote Edward Alexander of Howe in his biography (*Irving Howe*, 9).

27. Hilton Kramer, "Socialism Is the Name of Our Desire," in *Twilight of the Intellectuals* (New York: Ivan R. Dee, 1997).

28. The phrase—intended facetiously as a counter to all "the quasi-religious eulogies"—is Jeremy Larner's in his memoir of Howe in the Fall 1993 issue of *Dissent*.

29. Alexander Cockburn, "A Few Tasteless Words about Irving Howe," *Nation*, May 14, 1993.

30. Howe's friends and junior colleagues certainly embrace the analogy. As Josephine Woll wrote in *Dissent* (Fall 1993): "For Irving, Orwell was the model of a writer. For me, Irving was."

31. See my *George Orwell: The Politics of Literary Reputation* (1989; repr., New Brunswick: Transaction Publishers, 2002).

32. His biographer Gerald Sorin calls Howe "a hero of sorts," applying Howe's remarks on Silone's "heroism of tiredness" to Howe himself (*Irving Howe*, xiv).

33. Irving Howe, *Leon Trotsky* (New York: Viking, 1978), 161.

34. On Howe's high regard for Norman Thomas—as a politician and speaker rather than a writer—see *A Margin of Hope: An Intellectual Autobiography* (New York: Harcourt Brace Jovanovich, 1982), chap. 5.

35. Howe, *Leon Trotsky*, viii.

36. Howe, *Leon Trotsky*, 192–93.

37. Howe wrote in his preface to *Leon Trotsky*: "I have remained a socialist. I have found myself moving farther and farther away from [Trotsky's] ideas, yet he remains a figure of heroic magnitude" (viii).

38. Howe also used the phrase in the 1980s and '90s to characterize radical professors who favored multiculturalism and postmodernism over the classical literary canon and the traditional liberal arts curriculum.

39. One measure of the influence of Howe's 1954 essay is that a book by Alan Valentine appeared later that year under the title *The Age of Conformity* (Chicago: Regnery Press, 1954). An essay also appeared in the *American Scholar* in 1956: "American Literature in an Age of Conformity," by John W. Aldridge.

40. Quoted in Sorin, *Irving Howe*, 161.

41. Irving Howe, *Decline of the New* (New York: Harcourt Brace Jovanovich, 1970), 290. The essay was first published as "Silone and the Radical Conscience," *Dissent* (Winter 1956): 72–75. It was revised and reprinted in *Politics and the Novel* and *Decline of the New*.

42. All this is from the essay "Silone: A Luminous Example," in *Decline of the New*. A further measure of Howe's regard for Silone is that he and Lewis Coser dedicated *The American Communist Party* (1958) to "Ignazio Silone and Milovan Djilas—two men who more than any other stand for the attempt to create a non-Communist radical opinion in Europe."

43. Howe, *Decline of the New*, 290.

44. Howe, *Decline of the New*, 284.

45. Howe, *Decline of the New*, 285–87. This tension between the attractions of power and purity was one that Howe also carried throughout his life—as a radical who wrote for Henry Luce and *Time*, as a critic of conformist bourgeois life who became a chaired professor of English, and so on.

Howe obviously found inspiration in Silone's public example of how to creatively maintain and balance these oppositions. What then would Howe have had to say concerning recent revelations about Silone's preference for means over ends and his choice of expediency over morality as an Italian socialist? Silone's radical credentials and noble image have been soiled by evidence discovered in the 1990s, in the files of the Italian Fascist secret police, that he was an informant for the Fascists in the

1930s. Other documents establish that Silone was knowledgeable about CIA funding of the Congress for Cultural Freedom and other anti-Soviet cultural activities of the Western intelligence services in the "cultural Cold War"—activities that Howe castigated in "This Age of Conformity" and in *Dissent's* pages throughout the 1950s and '60s. In light of these findings Howe's praise of Silone sometimes rings most ironically: "The memory of [Silone's] refusal to accommodate himself to the fascist regime stirred feelings of bad conscience among literary men who had managed to become more flexible. Alas, men of exemplary stature are often hard to accept. They must seem a silent rebuke to those who had been less heroic or more cautious" (*Decline of the New*, 288).

46. The recurrent theme of Howe's essays in part 4 of *Decline of the New*, which consists of three substantial essays, is heroism. Orwell is his "intellectual hero" (269), Silone is his "hero of tiredness," and T. E. Lawrence exemplifies the entire "problem of heroism" (294–325).

47. Howe, *Decline of the New*, 293.

48. Wilson was one of the senior lecturers invited to teach the Christian Gauss seminars in the spring of 1953. Howe was selected as a junior lecturer, and he attended several of Wilson's sessions. Years later Howe turned down a submission to *Dissent* from Wilson, who, rather than hold a grudge, "teased him about being turned down by a magazine that didn't even pay" (Sorin, *Irving Howe*, 94, 147).

49. Irving Howe, "A Man of Letters," in *Celebrations and Attacks*, 221.

50. Howe, *A Margin of Hope*, 168.

51. Edmund Wilson, *The Triple Thinkers: Twelve Essays on Literary Subjects* (New York: Oxford University Press, 1948), 71. See also Janet Groth, *Edmund Wilson: A Critic for Our Time* (Athens: Ohio University Press, 1990); David Castronovo, *Edmund Wilson* (New York: F. Ungar, 1984), 33–42; and Jeffrey Meyers, *Edmund Wilson* (New York: Houghton Mifflin, 1995).

52. The collection's title derives from Wilson's essay "The Politics of Flaubert," and it was intended to provide Wilson with a unifying theme for his numerous fugitive pieces addressing such disparate figures as Paul Elmer More, A. E. Housman, Christian Gauss, John Jay Chapman, Karl Marx, and Ben Jonson. In addition to the aforementioned quartet of nineteenth-century figures (Pushkin, James, Shaw, Flaubert), the highlights of *The Triple Thinkers* are the introduction to Pushkin (including Wilson's own prose translation of "The Bronze Horseman"); the theoretical studies "Marxism and Literature" and "The Historical Interpretation of Literature"; and Wilson's interpretations in "Morose Ben Jonson," in which he subjects the Jacobean dramatist to speculative psychobiography.

53. I am well aware that the unpolitical Flaubert would have been unlikely to characterize either Howe or Wilson—at least during the latter's Marxist phase in the 1930s, when the first edition of *The Triple Thinkers* (1938) was published—as

a "triple thinker." Flaubert opposed socialism, the ideal of social equality, mass education, universal suffrage, and revolutions in general. Wilson quotes Flaubert's 1853 letter to Louise Colet: "The triple thinker . . . should have neither religion nor fatherland, nor even any social conviction" (*The Triple Thinkers*, 73–74).

54. Howe's triple thinking flowed, therefore, from his involvement in three different worlds, that is, from the seriousness he brought to politics, literature, and Jewish life. But he was hardly orthodox in any of those worlds. He was political, but his radicalism marginalized him in liberal and conservative America. He loved literature, but his disdain for professionalized "lit crit" made him an outsider in the literary academy. He was Jewish and valued his roots, but he could not accept a rejection of universalism and nationalism at the expense of the Palestinians. His insights and his own outsider status were linked. Howe's boundary crossing helps explain not only his originality and intellectual contributions but also his many conflicts and enemies.

55. See Irving Howe, "The New York Intellectuals," *Commentary* (March 1968).

56. During the reception after his 1986 lecture at Virginia, Howe chatted at length about *Politics and the Novel* (1957) with several of us, about whether it might be timely to reissue his landmark study. "There's been nothing like it since then," a few of us agreed. And in fact Howe did come to reissue it in 1992—perhaps gently nudged by our enthusiasm for the book.

57. See Irving Howe, "Ballet for the Man Who Enjoys Wallace Stevens," *Harper's*, May 1971, 102–9. See also Sorin, *Irving Howe*, 177–78, 222–23, 270, 286.

58. Daniel Bell, "Remembering Irving Howe," *Dissent* (Fall 1993): 517.

59. Irving Howe, "The Range of the New York Intellectuals," in *Creators and Disturbers: Reminiscences by Jewish Intellectuals of New York*, ed. Bernard Rosenberg (New York: Columbia University Press, 1982), 287.

60. See Sorin, *Irving Howe*, 146–47.

61. Leon Wieseltier, memorial address, delivered May 24, 1993.

62. Irving Howe, *Thomas Hardy* (New York: Macmillan, 1967).

63. Howe's supporters on the organized Left in the 1970s could best be described as coming from the Democratic Socialist Organizing Committee (DSOC), a group that merged with a small New Left group called the New American Movement (NAM) in the early 1980s. It is important to acknowledge Howe's political involvement in this strain of American socialism, even though literary criticism and *Dissent* became more central to his life and work than organized socialism after the late 1940s.

64. Irving Howe, *World of Our Fathers* (New York: Harcourt Brace Jovanovich, 1976), 645.

65. Just a year before his death, in his preface to the 1992 edition of *Politics and the Novel*, Howe wrote that his 1957 study "was written at a moment when I was drifting away from orthodox Marxism. . . . I still hold firmly to the socialist ethos which partly inspired this book, but the ideology to which these essays occasionally return no longer has for me the power it once had." See *Politics and the Novel* (1957; repr., New York: Columbia University Press, 1992), 7.

66. On the genre of the anecdote, see my *The Politics of Literary Reputation* (1989; repr., New York: Transaction, 2001).

67. Dickstein is quoted in the *New York Times* obituary on Howe, May 7, 1993. Also see Nicholas Howe, introduction to Irving Howe, *A Critic's Notebook* (New York: Harcourt Brace, 1994), 12.

68. Howe, *A Critic's Notebook*, 316.

69. Howe, *A Critic's Notebook*, 315–16. Occasionally Howe also lost his precarious balance between the esthetic and the ethical, with the latter overwhelming the former. And indeed, maintaining his much-prized "moral poise" depended chiefly on keeping his literary poise. Howe was blessed with a power rarely given to a critic, a power difficult to control: he had the literary equivalent of "perfect pitch." His ear for good prose style was nearly faultless. He possessed both an exquisitely fine sense for the rhythm and cadence of sentences and a superb judgment about *le mot juste*. These talents proved ideal equipment for a literary critic.

But Howe's concentrated energy could become a sharp weapon when it contracted and overfocused on the foibles of an adversary or homed in on isolated details of an ideological dispute. He was marvelous when he related a political element to the big picture, but he could be cutting and wounding when he became preoccupied with small concerns. Under such circumstances, he could use morality as a club. Such was arguably the case with Tom Hayden and the young New Leftists whom he blasted when they visited him and *Dissent* in 1965. On that episode, see Todd Gitlin, *The Sixties: Years of Hope, Days of Rage* (New York: Bantam Books, 1987), 171–76.

70. Irving Howe, "The Fate of Solzhenitsyn," in *Selected Writings* (New York: Harcourt Brace Jovanovich, 1990), 459, 463.

71. Irving Howe, introduction to *The Best of Sholom Aleichem*, ed. Irving Howe and Ruth R. Wisse (Washington DC: New Republic Books, 1979), xvii. Aleichem was also a "culture hero" of Howe, but less a personal, intellectual hero (unlike Trotsky, Orwell, Silone, and Wilson) than a nineteenth-century spirit of the age. Howe wrote of Aleichem: "I think of him as a culture hero in the sense that Dickens and Mark Twain were culture heroes. For he embodies the culture of eastern European Jews at a time of heightened consciousness" (12). See also Howe's essay "Sholom Aleichem: Voice of Our Past," collected in both *A World More Attractive* (New York: Horizon, 1963) and *Selected Writings*.

72. Irving Howe and B. J. Widick, *The UAW and Walter Reuther* (New York: Random House, 1949), 199. Howe's portrait of Reuther resembles a description of Howe's own former commissar self, in thrall to Trotskyist sectarian politics—a life that Howe, by 1949, had largely ended: "Reuther eats, sleeps, and talks union. He is as close to a political machine as any man alive today. He has forgotten how to relax and how to play. Reuther is characteristic of a generation of radicals that came to feel leftist politics is a dead end but could not throw off the moral compulsions that had led them to such politics" (201). By all accounts of his acquaintances, this passage could also describe Howe's own struggle at midcentury to work through his Trotskyist past.

73. Fittingly enough, in the last article he published in *Dissent* during his lifetime, Howe proposed "two cheers for utopia"—two, not three—yet genuine, heartfelt cheers nonetheless. Irving Howe, "Two Cheers for Utopia," *Dissent* (Spring 1993): 131–33.

74. Howe, "Writing and the Holocaust," 34.

75. Howe, "This Age of Conformity," in *Steady Work* (New York: Harcourt Brace Jovanovich, 1966), 319. The essay originally appeared in *Partisan Review* (January–February 1954).

76. Howe, "This Age of Conformity," 323.

Socialist

1

Mark Levinson and Brian Morton

A Man of the Left

Mark Levinson and Brian Morton were coeditors of *Dissent* magazine's book review section from 1988 until 2000. Levinson continues to edit the book review section and is also the director of policy at UNITE HERE, a union of apparel, textile, hotel, and laundry workers. His writings have appeared in *Dissent*, the *American Prospect*, the *Nation*, and the *New York Times*.

Morton teaches at Sarah Lawrence College and New York University and is the author of the novels *The Dylanist*, *Starting Out in the Evening*, and *A Window across the River*.

In one of his essays Ignazio Silone says that, as a child, he once laughed at the sight of a man being dragged through the street by the police. His father reproved him harshly, telling him never to make fun of a man who has been arrested. "Because he can't defend himself. And because he may be innocent. In any case because he is unhappy."

Irving Howe wrote that he found that last sentence "overwhelming, worthy of Tolstoy." Anyone familiar with Howe's work will understand why it moved him. At the heart of Howe's long intellectual career was a basic sentiment, one that never wavered. You could call it a sense of outrage at the insults suffered by people without power; you could call it a sense of identity with the insulted. You could call it, simply, a feeling of brotherliness.

Howe died suddenly [in May 1993] at the age of seventy-two. For the small community of the democratic Left in America the loss is bone deep. Howe sustained a thorough engagement with the idea of socialism, as both problem and goal, for over fifty years; in the light he provided, many of us learned to see.

The child of immigrant parents, Howe grew up in the Bronx at a time when "socialism, for many immigrant Jews, was not merely politics or an idea, it was an encompassing culture." He joined the Socialist Party of Norman Thomas in 1934, at the age of fourteen. When a few hundred Trotskyists were expelled from the party three years later, Howe went with them, attracted by the élan of thinkers like Max Shachtman and James Burnham—and not least by that of the "Old Man" himself. Though Howe spent only a few years in Trotsky's orbit and came to think him mistaken— worse than mistaken—on fundamental matters, Trotsky remained for him a figure of heroic and tragic dimensions.

In 1940, in the wake of a split with Trotsky over the nature of the Soviet Union, Howe followed Shachtman into the Workers Party, later renamed the Independent Socialist League. (He remained a member until 1953.) The debates with Trotsky led Howe to a belief that democracy was a sine qua non for any society that could be called a workers' state—for any decent society of any kind. For the rest of his life he never swerved from the conviction that socialism would be democratic or it would not be socialism at all.

In the late 1940s Howe began to contribute literary criticism to mag- azines such as *Partisan Review*. His two callings, politics and literature, enriched each other in a complex way. Howe never reduced literature to politics: his lifelong love affair with some of the great literary conservatives, from Dostoevsky to Conrad, is enough to make that clear. But the two passions grew from the same root. Literary criticism, as he practiced it, was a meditation on the widest, most serious concerns. In evaluating a novel, he once wrote, the questions he asked were, "How much of our life does it illuminate? How ample a moral vision does it suggest?" These are the same questions, we imagine, that he would ask of a work of political thought.

At the same time, along with the poet Eliezer Greenberg, Howe began translating Yiddish poetry and fiction into English; among the writers the two "discovered" was Isaac Bashevis Singer. Howe's engagement with Jewish culture was a labor of love and of rescue, culminating in 1976 with *World of Our Fathers*, his rich evocation of the experience of immigrant Jewry in America. He came to identify most closely with the tradition of secular Jewishness—the effort to preserve a distinctive Jewish culture in the space between faith and assimilation. He believed it a tradition in irreversible decline, but no less precious for being a lost cause.

By the early 1950s Howe was making his way into the world of the "New York intellectuals." The term refers to a loose-knit group of writers, mainly first-generation American Jews, most of whom—originally at any rate—were anti-Stalinist radicals in politics, modernists in literary taste. Their "speciality was the lack of a speciality"; their chosen literary form was the essay: "wide-ranging in reference, melding notions about literature and politics . . . taut with a pressure to 'go beyond' its subject, toward some encompassing moral or social observation." They were the kind of writers whose passing Russell Jacoby laments in *The Last Intellectuals*: generalists who wrote for a general audience in lucid, accessible prose. As an editor of *Dissent* Howe retained his passion for clarity, fighting an endless rearguard action against the creeping incursions of academic prose.

By 1954 the American socialist movement had run aground. McCarthyism was at its height, and American intellectuals were announcing their reconciliation with commercial society. European social democracy had come to accept the welfare state as the limit of its aspirations, and Stalinist totalitarianism had left a deep, perhaps indelible stain on the very idea of socialism. To Howe and a few colleagues it seemed a good time to launch a socialist magazine.

Dissent was begun, Howe wrote, because "some of us rebelled against the sterility of the sects that still remained from the thirties, even as we wanted to give new life to the values that had petrified in those sects." Their immediate task was to combat Stalinism abroad and McCarthyism at home; beyond that *Dissent*'s editors agreed that if socialism was to have a future, a serious reconsideration of its premises was required. Early issues of the magazine featured theoretical articles by Howe and Lewis Coser, Silone, George Lichtheim, and others, attempting to reclaim the honor—moral and intellectual—of the socialist idea.

A sense of homelessness can stimulate the mind. Howe and the other editors of *Dissent* recognized that they could no longer live off the intellectual inheritance of European socialism; their engagement with the problems of socialism in crisis led to a creative rediscovery of the problems of the United States. In its first years the magazine sought to puncture the complacency of the "American celebration" and explored questions of poverty, bureaucracy, mass society, and "alienation" long before these became themes of the New Left.

During the early days of the New Left, Howe and other *Dissent* editors were attracted to its generous spirit, its undogmatic native radicalism, its readiness to take risks. For a moment it seemed that two generations of the Left would link hands. For a moment.

A clash of ideas, generations, styles, wills, egos—Howe and New Leftists like Tom Hayden exploded on contact. They seemed determined to misunderstand each other; it was as if they misunderstood each other on principle. When New Leftists spoke of their hopes for a participatory— as opposed to a representative—democracy, Howe was reminded of the Stalinists of his youth, with their contempt for "bourgeois democracy."

When Howe argued that anticommunism (in the name of socialist values) was an essential element of democratic radicalism, many in the New Left saw him as a curdled cold warrior.

"Perhaps I should not have gotten so emotionally engaged in disputes with the New Left," Howe wrote later. "But I did. . . . I overreacted, becoming at times harsh and strident. I told myself that I was one of the few people who took the New Left seriously enough to keep arguing with it. Cold comfort."

What needs to be said about all this is that Howe argued with the New Left *as a man of the Left*. He objected not to their radicalism but to what he saw as the primitiveness of their radicalism. He was never tempted to join the rush toward neoconservatism; socialism, always, remained "the name of his desire." In the years that followed he continued to publish *Dissent*, criticizing the deepening social meanness of 1970s and '80s America and trying to keep alive the idea of democratic utopianism. Determined not to relive the mistakes of the 1960s, he worked hard to make *Dissent* a place where contributors and editors—now including many from the New Left—could disagree in an atmosphere of tolerance and respect.

In 1989 Howe and *Dissent* celebrated the fall of Communism in Eastern Europe. The next day, so to speak, he was casting a skeptical eye on Eastern European intellectuals' embrace of "free markets." There was no contradiction in this.

In 1990 Howe attended a conference in Mexico on the theme of the "World after Communism." When he returned he wrote an informal report about it for a few friends; it seems worthwhile to quote from it at length. He wrote of a

> considerable turn to the right among leading intellectuals. . . . Thoughts of social transcendence or major social change have been abandoned. The buzz word, used without much discrimination, is "markets." . . . The very mention of socialism brings pained looks, responses of irritation and boredom—"that old stuff." Argue that you mean by socialism something sharply, utterly different from Communist dictatorship, and it gets little or no response. I was looked upon, not with hostility, . . . but as a sort of amiable fossil. . . .
>
> The conclusion we can draw is that we are going to be fairly isolated these next several years. . . . But we will persist!
>
> One thing more: I visited in Coyoacan the house in which Trotsky was killed. . . . What struck and moved me was the spartan atmosphere of this house. . . . Trotsky worked in a very small room, with a simple little table. Old typewriters, very modest furnishings, all together about

the size of a smallish apartment. How telling a contrast in its modesty this seemed to the opulent, extravagant atmosphere surrounding the conference!

People who knew Irving used to joke about his abruptness. When he called on the phone, he'd ask you if you "had a minute"—and within precisely one minute his business with you was done. He would signal the end of the conversation not by saying good-bye but simply by hanging up.

These habits never bothered us. It was a pleasure to get hung up on by Irving: he was usually eager to get back to work, and he took it for granted that you were too.

2

Ronald Radosh

Journey of a Social Democrat

Ronald Radosh, Adjunct Senior Fellow at the Hudson Institute, is professor emeritus of history at the City University of New York. He is author of *Commies: A Journey through the Old Left, the New Left, and the Leftover Left* (2001) and *Divided They Fell: The Demise of the Democratic Party, 1964–1996* (1996) and coauthor of *The Rosenberg File* (1983, 1997) and *The Amerasia Spy Case: Prelude to McCarthyism* (1987). He contributes frequently to the *New Republic, National Review*, the *Weekly Standard*, and other publications.

Irving Howe was one of our greatest intellects, a man of passion and intelligence who epitomized the now-lost world of the 1930s and 1940s "New York intellectuals," a term he himself coined in a 1968 essay. He was by profession a literary critic who wrote about Céline and Emerson and, of course, the world of the Yiddish community in which he grew up and from which he brought the world's attention to a then-unknown Isaac Bashevis Singer. But Howe was also a student of culture who could not separate himself from the turmoil of his own world. As he once put it, the socialist movement was his school and his university. He grew up in its milieu and, until his recent death, never left its ranks.

Howe's recent biographers have furnished us a full picture of Howe's life. But let me supplement them here with some thoughts about his accomplishments and failures. Howe, of course, tried to do this himself in his 1982 autobiography, *A Margin of Hope*. Herein he presented his own estimate of the meaning of his life's course. As usual with Howe there is much wisdom to be found in its pages. Howe understood, as so many of his contemporaries did not, that in the search for utopia lay the seeds of the totalitarian mentality. Writing about the Spanish Civil War, Howe reflected on the dire fact that it was a group of brave and idealistic young American Communists who went to fight for the Loyalist regime while others temporized. But in so doing they became pawns of Stalin's secret police, which revealed to Howe "the tragic character of those years: that the yearning for some better world should repeatedly end in muck, foul play, and murder."

After a youthful Trotskyism and a political baptism in the sectarian world of the late Max Shachtman's Workers Party and Independent Socialist League, Howe was to settle into the less dogmatic and more open world of moderate social democracy. Indeed, he would often say to me, in my own dogmatic socialist phase as a member of Michael Harrington's Democratic Socialist Organizing Committee and later the Democratic Socialists of America, "Why do you and the others have to call yourselves socialists? Isn't social democracy enough for America—indeed, isn't that but a remote possibility?" These words, it turned out, are similar to what Elliot Cohen of *Commentary* said to Howe in the early 1950s, when Cohen told him that whatever kind of revolutionary Howe thought himself to be, he really had a "social-democratic temperament." It was, Howe remembered, one of those transforming moments of recognition that he had long resisted. And to his successors he tried, sometimes fruitlessly, to impart this same message.

In the new postwar world, having left the Leninist sects of his youth, Howe founded *Dissent*, which was to become his final legacy to the world. It was in its pages, as well as in those of *Partisan Review* in the 1950s—a decade, Howe wrote, of "suffocating complacency"—that he was to make his mark. The very introduction of his journal made a point he had made earlier in *Partisan Review*: America had to come out of an "age of conformity," and Howe cautioned intellectuals against accepting the entrapments of power and thereby abandoning their function as intellectuals. Unlike others around him, Howe warned that the intellectual atmosphere of freedom was "under severe attack," and that meant no temporizing with McCarthyism in any of its manifestations. By tying the intellectual to the newly emerging civil rights movement and other currents of change, *Dissent* itself came to symbolize the promise of a new epoch.

At a critical juncture in the early Cold War, Irving Howe realized that for all its imperfections—some of which he was most keenly aware of— the West faced a justifiable and serious danger from the Soviet Union. At a time when the bulk of the so-called Left was still mesmerized by the remnants of the wartime Popular Front in the guise of Henry Wallace's "Progressive" movement, Irving Howe argued time and time again that the fear of Communist power was well-founded, that were Stalinism to win, the most precious values of the West would be destroyed. That meant one had to support both the Marshall Plan and the forces of liberal anticommunism in Europe—precisely those forces that the international Left was dubbing the agencies of American imperialism.

It was precisely his anticommunism, however, that allowed Howe to respond forcefully at yet another critical juncture: the birth of the 1960s New Left. Howe and his associates had worked tirelessly for the reemergence of a Left rooted in the American democratic culture. But when the New Left rose from the ashes, it reeked of anti-Americanism and a rather crude Marxism, and its young adherents tended to romanticize and support any Third World dictatorship whose leaders used the rhetoric of Marxism-Leninism. Howe looked at this New Left and, reflecting on his own generation's bitter experience, saw a new version of the old "after Fascism—us" of the Third Period Communists. In a critical and biting essay, "New Styles in Leftism," Howe hit fiercely at the new currents of authoritarian leftism that soon would get the name "radical chic." Here he took on those who abided by the "heritage" of Stalinism, which still existed for those who endorsed the cult of Mao and Fidel and for those who thought that the "wish to shock" was a new form of social revolution.

For these thoughts Howe became anathema to the New Left. At a now-famous meeting in one of those old Workman's Circle lecture halls, Howe debated Tom Hayden, then the young leader of Students for a Democratic Society (SDS); author of the Port Huron Statement (the early New Left's manifesto); and spokesman for those who rejected anticommunism, as Hayden and Staughton Lynd put it, as "the equivalent of rape." While Howe made his points, Hayden turned pale and stormed out of the hall, indicating by his action that a major rupture had taken place, that the breaking of the tie between the old socialists and the emerging young movement was now complete. For Howe, Tom Hayden and his supporters lacked "historical sense." He was right, and they would never forgive him for the espousal of his principles and for the passion with which he enunciated them.

Years later Howe would write that perhaps he had "overreacted, becoming at times harsh and strident," that perhaps he did not have to act in such a contentious fashion toward the New Left. But Howe was right then, and his criticism of the New Left holds up twenty-five years after the short life span of the Movement. And this, indeed, brings me to the path taken by Howe during the last fifteen years of his life. An opponent of Reaganism, he became bitter about what he saw as the new greed prevailing in our culture, and this became somewhat of an obsession. Howe could never resist taking a potshot at the hated neoconservatives, his former comrades who had drifted away from their roots to embrace the new conservative mood. To be fair, they were not too kind to him either. Writing in the *New Criterion*, Hilton Kramer chastised Howe for clinging to the dream of a socialist project whose time had passed. After all, in Howe's own publication

Robert Heilbroner had acknowledged that it was economic thinkers of the Right, Hayek and Von Mises in particular, who had proved more prescient about socialism than any of the Left had. And Marxist historians like Eugene Genovese had written—in the journal Howe had come to disdain most, *Commentary*—that socialism had finally "met its Waterloo"; rather than face the meaning of this successful counterrevolution, Genovese wrote, its adherents preferred "to happily dwell on the evil legacy of Ronald Reagan."

That was precisely the path and tone adopted by Howe from the 1980s on. Kramer, however, was unfair to say that Howe tried to hide his esteem for Trotsky, an accusation that hinted that Howe had supposedly hidden ultrarevolutionary roots. Trotskyism was a ghost Howe had long since abandoned. As he wrote in his short book on Trotsky, Trotskyism had become a "petrified ideology." Yet in his obsessive dislike for his old comrades who had turned to the new neoconservatism, Howe could not acknowledge the role played by Reagan in helping along the demise of the Soviet Union nor give his administration any credit when it was due. Evidently Howe could not see that there was anything to be said in criticism of the inadequacies of the New Deal liberalism that had emerged from conservative circles nor acknowledge the obvious failure of so many old liberal bromides.

All of this might have been expected. But sadly Howe also seemed to repudiate many of his old, most basic criticisms that had held up with time. An opponent of American policy in Central America, he could not criticize the Sandinistas when it would have helped, preferring to see them, as he once put it at a *Dissent* meeting, as a "new formulation." He even seemed to believe that it was futile to criticize black support for Communism, since Communists in South Africa and elsewhere fought for black freedom when other whites were silent. That Howe himself had answered these specious arguments years earlier seemed to matter little.

At one point during the Vietnam years Howe and his comrades had sought a third force—a social movement in Asia and Europe that would provide a way to reject both capitalism and Communism. He worked for the success of such a group in Vietnam, only to find it nonexistent or incapable of gaining political success. The effect was to blind his judgment when it came to an entirely new epoch. Thus the man who once endorsed Joseph Buttinger's work against both Communist and French imperialism now was saying, as he said to this writer, "I have learned that there is no third force." The implication—for Nicaragua especially—was that one had to choose the Sandinistas. Here Howe was endorsing the then-conventional wisdom of the very New Left he had earlier rejected. That this put him at odds with his Latin American counterpart, the social-democratic poet and writer Octavio Paz, was something he did not mull over. It also had political ramifications for Howe's chosen political course, enabling him to finally reconcile with those very elements of the New Left that had for so many years wanted nothing to do with him. This was acknowledged in an approving *New Yorker* piece, whose author observed that those former "student radicals grew a little older and saw the value of a more tolerant, less dogmatic, more democratic approach to the remaking of society," and thus Howe was there to now "welcome his young critics back." True, perhaps, for a few. But careful readers of *Dissent* could notice many examples of the kind of Left-think articles and specious arguments that had been absent in the journal's formative and influential years.

Still, Howe's contributions and his erudition, his thoughtfulness and his commitment to democracy will be sorely missed. Even when he disagreed, as was often, he opened the pages of his journal to that very disagreement. Howe could not allow himself to give up the socialist project. Indeed, he inexplicably reaffirmed it after having himself abandoned it years ago. But in his belief that it was the duty of the intellectual to articulate democratic values and to reject authoritarianism, he has left us a lasting legacy. Howe knew that the wave of the future was simply democracy and that to speak on behalf of its ideal could unite conservatives, liberals, and radicals. In a time of new beginnings, when the Cold War has ended and those on opposite sides of the fence are beginning to work together in a new framework and period, that is a legacy still worth cherishing.

3

Ian Williams

An Ex-Maoist Looks at an Ex-Trotskyist:

On Howe's Leon Trotsky

Ian Williams's first book, *The Alms Trade*, was published in 1989, and his second, *The UN for Beginners*, was published in 1995. He has also contributed to many other publications on politics and international affairs.

Born in Liverpool, he graduated from Liverpool University despite several years' suspension for protests against its investments in South Africa. His variegated career path includes a drinking competition with Chinese premier Chou En Lai and an argument on English literature with Chiang Ching, a.k.a. Mme. Mao. He eventually became a full-time labor-union official until the early 1980s, when he moved into full-time writing after winning a Nuffield Fellowship to study Indian unions.

In 1987 he was a speechwriter for U.K. Labour Party leader Neil Kinnock during the elections. He has been a regular contributor in Britain to the *Guardian*, the *Scotsman*, the *Sunday Herald*, the *Daily Telegraph*, the *Financial Times*, the *New Statesman*, the *European*, the *Observer*, and the *Independent*, of which he was one of the founding contributors.

Since 1980 he has lived in Manhattan, where he has written for on-line media such as *Alternet*, *Salon*, and the *Institute for War and Peace Reporting*; he has also been a columnist for the *New York Observer* and a contributor to the *Nation*, *Newsday*, *Dissent*, the *Wall Street Journal*, the *Village Voice*, *LA Weekly*, and *New York*. Internationally he has contributed to media across the world, from the *Jamaica Gleaner* and the *Jordan Times* to the *South China Morning Post* and the *Australian*. In addition to writing, he frequently comments on politics and world affairs on TV and radio outlets: ABC, CNN, BBC, ITN, CNBC, MSNBC, Fox, and so on.

A quarter of a century since he wrote it, Howe's biography of Trotsky raises far more questions than it can directly answer. How could a devoted democratic socialist describe a founder of the Bolshevik Party and thus of the Soviet state as "one of titans of the century," not least when the author also recognizes that Trotskyism is "without political or intellectual significance: a petrified ideology"?[1]

Outcast and unarmed, the prophet's strong residual attraction for someone as intellectually and politically rigorous as Howe bears scrutiny. Throughout this biography he is in a state of quantum indeterminacy about his subject, shifting from a state of intellectual criticism to one of emotional attachment, often in the same paragraph. We read detailed condemnation of the totalitarian state that Trotsky helped bring to birth, and of the failure of his political movement, and of his failed predictions, yet Howe interlards this with general superlatives about his subject's heroic virtues.

Howe is not alone in this. There is, it seems, a special romantic Trotsky in the hearts of a certain generation of the American Left in particular: a proto-Che, a revolutionary and man of action who was yet an intellectual and man of sensibility. It is a mythic construct, as befits a mythical figure, or perhaps, in this more sordidly commercial age, a spectacularly successful example of rebranding. In either case somehow the American Left has absolved Trotsky of any moral responsibility for the events in the Soviet Union after his exile and indeed tends to overlook his direct responsibility for the formation and, more important, the subsequent development of the Soviet regime.

Coming from Britain to the United States, one cannot help but be impressed, or rather somewhat depressed, by the influence of Trotskyism on the American Left. Admittedly the Left in much of the world is now hardly at the apogee of its influence, in contrast to the hopes many of us had at the fall of Berlin Wall, when we imagined a new promise for the core collectivist values of democratic socialism, untrammeled by the sordid reality of "actually existing socialism" of the East European variety.

But here in the United States it seems that Leon Trotsky's attempt to pass himself off as a democratic socialist was in large measure swallowed by the noncommunist Left. The Dewey Commission, headed by the philosopher John Dewey to examine the charges against Trotsky at the Moscow trials, established that the accusations were ridiculous but would perhaps have done better to go on to scrutinize Trotsky's own behavior in power. Although Dewey, according to Howe, had serious misgivings about the exile's democratic credentials for liberal sainthood, it would appear that many American socialists took the commission's report as a clean bill of political health for the exiled leader.

Within a few short years much of the noncommunist American socialist movement was deeply under the influence of the "Old Man"—what remained of it, that is, after his followers had joined the Socialist Party and their infectious polemical sectarianism had spread through it, splitting it into sects. As a result, instead of being a cluster of tiny cults breeding on the edge of a mass social-democratic party, as in Europe, in a sense "Trotskyism" in the United States killed the host and replaced it.

The Bolshevik exile joined the mainstream of American socialism, particularly among those intellectuals, such as Howe, who still kept the red flag fluttering from their ivory towers, and this certainly contributed to socialism losing its admittedly slender chance to enter the mainstream of American politics. For American workers and liberals the choice was between Communist-dominated activism and fervent loyalties to smaller and smaller sects dominated by and named after obscure political leaders in unconscious imitation of the Hasidic sects following East European rabbi families decades after the *shtetl* was gone: Pabloites, Shachtmanites, Mandelites, each wishing on the other the fate of the Amalekites. No wonder most of the natural constituency for social democracy chose to go with the Democrats.

However, even among those, often academics and intellectuals, who tried to keep alive the ideals of democratic socialism in America, Trotsky seemed to remain respectable when other manifestations of the Soviet "experiment" were beyond the pale. Although he himself sought sedulously to project himself as the pretender to the throne of Vladimir Ilyich temporarily occupied by Stalin, many of his admirers solipsistically cast him in their own image, whether anti-Soviet or democratic socialist.

The resilience of Trotsky's attraction is shown by the continued respect that even the neocons and others who began their political life in his movement feel for him, although they have left socialism behind. Howe's book, inadvertently, sheds some additional light on this conundrum: how people ranging from the tiniest and most fissured sects advocating world revolution and the impending downfall of capitalism to powerbrokers in the Reagan and Bush administrations—and staunch anti-Leninist social democrats in between—can still have mental icons of the Old Man hanging inside their skulls.

In Britain, by contrast, Trotskyist movements were peripheral to the Labour Party, buttressed as it was by a long tradition of indigenous socialism; spurning foreign models; and nurtured on unions, Fabianism, and Methodism. The cyclical Trotskyist attempts to infiltrate the Labour Party, usually through its youth movement, were regularly defeated. They made little or no impression in the unions, where indeed much of the burden of combating them was borne by the Communist Party, which had an industrial influence way beyond its membership. That was also why many on the left of the Labour Party tended to travel in parallel, if not necessarily in fellowship, with the Communist Party, since its union influence gave it some sway in the Labour Party, where unions had a block vote.

Even so, in Britain, with the intellectual and emotional support of a mass socialist tradition, it was entirely possible to be a radical left-wing socialist and yet to regard Trotsky, Lenin, and Stalin as cut from the same absolutist and totalitarian cloth.

Howe's biography of Trotsky reflects much of the American Left's ambivalence. His clarity and honesty continually bring him back to a recognition that Trotsky never renounced Leninism and that, in the end, the latter gave birth to Stalinism. But the intellect he brings to bear on this is blunted, one suspects because of Trotsky's appeal to the intellectuals, like Howe, rather than to the intellect.

Howe published the book in 1977, when Trotsky was important because, in effect, so many intellectuals thought he was. Even if Trotskyism and Trotskyists were of marginal importance to any meaningful political movement in the United States, the Soviet Union still stood, apparently strong, and in a bipolar world his views on the origins and development of the Bolshevik state system had relevance for socialists assessing means to the socialist future.

It also followed a period in which Howe was wrestling for the souls of younger socialists in the New Left, trying to prove to skeptical SDS revolutionaries that it was possible to be anti-Soviet and still a radical socialist. Although he did not pull his punches in those debates, it would not have helped to throw Trotsky, a Left icon, out with the Stalinist bathwater. In those days before the Reagan/Thatcher counterrevolution the achievements of social democracy in Western Europe were not the stuff to stir the blood of the young with hope. "The West is Red" was not a slogan to conjure with.

Indeed, by the time Howe wrote, Trotsky may have had a rival in Mao Zedong, but the latter, although an intellectual with some of the necessary romantic qualifications, suffered several disabilities. He had missed martyrdom and had hung around too long to be distanced from any "mistakes" in the Chinese system. Indeed, he was not Jewish! What is more, Mao was not part of the Western intellectual tradition that had formed Trotsky and Howe. "Somewhere in the orthodox Marxist there survived a streak of nineteenth-century ethicism, earnest and romantic," Howe claims, with the added advantage that Trotsky was "frank and courageous" in the face of power (5).

Howe introduces himself as still a socialist and admits to a "brief time" under "Trotsky's political influence," although in the forty years since "I have found myself moving farther and farther away from his ideas" (viii). So why was a social-democratic writer writing about an exiled Russian whose ideas he no longer espoused? Howe explains that Trotsky "remains a figure of heroic magnitude, and I have tried to see him with as much objectivity as I could summon" (viii). It was perhaps not enough.

Heroes were in demand both when Howe was growing up and when he wrote his biography. The intellectually voracious radical Jewish culture of the 1930s and '40s thought that ideas mattered and that they could change the world. Is it too far a stretch to remember that this was the milieu that gave birth to Superman and other comic-book superheroes? Lev Davidovich Bronstein, the Russian Jewish intellectual, may never have stepped into a phone booth like Clark Kent, but he did transform himself into a Colossus, bestriding the globe. This was surely in the mind of Howe, who was rediscovering his Jewish roots and had recently written *World of Our Fathers.*

It perhaps made marginally more sense to lionize Lev Bronstein than it did to cry when Stalin died, as some Jewish communists did—just before "Uncle Joe" was about to try for a second run at the Final Solution, by many accounts.

The era and the people also gave birth to science fiction writers such as the explicitly Marxist Futurians in New York, with writers like Frederick Pohl and Cyril Kornbluth, who ran dystopian thought experiments on society, and Isaac Asimov, who created a history of the future in broad galactic sweeps, reminiscent perhaps of Trotsky's depictions of the recent past. Big solutions, all-inclusive tidal waves of history, the certainty of true believers were all in the air in Howe's formative years.

Howe rhapsodizes, as enthralled by the man as he is disturbed by the result: "His personal fearlessness, his combination of firm political ends with tactical ingenuity, and his incomparable gifts as an orator helped to transform him, at the age of twenty-six, into a leader of the first rank: he had entered upon the stage of modern history and only the ax of a murderer would remove him" (20). It is interesting that one could write a short and entirely accurate encomium of Adolf Hitler in almost exactly the same vein, if one chose to eschew ethical judgment of the use of these singular talents and its consequences.

These occasional intrusions of hagiography into Howe's treatment perhaps highlight the path that many followers of the Old Man took to neo-conservatism, even if it is not a journey that Howe himself ever chose to take. They help explain why Trotsky remains a hero even for those who have abandoned his socialist ideas. Trotsky was an intellectual who was a man of action. He had fomented revolution; he had waged a war that looked romantic the farther away from it the observer was in space and time. He wrote about his own times and deeds with verve and with the broad brush of certainty that appeals to intellectuals haunted by quibbles and details. And what's more, he was dead, martyred. No wonder people like Howe could see the warts, describe them, and yet simultaneously paint them over.

However, Howe's hero never renounced the Bolshevik's methods, and he never seriously addressed, let alone apologized for, his own role in developing the totalitarian state that hounded him to his death. But it had begun its execution of opponents while he was one of its leaders. Indeed, in his arrogance Trotsky never explained quite why he had been so politically maladroit in his assessment of the trend in the party represented by Stalin and why the latter, whom he despised so roundly, so roundly defeated and ousted him.

"If there is a single text that supports those who believe Leninism and Stalinism to be closely linked or to form a line of continuous descent, it is *Terrorism and Communism*," Howe declares regretfully (74). He is clearly still not prepared to make the connection unequivocally in this biography. He deems it "perhaps profitless" to try to identify the precise time when "the revolutionary dictatorship of Lenin gave way to the totalitarianism of Stalin" (88). It is interesting that Howe himself is in effect distinguishing the two, when by then his general drift of political thought was rather to conflate them.

It is equally interesting that Howe's other great mentor was George Orwell, whose emphasis on an intellectual tradition, on democracy and decency, anticipated Howe's and was so much clearer, so much earlier, about this issue. Orwell, for example, took Arthur Koestler to task for his residual loyalty to the party "and a resulting tendency to make all bad developments date from the rise of Stalin," whereas "all the seeds of the evil were there from the start, and . . . things would not have been substantially different if Lenin or Trotsky had remained in control."[2]

Trotsky himself made the break with his past, says Howe, during the last decade of his life, when he "offered a towering example of what a man can be" (130). He adds, "A later generation . . . may be forgiven if it sees the issue of democracy as crucial and regards Trotsky's sustained critique of Stalinism as his greatest contribution to modern thought and politics" (121).

However, an even later generation could equally be forgiven for regarding as lacking and somewhat insubstantial any critique that sedulously avoids considering the roots of totalitarianism in the theory and practice espoused by the ruling party when Trotsky was one of its architects. *Terrorism and Communism* would have allowed him to be cast as Squealer as much as Snowball.

Accurate as his current allegations about Soviet practices may have been, Trotsky was far from the first to identify the regime's faults, and the absence of any hint of self-criticism could make it look like a Tweedledum-Tweedledee bout in which the only serious question was whether he or Stalin should be master.

In contrast, Howe's critique of Bolshevism is measured and analytical rather than bell-book-and-candling. He distinguishes between the freedom of internal debate among the original Bolsheviks under Lenin and in the later Stalinist and post-Leninist organization and so to some extent discounts the inevitability of what happens when a party of true believers becomes possessed of exclusive state power. Few, if any, of the sects that claimed to follow Trotsky showed overmuch toleration for dissent in their ranks, even if they, perhaps fortunately, never achieved state power to enforce their discipline. In fact the younger Trotsky was more astute than both Howe and the later Trotsky in foretelling the way that things would go when the Central Committee substituted itself for party, class, and state.

Howe recognizes this in a strangely muted way. In describing his subject's failures he says, "this is not to excuse the principled failure of Trotsky to raise the issue of multi-party socialist democracy, it is, at best, to explain it" (125). This is strange wording, since by all of Howe's normal standards the failure to raise such an issue was deeply *unprincipled.*

Where Howe went part of the road with the neocons in the early stages was in the strain of Trotskyism identified above all by anticommunism, or anti-Stalinism, developed by Max Shachtman, who took the Old Man's critiques of the Soviet system to new and higher levels of dissociation and whom Howe acknowledges as a major influence.

The followers of Shachtman and their neocon political progeny had little or no difficulty in seeing Communism and the Soviet Union not as some redeemable wayward revolution but as an absolute evil to be crusaded against. That proto-neocon passion against the Evil Empire reached a crescendo by the fall of the U.S.S.R., ironically almost putting retrospective truth in the Stalinist canards about Trotskyism's alliance with fascism, in light of neoconservative support for U.S. alliances with right-wing dictatorships against the greater enemy of Communism.

What did the neocons take from Trotsky? Certainly we know that politically they abandoned Trotskyism, in the sense of the revolutionary socialism that their hero would have considered his essence. However, there are strongly idiosyncratic characteristics of the Old Man and his movement that seem to be adoptable and transmittable even when pithed of their ideological core. As Howe, in his introduction, mentions, his hero's ideas "take on vibrancy only when set into their context of striving, debate, combat" (vi). As he points out, Trotsky's oratory earned "the dislike, even hatred, of many opponents because of what they saw as the polemical ruthlessness and arrogance of his style" (41).

We miss from this an appreciation that the later Howe had himself become one of those opponents, an advocate for democracy and openness, for democratic socialism as opposed to the burgeoning totalitarianism of Bolshevism, who would surely have been cast rhetorically into the dustbin of history by his subject, depicted here as a Leftist Rush Limbaugh.

However, no one who has had dealings with the various strains of Trotskyism in later years would have any difficulty in identifying this robustly unforgiving polemicism as an integral part of Trotskyist practice, even more so than that of their Stalinist antagonists.

Indeed, Howe reports that Trotsky in 1920 condoned "acts of repression that undercut whatever remnants there still were of 'Soviet democracy.' Worse yet he did all this with a kind of excessive zeal, as if to blot out from memory much of what he had said in earlier years" (70).

Trotskyism's obsession with the Soviet Union, its inability to shed the baggage of Bolshevism, led for decades to a strange sterile dialectic, all antithesis and no thesis, in which negative polemics and Talmudic exegesis of the Master's texts substituted for engagement with the realities of political and social life, with perhaps a penchant for infiltrating and suborning other political entities.

It is fascinating to see how that passion has survived the demise of its target. The "striving, debate and combat," the deep self-certainty of the Trotskyist sects, the polemics with no quarter, the eschewal of all thought of consensus and compromise as betrayal of the truth are recognizable characteristics of the neocons—and to some extent of neo-neocons such as Christopher Hitchens, who, like Howe, has Trotsky and Orwell as twin icons. Could it be some common thread of worry for politically motivated intellectuals, *un impuissance des clercs*, a feeling that, despite the aphorism, the pen usually wilts in the face of the sword?

However, so much negative passion demands a thoroughly unworthy opponent, and radical Islam seems to have provided the neocons with more than enough target for their redirected revolutionary ire now that they have lost their primary target. Ironically some at least of their cousins who stayed in the nominally socialist fold have equally eagerly acted as apologists for the Islamic states against "imperialism."

Howe recognizes the inherent idealism, in the Platonic sense, that Trotsky displays. Somewhat at odds with his own generally more approbatory treatment, he quotes approvingly Joel Carmichael's "shrewd" assessment of his subject: "It was no doubt his lofty—indeed in the philosophical sense 'idealist'—view of politics that made Trotsky misunderstand what was actually happening. . . . It astigmatized him, as it were, with respect to the power of the actual apparatus, and made him regard himself as Bolshevik paragon merely because of his identification with the Idea of the Party: he disregarded his failure to be identified with its personnel" (92).

Certainly it could be argued that the neocons inherited from Trotsky the passion for the importance of ideas, and of fighting for them, that that intoxication, transferred from the heady intellectualism and sectarianism of the sundered American socialist movement, has transformed American conservatism, which had previously tended more naturally to empiricist defenses of the status quo or to golden days.

Almost equally integral to Trotskyism was the ability to hold huge, inspiring, eloquent—and utterly wrong—"Ideas" and to hold on to them in the face of uncooperative reality. Even the levelheaded Howe treasured Trotsky's "heroic" ability to be stunningly wrong in a spectacular, albeit imaginatively attractive way. In dealing with his "boldest" theory, of Permanent Revolution, Howe asserts that "the full measure of its audacity can be grasped even today by anyone who troubles to break past the special barriers of Marxist vocabulary" (28). However, while Howe is mesmerized with the "brilliance" of Trotsky's historical prognosis, he goes on to admit that history neglected to follow the course so brilliantly laid out for it. Nor does the idea that a minority working class cannot bring about socialism seem that audacious in the light of the historical experience of so many failed statist pseudo-socialist experiments in the Third World.

Indeed, Howe admits that Trotsky "failed to anticipate the modern phenomenon of the totalitarian or authoritarian state, which would bring some of the features of permanent revolution into a socioeconomic development having some of the features of a permanent counter-revolution" (33). As failures go, this goes a long way. Howe is too kind when he concludes that "Trotsky's theory remains a valuable lens for seeing what has happened in the twentieth century—but a lens that needs correction" (33). A lens that fails so signally surely needs recasting and regrinding in its entirety.

Toward the conclusion of his biography Howe tempers his romantic attachment and becomes less uncritical, seeing his subject emerging as "a figure of greatness, but flawed greatness, a man great of personal courage and intellectual resources, but flawed in self recognition, in his final inability or refusal to scrutinize his own assumptions with the corrosive intensity he brought to those of his political opponents" (135).

More than a quarter of a century after Howe's biography, six decades after Trotsky's death, and ten years after the curtain came down finally on the Bolshevik experiment, things can be seen in a different light. Trotsky's role "on the stage of modern history" has shrunken into perspective. He lost the arguments in the Soviet Union: capitalism did not collapse catastrophically, the industrial proletariat in the world did not move to revolution. The reformers and social democrats he despised built societies that, even after Thatcherism and the Third Way, still offer workers more in the way of freedom, security rights, and prosperity than any other societies that have existed on the face of the earth.

Trotsky may not be in the "dustbin of history" to which he consigned his democratic-socialist opponents in the Leningrad Soviet (52), but he is now a bit player who exited, stage left, in a show that was a hit for a while but has now closed with no prospect of ever reopening. He is more reminiscent of Rosencrantz and Guildenstern than of Hamlet.

Ironically the only admirers of Trotsky to achieve any degree of power are the neocons, those who have joined with the world's biggest imperialist power to remake the world in some neoliberal capitalist image. It is an achievement, but it is a severely qualified one. Howe, who knew just how ineffectual the squabbling Trotskyist sects were—"not distinguished for an ability to engage in fresh thought politically, or reach the masses of workers practically" (191)—would be amazed, possibly even amused, if he were around to see the heights reached by his former comrades, even if one suspects he would think they were climbing the wrong mountain.

After all, once the socialism was stripped out, which was quite easily done in the face of popular indifference, what was left of Trotskyism but the failed predictions, the ability to hold a deep belief, with quasi-religious fervor, in a secular idea in the face of all advice and empirical evidence to the contrary? Having infiltrated the conservative movement, Trotsky's heirs, still an antithesis looking for a thesis to batter, have substituted Islam, or Islamic fascism, to fill the gap in their universe left by the disappearing Soviet Union.

They have a mission to remake the world, but instead of Trotsky's Red Army swooping to bring socialism to ungrateful Poles and Central Asians, it is now the U.S. military bringing democracy and free markets to lesser breeds hitherto without the law. And with the ruthless romanticism of the revolutionary, they think the price in blood is well worth paying, that history will absolve them.

Howe never succumbed to such temptations, retaining an attachment to socialism and democracy that eschewed such misplaced millennial visions. Somehow he contrives to admire the man while deploring his deeds; his philosophy; and, when it comes down it, most of his life work. But his uncharacteristic partial abandonment of his usual sharply critical spirit when it came to Lev Davidovich Bronstein—the Red intellectual who could, and briefly did—demonstrates the dangerous seductions of hero worship. It is difficult to steer a course between the Scylla of damnation and the Charybdis of canonization when dealing with historical figures, and if so rigorous a thinker as Howe steered so close to the rocks as he did with this biography, it is a warning to others to try harder for some objectivity.

Notes

1. Howe, *Leon Trotsky*, 193, 192. Subsequent references will appear in the text.

2. George Orwell, "Catastrophic Gradualism," in *Collected Essays of George Orwell* (Harmondsworth, U.K.: Penguin, 1970), 4: 5.

4

Samuel Hux

Our "Uncle Irving":

Howe's Conservative Strain

Samuel Hux attended the University of North Carolina at Chapel Hill and taught at the CUNY Graduate Center. He became acquainted with Irving Howe as a contributor to *Dissent*, for which he began writing in the 1970s. Hux has also contributed to *Modern Age* and other conservative publications. He calls himself "a socialist conservative," by which he means that he is conservative in temperament and a social democrat in his politics.

"Uncle Irving" . . . Or so my colleague Elaine Hoffman Baruch and I referred to Irving Howe—a private joke whose origins I have forgotten. Once at a *Dissent* editorial meeting, which I attended as a frequent contributor, a female member of the board objected to an essay by Baruch that Howe thought extraordinary (it failed some rad-fem test, as I recall): "I don't want to see anything else by that person in this magazine!" Howe cast me a quick apologetic glance, then said, "Now, Cynthia . . . no more of that." I suppose that might sound somewhat avuncular—but I think he was "Uncle" Irving because ordinarily he was not anyone's idea of mother's brother. Not that I endorse one popular image of Howe as insensitive and abrasive, wearing that "iron smile" Robert Lowell pasted on him in the poem "The New York Intellectual." Those who found him abrasive (at least in the years I knew him) knew only the public, polemical Howe, in which role he could be devastating. In fact Irving could be quite *courtly*, although I think he would have bristled at the suggestion.

For a while I was a neighbor of the Malcolm Cowleys, then in their eighties; Irving asked that I pass on his best regards. I saw Mrs. Cowley at the market and did just that. "Oh, he's *such* a gentleman," she said. "Do you know that the last time I saw Irving he told me my dress was the most beautiful he'd ever seen?" Well, I suppose it's not too difficult to charm an elderly woman who, incidentally, once was a fashion critic. But I found it fascinating to observe Irving's demeanor toward another octogenarian lady one evening, the widow of one of his close friends: gentle, solicitous, and *protective*, fearing overzealous attention to a distinguished and brave woman (an American courier for the anti-Nazi Austrian underground). I was fascinated because the first time I met Irving Howe he struck me as incredibly awkward.

In 1972 I mailed *Dissent* an essay on some higher-education matter. He phoned: not for us, but would you like to meet at a delicatessen and discuss another possibility? I was on time and found Howe already there, pacing back and forth on the sidewalk. He was pleasant enough as long as we were discussing the subject at hand, but when that was settled before the spartan repast was finished, I felt he couldn't wait to be gone: my questions or comments on whatever else was on my mind received the briefest of answers or responses, a sort of metaphorical drumming of fingers on the table, and in a few minutes I was as eager to escape as he was. Many years later, when I saw him at the ballet one evening (a very regular occurrence), we talked about the program until he'd said what he had to say and saw that I had too and then, seeing his wife beckoning, walked away without a by-your-leave. (A couple of weeks later he was profusely apologetic.) But by this time I knew him well enough to take no offense. He was the busiest man I have ever known. One of his associates remarked in a eulogy that "often he managed to slight a friend without knowing it." Rudeness? Perhaps. But a surprising and deep innocence, I judge.

Irving's was a formidable intellect. He was more than a little frightening, he could make one nervous—and I think he was sometimes nervous in response to the nervousness he didn't know he generated. Sometime in the late 1970s he read a paper on George Eliot at a conference at the CUNY Graduate Center sponsored by my college and organized by Elaine Baruch. His paper presented, he sat on the stage while the other speaker, a beautiful young scholar, read hers. He paid absolute attention but hunched forward in his chair, twirling his glasses. The young woman grew more and more nervous, repeated sentences, stumbled verbally—a painfully embarrassing performance. At lunch afterward Irving wondered what was wrong with her since she had a worthy essay. I answered, "Irving, you scared her to death." He clearly did not believe me.

I imagine that by now the reader may be thinking: All well and good, but why, might I ask, a testimonial to a socialist from a cultural conservative? Well, the answer to that question is the subtext of this essay. But to make that answer clear I'm going to have to be a little rude myself (not innocently so) and violate the ethics of the encomiast by talking about myself as well as about my subject. After all, it is only by virtue of his impact upon me that he becomes my subject. That is, I have to take myself as seriously as I take Irving Howe, or as seriously as he took me . . . or rather, almost. He once called me "brilliant" (behind my back). With no false modesty, I know that's undeserved; I know the difference between smart and brilliant. But I'll be pleased until the day I die that he thought highly enough of me to bother to exaggerate. He occasionally praised what he called (to my face, or rather, in correspondence) my "Huxian insights." But he occasionally was critical of my "Huxian voice," which always frustrated me, for I thought (something I never told him) that my polemical style was a reflection of his; in any case I early on, before I met him, chose him as a model. And after I met him I would often find when writing an essay that I was imagining it as a conversation with Irving: he was my "designated reader," so to speak. And often when reading something of his I thought, "I know exactly where you are going." This was partly because of his lucidity but partly, I thought, because our modes of thinking were akin (which of course is a different matter from having the same ideas). So I was stunned when he wrote me once that "people often praise conversational prose, but really conversational prose is hard to read."

I don't want to exaggerate my closeness to Irving. Only with qualification can I say, "He was my friend." I knew him well. He did not know me anywhere nearly so well. That's only as it should be. I am scarcely an egalitarian demanding reciprocity. We lunched together perhaps three times, and there were maybe as many parties. We ran into each other at cultural events and conferences. But the relationship was primarily professional, intellectual: editorial correspondence and phone calls, *Dissent* meetings. Nonetheless, his impact on me was profound, and I will regret as long as I live that we were not closer than we were.

I knew *of* Irving Howe, of course, long before that delicatessen conference in 1972. Sometime in the late 1950s I drove from Chapel Hill, North Carolina, where I was a student, to Durham on some forgotten errand and ended up in a tobacconist's shop that also stocked newspapers, pornographic magazines, and . . . *Dissent* (nothing else, no other journals at all). Intrigued, I bought it and thus first encountered Irving Howe. The first book of his I read was not *Politics and the Novel*, which introduced him to so many people, but probably his least-known work, *The UAW and Walter Reuther* (with B. J. Widick); the second was *The American Communist Party: A Critical History* (with Lewis Coser). Howe was for me, that is, a social critic and historian who incidentally also wrote literary criticism, which I caught up with later in graduate school and as a young faculty member:

Politics and the Novel, William Faulkner, and so on, and the essays, which would be collected in *A World More Attractive, Steady Work, Decline of the New,* and others. Even today, when thinking of Howe, I'm as likely to recall his political scholarship, like *Leon Trotsky* and *Socialism and America,* as I am to reflect upon the literary; and I'm certain that his greatest work was social history, *World of Our Fathers,* and that his second greatest was of the same genre, for *A Margin of Hope: An Intellectual Autobiography* is the portrait of a distinctive world as much as it is memoir.

I took a degree in literature only because I thought I'd be better at it than at the history I was more interested in or the philosophy I loved more. I imagined a career of teaching what I thought I'd teach best and writing on whatever interested me or engaged my affection, and as a writer I wished to be an essayist rather than a specialist writing for others in his field. But I was terribly innocent about the specialist demands that would be made in the profession, and when I discovered them, I began to admire Howe even more as a man who refused to specialize and even made a success of that refusal. I also refused. But unless one is blessed with Howe's enormous energy and his genius for time management, churning out essays in literary criticism followed by political polemics followed by philosophical reflections followed by historical speculations and so on, while never carving out a recognizable niche, is no prescription for academic stardom. I could then say that Howe's example, which few are capable of emulating, had a negative impact upon me; but I don't regret it for a moment.

I should add to the penultimate sentence above: unless one is blessed with Howe's talent. I'm not sure he was a great critic, but he was an excellent, *strong* critic, and his strength lay partly in his avoidance of all critical fashions and schools. If he had a method, it was the challenge recommended by T. S. Eliot: be very intelligent and sensitive. And I would recommend to today's obsessive "methodists," the deconstructionists and post-whatnots, with their immense and unearned philosophic pretensions, a reading of Howe's posthumous *A Critic's Notebook,* where one finds a man with no such pretensions at all (he once told me he thought he was philosophically tone-deaf—which he wasn't) examining the inner nature of fiction with an extraordinary phenomenological care. There is a logic to Howe's last work being a series of *pensées* on fiction (or *shtiklakh* as he called them— "morsels"), for his literary criticism was overwhelmingly devoted to novels, both in periodical essays and reviews and in books (Sherwood Anderson, Faulkner, Thomas Hardy). But I thought his rare efforts in the criticism of poetry, a genre he's hardly associated with, were the equal of his fiction criticism; and what characterized one characterized the other: a respect for the aesthetic, but with a loyalty to the historical, a conviction that criticism is a moral discipline, and an allergy to cant.

Howe was of course a political partisan, but his literary criticism was never a vehicle for special pleading. Nor was his criticism of historical texts and memoirs: he drew a firm line between his polemical pieces and his reviews of politically charged books for which he had scant sympathy. He did not disguise where he stood, but what he demanded from the subject were matters of tone, honesty, and coherence. And happily for reader and often for subject, he failed to draw a firm line between his critical approach to creative literature and to the nonfictional. That is, for a man who knew so well the difference between history and literature, his nonliterary criticism is very literary: "Toward the end, Whittaker Chambers seems to have gone a little mad. It is not hard to understand why, and if one brings to life a fraction of the imaginativeness we all so devoutly accord to literature, it is even possible to sympathize with his condition." A man deserves, surely, the same attention we'd give a text (especially since: "That Whittaker Chambers told the truth and Alger Hiss did not, seems to be highly probable"). I could discuss Howe on other historical subjects: his "T. E. Lawrence: The Problem of Heroism," for instance, is the best introduction to that figure I know of; I have tactically alluded to Whittaker Chambers instead as a kind of ironic transition to all that now follows. For it was Chambers who explained to William Buckley, "I am not a conservative. . . . I am a man of the Right."

I want to make a proposal about which I am serious only within strict limits, by which I am being intentionally provocative (which habit is one of Howe's legacies), and for which Irving would probably curse me: Irving Howe as conservative. I don't mean the kind of charge that always irritated Irving, made by New Leftists, Marxist ideologues, and the occasional *marxisant* pisher, that he was "moving to the Right," was a "mere" social democrat unlike the more courageous Big Thinkers of the Left. I mean . . . well, we'll see what I mean.

The first essay I wrote for *Dissent*, a direct consequence of that 1972 delicatessen conference, was entitled "Liberal Education and Radical Values" (Fall 1972). Its argument was Irving's as much as mine: that the with-it Left's whoring after "relevance" and disregard for the cultural tradition of the West not only made for a poor education but was a condescending insult to the minority and working-class students the radicalized professors professed to be so concerned about. As I reread it I find really very little that would have made it inappropriate for submission to a journal like *Modern Age* had I known at the time what my political philosophy *really* was. I knew there were conservatives I admired, and there were more I grew to admire during the 1970s: Michael Oakeshott, for instance, whom I was inspired to read by an appreciative essay by Hanna Fenichel Pitkin in (ironically) *Dissent*. But there were conservatives my mentor Uncle Irving admired, and he *knew* what his political philosophy really was. Howe's kindly feelings toward *traditionalist* conservatives are documented (see *A Margin of Hope*, 225–27): Clinton Rossiter, Russell Kirk, and especially Peter Viereck. Still, he could be impatient with them as well: in a letter to me he referred to Kirk's thought and disposition dismissively as "georgics." (To be fair, this was probably in part a function of Irving's incorrigible urbanism: another time he wrote me that "the city is in my blood, like a poison.")

I submitted nothing else to *Dissent* for a few years (although I read everything of Howe's that came out); I was having some difficulty judging my professed socialism in the light of my growing conservative urges. One result of a kind of dialogue with myself was an essay in *Moment* in 1978, "Confessions of a Socialist Conservative," in which I argued that a *temperamental* conservatism was perfectly consistent with a profession of social democracy and confided that "it doesn't seem to me that mainline political conservatism [I really meant the Republican Party] is very temperamentally conservative." Irving saw that essay and invited another contribution to *Dissent*, and there began a fairly intense relationship with that journal that lasted for seven or eight years, until it more or less petered out in the late 1980s, by which time I was beginning to *feel* in my soul what I already knew intellectually: that a profound distrust of capitalism did not necessitate one's being a socialist.

In Irving's "invitation" he remarked, "If you had a sense of the Left a little richer than you seem to, you'd know that the tradition from which people like myself come, though it was disastrously mistaken and worse on many counts, nevertheless did share with serious conservatives a feeling for the past, a respect for inherited culture." I was a little miffed by the first clause because I thought my early contribution to *Dissent* showed just that rich sense and because the continuation of the sentence quoted above was in fact one theme of that 1972 piece: "we said that we wanted that tradition to be made accessible to everyone, not just the rich." In any case my temperamental conservatism was acceptable in a contributor: "It's OK with me if you come out in behalf of conservative values as long as you attack [in a symposium entitled 'Against the Neoconservatives'] what are now called conservative politics."

Now of course Irving's acceptance of my temperamental or cultural conservatism and his resistant admiration of some more thoroughgoing types do not make him a "conservative." Rather, it was his *own* cultural conservatism that inspires me to risk that identification.

There is the matter of his taste and inclinations: for all his writing on "modernism" and "postmodernism," those tastes were admirably "retrograde"—his preference for nineteenth-century novels (or twentieth-century ones that leaned in that direction) and admiration for old-fashioned and out-of-fashion poets like Edwin Arlington Robinson.

There is the fact that so much of his work was that of the *conservateur.* He was an eloquent and always reliable defender of the Western cultural heritage throughout his busy career, especially against the countercultural idiocy of the 1960s and more recently against "political correctness" and "multicultural" tribalism (for instance, "The Value of the Canon," collected in Paul Berman's *Debating P.C.*). Even when he wrote about, or for, "progressive" causes like socialism he fell naturally into a kind of unprogressive mode, always testing his own views against the classical works and history of that tradition (as it was to him), about which he was immensely learned and which he was intent upon protecting from the more ignorant looters of the Left. As editor and translator for three and a half decades and four collections, he tried to insure that Yiddish literature not vanish with the language; as historian he tried to insure that "the world of his father" survived in memory.

And there is the matter of small gestures, habits, personal style that could be evoked only through an anthology of anecdotes and that I will sum up as moral and intellectual good manners.

Now, really, I understand that none of this makes Howe a conservative in any popularly understood sense. And knowing that Irving would not like this identification at all, I'll now drop it—but only to ask a question.

Before getting to that question, however, it may be of interest to consider why Irving would not like this identification, aside from the obvious fact that "socialist" was good enough for him, for I think there's something beyond the obvious. He found a *National Review* caricature of him as a nineteenth-century figure out of touch with the modern, to which I alerted him, "a great comedy"—but I'm certain he wouldn't find my remarks amusing. While *conservative* could be a term of respect for Irving when he was referring to men like Rossiter, Kirk, and Viereck, whom he called "civilized and moderate men," the courtesy was not extended to the more capitalistically oriented conservatives whom he judged ascendant and more populous. Then again, the putative conservatives he knew best, I mean from personal experience, were his ex-colleagues, the "neoconservatives" whom he considered "frantic ideologues with their own version of P.C., the classics as safeguard for the status quo"—and he worried about *their* ascendancy. So out of respect for Irving's sensibilities I'll modify my identification of him with this compromise: he had his strong traditionalist side.

Now . . . suppose we were talking about someone who shared Howe's cultural values and disposition; who was not, however, a famous old soldier of the Left; yet who held economic views similar to his. What were those views? Once he shed the orthodox Marxism of his Trotskyist youth and passed through the somewhat vaguely defined socialist values of his middle age, he began to identify with the "market socialism" of the Glasgow economist Alec Nove (*The Economics of Feasible Socialism*), whose "feasible socialism" is not greatly different in spirit and nuance from, and is substantially akin in desired outcome to, my beloved Chesterton's distributism (which proposition could be a subject for an essay itself). Would you be comfortable calling that someone a conservative? I would. I'd have far less difficulty than in so honoring that foreigner to "the politics of prudence," Newt Gingrich, who may be a man of the Right but who is a conservative I don't know how, unless someone has invented the category of "cybercon," and who must be the sort of "conservative" who leads that Hungarian American Tory John Lukacs (in *Confessions of an Original Sinner*) to distance himself as a "reactionary." And I have much less trouble with my imaginary figure than I have with our friends the libertarians/right-wing anarchists/anarcho-capitalists, who in their profound distrust of government seem willing to accept the highly *un*conservative dys-culture that an unpoliced capitalism would be likely to engender.

In October 1987 I took part in the written "Symposium on Humane Socialism and Traditional Conservatism" in *New Oxford Review* along with fourteen others, including John Lukacs and Russell Kirk. Kirk referred to the anarcho-capitalists—as was his wont—as "ideologues of solipsism." Lukacs wrote that "*all* of the important conservative thinkers of the last 200 years have been anti-materialist and therefore, by definition, anti-capitalist." But we all know, don't we, that most Americans, not to say most conservatives, identify conservatism with enthusiasm for capitalism. And we all know, or ought to, that conservatives have often facilitated that misidentification, although, as David Frum has written recently of Russell Kirk, "As long as he lived, by word and example he cautioned conservatives against over-indulging their fascination with economics." Then Frum concludes, "He taught that conservatism was above all a *moral* cause: one devoted to the preservation of the priceless heritage of Western civilization." Which is what Irving Howe was about.

That *New Oxford Review* symposium was an invitation to the kind of dialogue—people left and right who fear the cultural and social consequences of corporate giantism—that is implicit in Eugene Genovese's recent *The Southern Tradition*. I sent a copy to Irving—and that was the only correspondence from me he never acknowledged. I don't *know* why, but I suspect why. So again, I'm not really going to try to induct Irving posthumously.

Nonetheless, he helped me find my way to my own conservatism. A more direct route, the Southern way Genovese writes about, was blocked for me by the racial politics that obscured those virtues Genovese is now excavating; and in the Chapel Hill of my youth I don't recall any professor ever talking about the Agrarians, whose ideas ("rural distributism," as it were) make more and more sense to me every year.

To say Irving helped me find my way involves two questions: *how* he helped me and *what* I found. The *how*: that's largely implicit in all I've said so far, and I hope that the narrative speaks as well as some belabored explanation would. But it is partly that, as I've confessed already, when I wrote I found that often I was imagining a dialogue with Irving; he was my "designated reader," although I should have said "designated contestant," for my imaginary dialogues were more often than not arguments. The *what*: I am a conservative, but I would be quite uncomfortable calling myself a man of the Right: there seem to be so many unconservative people there, just as there are so many illiberal people on the Left. I read and hear much about a "culture war" going on in this nation, but because of the example of Irving Howe I cannot buy the notion that the warriors fall neatly to the left and right. This is important to me because I think that (for all the obvious interdependence) culture is ultimately vastly more important than economics. And because I knew Irving, no one will ever convince me that a "cybercon" lecturing about "revolution" (without the sense of tradition to say "counter-") and his followers, self-designated "bomb throwers," are my friends while some people I used to be associated with are not.

One last matter. Some years ago a Burkean friend asked me if I were still a socialist. "I'm too conservative to change," I replied. Well, I wasn't *that* conservative, but Irving was. Of course there's one change we all must face, and I sorely miss Irving's presence on this earth. When he died I somehow misheard the location of his memorial service, showed up at the wrong place, and never got to say good-bye. I have been wanting to pay my respects ever since.

5

Marshall Berman

Irving and the New Left:
From Fighter to Leader

Marshall Berman: born, Bronx NY; displaced by Cross-Bronx Expressway; NY public schools; Columbia (Lionel Trilling, Steven Marcus, Daniel Bell, Peter Gay, Jacob Taubes, Susan Sontag); Oxford (Isaiah Berlin, James Joll, Iris Murdoch, Norman Birnbaum); Harvard (Mike Walzer, Judith Shklar, Barrington Moore, Stanley Hoffmann); New Left, especially movement against Vietnam War; tear gas, arrest, overall sense of pride—"my generation stopped an imperial war"; taught since 1967 at CCNY and CUNY, distinguished professor since 2001; visiting professor at Stanford, New Mexico, Harvard; author, *The Politics of Authenticity* (1971), *All That Is Solid Melts into Air: The Experience of Modernity* (1982, 1988), *Adventures in Marxism* (1999); working on new book, *One Hundred Years of Spectacle: Metamorphoses of Times Square*; dozens of articles on culture and politics, on New York and urbanism; helped write and appeared on PBS documentary *History of New York* (1999, 2001); worked on editorial board of *Dissent* since circa 1980.

I first met Irving in 1965, after he had invited me to expand a letter to *Dissent* into an article—I thought, "Once in a lifetime, how can I go wrong?" We met for coffee at one of Broadway's many vanished cafeterias. Irving liked what I wrote, was personally very nice (he even gave me a Ninety-second Street "Y" ticket that he couldn't use for the great Yiddish poet Glatstein), but he couldn't seem to stop hectoring me and "my generation": he said, You've all grown up all wrong. I had grown up on *Dissent*, so I felt pretty let down.

The late 1960s were not good years for *Dissent*. The editors seemed more upset about kids at antiwar demos carrying Vietcong flags than about

American bombs ravaging Vietnam. I thought Irving and his intimates had wholly lost the sense of balance and proportion that they were always (quite rightly) urging on others. I even let my student subscription (was it two dollars?) lapse. I did what I had to do—tear gas, court appearances, and so on—but I felt sad.

Then, in 1971 or so, Irving published a piece about the New Left and "the crisis of civilization." It argued something like this: Now that the New Left is safely dead, we can admit what it and we had in common. Indeed, we can even admit the ways in which it surpassed us. New Leftists were like the best Russian intellectuals of Dostoevsky's day: their politics, even when misdirected, was part of a passionate search for meaning in life; we tended to act as if all questions of meaning had been decided already. We were wrong, he said, and the social democracy of the future will have to incorporate the quest for meaning into its politics if it is to stay alive.

I called Irving up, told him how moved I was by his piece, how great I thought it was, how I wanted to stay in touch. Then, as often, he was embarrassed by naked emotional display, but he said he was glad I had called, and "now maybe you can write for us again." In 1978 he gave me what I knew was an unusual amount of time and space for a long *Dissent* piece, on Marx and modernism, which ever since that moment has played a central role in my life.

Irving Howe often drove me crazy, but he also inspired me. He stood up for the best human values at times when hardly anybody did. And he reached out and stood up for me. I'll always be grateful, and I hope I can always keep on giving back.

The hymns of praise that followed Irving's death overlooked one of his most special qualities: his capacity to change and grow at a time of life— his fifties and sixties—when most people stagnate or shrink. But we can't appreciate his growth without facing some of his other qualities that needed to be outgrown. I want to focus on Irving in the late 1960s and early 1970s: before he grew and after.

Before he outgrew, Irving acted out, and some of his most extravagant acting out was aimed at my generation. In 1965 he brought out an essay called "New Styles in Leftism," an assault on the New Left. Before and after it ran in *Dissent*, he went on tour and gave it as a lecture at colleges around the country (I heard it at Harvard in the spring and at the New School in the fall). This talk drew big crowds and strong responses; talk reached the shouting level within a couple of minutes and stayed that way for hours; people screamed at and denounced old allies, felt betrayed, discovered that they couldn't work together after all. Irving claimed to be speaking on behalf of sober rationality, but in fact he was striking deep emotional chords and raising the temperature of political discourse to a frenzy. (Events soon drove the fever even higher, but he did more than his share to keep it up.) His essay is commonly and correctly listed as an opening salvo in the great American "culture wars" that still rage on today.

"New Styles in Leftism" says two things: (1) the New Left is wrong to be obsessed with style; (2) the New Left has THE WRONG STYLE. Thesis one was absolutely right. Obsession with *echt*-radical style often estranged us from our deepest values: people who were really kindred spirits tore each other to pieces over how they dressed and danced and what they smoked and over who was really "truly radical," to the amusement of the *mamzers* who ran the world. But Irving seemed not only to lose touch with insight number one but to become the sort of person he unmasked, a man obsessed with style. He seemed complacently happy in a world of thesis two, where only people with THE RIGHT STYLE were allowed to play. For the next few years *Dissent* seemed to care more about somebody flying a Vietcong flag at a mass antiwar demonstration than about what American guns and bombs were actually doing to Vietnam. This struck me as tragic, rather than just dumb, because Irving was so smart, and his own insight into thesis one should have skewered all the varieties of thesis two, including the ones he seemed to embrace. I kept up my student subscription, but *Dissent* was hard to read. I remember saying, bitterly, that it should be renamed "The Joy of Sects."

But then Irving outgrew and overcame. In the October 1971 *Dissent* he published an essay called "What's the Trouble? Social Crisis, Crisis of Civilization, Both?" A clunky title, a complex piece, not reducible to sound bites, never reprinted, but maybe the best thing he ever wrote. Here, instead of dissing the New Left and the counterculture, as he had done for years, Irving tried to locate us in modern history's long waves. The mood of "What's the Trouble?" is reflective rather than polemical. If there is any polemic in it, it is directed at unnamed people in Irving's own circle "who, in the name of plebeian solidity, minimize[d] the significance of the new youth styles" and who thought the late-1960s counterculture was "unique to disoriented or spoiled middle-class youth." Against them Irving insists not only on the pervasiveness of youth rebellion—yes, even in the working class—but on its seriousness: "There are overwhelming cultural or pseudocultural experiences shared by the young of all classes, certainly more so than in any previous society. Movies, rock music, drugs . . . increasingly do create a generational consciousness that, to an undetermined extent, disintegrates class lines."

This idea—that mass media and drugs could shape consciousness and disintegrate class identities—would have been commonplace (indeed, would not even have been noticed) in a paper like the *Village Voice*. But when Irving said it in the very different context of *Dissent*, he was addressing a founders' generation then in its fifties and sixties and pointing out "overwhelming experiences" that it was refusing to face. He was arguing very hard not only against his readers' grain but (note that verbal emphasis, "increasingly *do* create") against his own.

Back then there were several older intellectuals out there who insisted on the primacy of mass media in contemporary life: Marshall McLuhan, Leslie Fiedler, Susan Sontag, Charles Reich, Herbert Marcuse. But their angle was that "the kids," the younger generation that had grown up on television, were uniquely whole, free human beings, liberated from the hang-ups of the literate (as in, "The kids don't need Shakespeare and Freud," etc., etc.). Irving was as scornful of this *narishkeit* as he was of the hate campaigns against "the kids" whipped up by the Nixon White House.

He argued that the youthful extravagances of the 1960s showed not that "the kids" were out of the civilized mainstream but precisely that they were *in* the mainstream: "Some of the more spectacular symptoms of disaffection we are now witnessing ought to be taken not as historical novelties revealing the special virtue or wickedness of a new generation, but as tokens of that continuity of restlessness and trouble that comprises the history of Western consciousness since the late 18th century."

Irving then discusses the modern welfare state. A state like this, he says, is not only a triumph of state-building but an achievement of "Western consciousness" and a great leap forward in human history. But even at its best, he says—and the United States is a long way from its best— a welfare state inevitably undercuts itself. This is because it is unstable enough to encourage the militant arousal of previously silent groups; the intensification of political discontents; and the reappearance, if in new and strange forms, of those tormenting "ultimate questions" with which modern man has beset himself for a century and a half. That these "ultimate questions" as to man's place in the universe, the meaning of his existence, the nature of his destiny now come to us in modish or foolish ways is cause for impatience or polemic. But we would be dooming ourselves to a philistine narrowness if we denied that such questions do beset human beings, that they are significant questions, and that in our moment there are peculiarly urgent reasons for coming back to them.

Suddenly Irving had shifted and deepened the focus of political thought to explore "those tormenting ultimate questions" about "the meaning of existence." We all must face those questions, he says, and ask—in the words of the great nineteenth-century Russian writers and in Irving's own italics—

"*How shall we live?*" At the climax of this essay Irving highlights Dostoevsky and his meditation on the idea of "The Golden Age": it can never be realized in the world, yet without it everyday life in the world can mean nothing at all. At the essay's end Irving insists that "the effort to force men into utopia leads to barbarism." But then at the *very* end he affirms that "to live without the image of utopia is to risk the death of the imagination."

This essay marked a creative breakthrough. Irving had spent years fighting the New Left, which was even more furious in its own fighting; but now that the New Left had eaten itself up and clearly wasn't coming back, Irving not only could see how valuable our movement had been but could say what it ultimately *meant* in greater clarity and depth than any of us had ever been able to. The New Left came into being not to promote a lifestyle but to confront the most urgent spiritual question, *How shall we live?* In the New Left's early days that was clear to many of us. (See the 1962 SDS Port Huron Statement.) But amid the war, the riots, the splits, the assassinations, "the tormenting ultimate questions" that brought our movement to life got buried in the mess our lives became. It wasn't just that Irving was reminding us why *we* were out there; he was generous enough to admit that we had reminded him of why *he* was out there. True, he could only see the light after our star died; but it was impressive that he could see it and say it at all. As the New Left disintegrated, Irving grasped its deepest drive and reason for being, and he internalized that drive and that reason and made them his own. He overcame the spiritual complacency that drove his 1960s life as a hit man and grew into a spiritual urgency that gave him new substance and depth.

"What's the Trouble?" is not only a fusion of deep thinking and deep feeling but a brilliant speech-act, a rich and complex work of communication. It helped transform *Dissent* from a sectarian base into an open political and cultural space, where democratic socialists who really meant it and survivors of the New Left—the Slightly Used Left, I used to call us then—could talk and listen and think and learn from each other, and have arguments without walking out, and imagine a golden age. It lifted Irving from a fighter to a leader.

6

Alexander Cockburn

Irving Howe, R.I.P.:

A Few Tasteless Words

Journalist and editor Alexander Cockburn is best known as a left-wing
political journalist and regular columnist for the *Nation*.

The slush about Irving Howe is ankle deep.

Tributes following his death [in May 1993] appeared in the *New York
Times* (Michael Weinstein, the salesman of "managed competition"; also
Leon Wieseltier); the *New Republic*; *Newsday*; the *New Yorker*; and the
Nation itself, by Ted Solotaroff ("He leaves the air vivid around him, in
Stephen Spender's words, signed with his honor"). This is not to mention
a column on Howe in the *Washington Post* by E. J. Dionne, surely the most
overrated political commentator of the late twentieth century, except for
Sid Blumenthal, Joe Klein, Michael Kramer, Mark Shields, and Charles
Krauthammer, who, be it noted, is *against* intervention in Bosnia.

Howe's prime function, politically speaking, in the last thirty years of
his life was that of policing the Left on behalf of the powers that be.

A glance at the obits tells the whole story. In the 1960s Howe "was . . .
denouncing the violent, authoritarian strains of the New Left" (Weinstein).
"About the authoritarian tendencies of the New Left, and the shabbiness
of many of its notions, nobody was more withering" (Wieseltier). "Howe
rejected the New Left cults of youth and expressive violence in the '60s,
the cults of Castro and Ho Chi Minh and Mao" (Dionne). "He vigorously
scolded the student Left for its intellectual laziness, authoritarian arrogance
and occasional barbarism" (Clarence Page, *Chicago Tribune*). Get the idea?

In other words, Howe was an assiduous foot soldier in the ideological Cointelpro campaign to discredit vibrant political currents electrifying
America and supporting liberation movements in the Third World, the only

significant general mobilization of a Left in the United States in the second half of the twentieth century. One of Howe's particular contributions was promulgation of the libel on the New Left, or "the Campus Left," as he affected to call it, as enemies of Israel and, ergo, anti-Semites. In 1984 Howe successfully organized the denial of endorsement of Jesse Jackson's candidacy in the primaries by the Democratic Socialists of America. In 1988 he tried again but failed.

In his later years he would be wheeled onto the op-ed pages to announce what "the Left" thought of Dukakis or Clinton, but by that time his prime sociological significance was as a magnet for money from the MacArthur Foundation. As Josh Muravchik, probably a Shachtmanite like Howe, and his one-time coeditor Carl Gershman once pointed out in an entertaining piece, the chances of an American receiving a MacArthur genius award are about a million to one. Become a member of the editorial board of *Dissent*, and the odds are ten to one. Judge the man by his epigones, for example, Paul Berman, who, being a certified MacArthur genius, presumably knows how to write the words "thank you." In the May 24 issue of the *New Yorker* Berman wrote an unsigned editorial about Carlo Tresca and Manuel de Dios Unanue, both journalists gunned down in New York, fifty years apart. Berman lamented anarchist Tresca's obscurity and referred to a small gathering held last March to memorialize him on the fiftieth anniversary of his death. But while he displayed detailed knowledge of Tresca, he found no occasion to mention the major source on Tresca, Dorothy Gallagher's biography, published in 1988, *All the Right Enemies: The Life and Murder of Carlo Tresca*.

Contrast Howe's unappetizing curriculum with the honorable career of Dave Dellinger, whose fine autobiography was just published and who, unlike Howe, has been a positive force down these tumultuous years.

7

Joseph Epstein

The Old People's Socialist League

A master of both the familiar and the literary essay, Joseph Epstein is also well-known as a provocative social critic. In 1997 Epstein stepped down as editor of the *American Scholar*, which he had edited for more than two decades. Epstein is known for his accomplished writing style and subtle wit. His characteristic self-portrayal in his essays is that of an ingenuous and often befuddled bystander.

Like Irving Howe, Epstein is a strong admirer of contemporary Russian and East European anti-Soviet critics. Nonetheless, although Epstein wrote for *Dissent* in the 1960s (and even introduced *The New Conservatives*, a 1974 *Dissent* collection edited by Howe and Lewis Coser), he occasionally became a vocal critic of Howe's politics by the 1980s, as the following negative assessment of Howe's career evinces.

> A wonderful man, Irving Howe. He's done so much for Yiddish literature and for me. But he's not a youngster any more, and still, still with this socialist meshugas. – Isaac Bashevis Singer, television interview, 1981

All things considered, the literary critic and political intellectual Irving Howe is having a good afterlife. Since his death in 1993 his reputation, at least in certain quarters, seems only to have grown greater. Every so often one reads a worshipful word about him in the *New Yorker* or the *New Republic* or the *New York Times Book Review*. In a recent book, *Achieving Our Country*, the philosopher Richard Rorty comes very near to apotheosizing Howe, ranking his essays with those of George Orwell and Edmund Wilson; praising "his incredible energy and his exceptional honesty"; and closing with the thought that, although "Howe would have loathed being called a warrior-saint, . . . this term does help catch one of the reasons he came to play the role in many people's lives which Orwell did in his."

And then there is the documentary film *Arguing the World.* This film chronicles the undergraduate careers of four New Yorkers—Irving Kristol, Nathan Glazer, Daniel Bell, and Howe—and follows their political peregrinations since college days. In it Howe seems to appear on-screen more than any of the others and to be talked about more admiringly; the last word is his; and, by virtue of the fact that he traveled the least far from his early political radicalism, he is subtly made to seem the hero of the story.

Howe is usually counted among the central figures of the group known as the "New York intellectuals": a circle of writers and critics who gathered around *Partisan Review* in the 1930s and later around *Commentary.* Born in 1920, he was in fact a bit younger than the main figures in the group and seems also in many ways to have been a psychologically less abstruse and more clearly driven character. Suffering no known writer's blocks, never (apparently) an analysand, he was an immensely productive writer—the author and editor of more than thirty books—as well as, starting in the mid-1950s, one of the founding editors of and the main force behind the quarterly magazine *Dissent.*

Before going on to consider his career, though, I need to acknowledge a debt to Irving Howe, who encouraged me when I was a young writer. For a special issue of *Dissent* on blue-collar lives Howe asked me in the early 1970s to write an article on the town of Cicero, outside Chicago. I was freelancing at the time, and the fee, five hundred dollars, seemed to me rather grand, especially given the proletarianized look of *Dissent.* Although Howe was not an impressive editor—*Dissent*, then as now, had a fairly high unreadability quotient—he did see it as part of his job to bring along younger writers. Certainly he attempted to do so with me. I wrote three or four more pieces for *Dissent* over the next few years, including an attack on the then-emerging movement of neoconservatism and an introduction to the magazine's twenty-fifth-anniversary issue.

I met Howe during this same period, when he came to Chicago to read from *World of Our Fathers,* his big book about the immigrant Jews of New York that was then still a work in progress (it would be published to immense acclaim in 1976). When he arrived at my apartment, I was rather surprised at what seemed his lack of physical vanity, especially in a man whose weaknesses were said to include women (he married four times). To a friend who asked about Howe's appearance, I said that he looked as if his shirt were out of his pants—only it wasn't. He was tall, but, after a New York youth in the socialist movement, there was nothing athletic or physically graceful about him. His tie was loose at the neck, his thin, receded hair barely combed. For a man who could command a rather elegant prose style, his physical style had about it something of the *shleppoisie.*

A kinder word, of course, would be *haimish*, or "old-shoe," and Howe did have a way in conversation of making me, a youngish contributor to his magazine, feel myself his contemporary and even peer. While staying in Chicago, he was also able to convince his host, the then-chairman of the English department at Northwestern University, to offer me a teaching job. Since I had no Ph.D., and no teaching experience whatsoever, this must have been an interesting piece of persuasion. I remained in the job for thirty years.

When my own politics changed, Howe and I never had an official falling-out, only a falling-away. He may have thought me, in the old leftist phrase that was a favorite of his, a "sellout"; more likely he did not think of me at all, except perhaps as another younger writer who had slipped away. I continued to read him, mostly in the *New Republic*, sometimes in the *New York Review of Books* or the *New York Times Book Review*. I was asked to review his autobiography, *A Margin of Hope* (1982), but found it rather a joyless book and declined. By then, in any case, I had come to read Howe rather differently. I read him through a political loupe and with a slightly skeptical heart.

But this brings me to a new intellectual biography by Edward Alexander entitled *Irving Howe: Socialist, Critic, Jew*. When, a few years ago, I heard that Alexander (a professor of English at the University of Washington in Seattle and politically a conservative) was planning this book, I thought, as Igor Stravinsky is said to have remarked whenever he was presented with some new avant-gardeish musical creation, "Who needs it?" Howe was not, after all, a major figure even among his contemporaries. But now that preparations are apparently under way to make him into the American Orwell, it is good to have all the facts of his intellectual life before us. Alexander has written a solid and useful book.

Because of constraints placed upon Alexander by Howe's family—he has not been allowed, for instance, to quote from Howe's letters—*Irving Howe: Socialist, Critic, Jew* is also a relatively impersonal book. Although they knew each other (according to Alexander, Howe used to refer to him as his "favorite reactionary"), and although, from time to time, personal exchanges figure in the narrative, this is for the most part, as Alexander says, "a biography of Howe's mind": an attempt to understand the various positions, political and cultural, taken by Howe over a lengthy and contentious career.

The three terms in Alexander's title—socialist, critic, Jew—have the priorities in precisely the right order. Howe was first a socialist; then a critic; and finally a Jew, secularist division, literary branch. The three categories often fed into one another: the socialist in Howe often set the program for the literary critic, and both socialism and criticism aroused his interest in Yiddish literature, thus bringing out the Jew. But socialism was paramount.

Howe came of age in the mean teeth of the Depression, and no doubt it was the central public event of his life, conditioning and coloring all else. His father's grocery store went bankrupt in 1930, when Irving was ten, and the family, as he would report in *A Margin of Hope*, began "dropping from the lower middle class to the proletariat—the most painful of all social descents." His parents now worked in the dress trade—his mother as an operator, his father as a presser—and Howe grew up with memories of dispossessed families, all their belongings on the sidewalk.

Much more important to the young Irving Howe than the storefront *shul* in which he had his bar mitzvah was the headquarters of the Workman's Circle, where he became attracted to what was in those days known as the "movement" and would soon become, as he later called it, "my home and my passion." At fourteen, as he tells it in *A Margin of Hope*, he began attending Sunday-night meetings of the Young People's Socialist League. He would in time acknowledge that his early socialism provided something akin to a replacement for the religion he never had; once he was under its spell, "everything seemed to fall into place: ordered meaning, a world grasped through theory, a life shaped by purpose."

Howe was never a member of the Communist Party; he claimed that, as a boy, he was much put off by the Communists' stringent discipline. But he did become a Trotskyist. One gathers that he never altogether lost his admiration for the figure of Leon Trotsky, who seemed to excite a great many intellectuals through his ability to wield, with stunning success, both pen and (as commander of the Red Army after the Bolshevik Revolution) sword. Howe was always an anti-Stalinist—anti-Stalinism was at the heart of Trotskyism—and he was later a strong anticommunist. But socialism itself, backed up by an early and thoroughgoing belief in Marxism, gave him all the rope he needed to tie himself in knots.

As an undergraduate at the City College of New York Howe studied English literature—"it struck me as the easiest major, where I could bullshit the most"—and was smitten, like so many other young men with literary flair, by the work of Edmund Wilson, whose "moral gravity moved me." He also changed his name (he had been born Irving Horenstein). He was hardly the only Jew in the "movement" to do so, the ostensible purpose being to secure a broader American audience for the views of these budding radicals. Thus Daniel Bell was originally Daniel Bolotsky, and Philip Rahv and William Phillips, the founding editors of *Partisan Review*, were born Ivan Greenbaum and William Litvinsky.

As a young man Howe, who had discovered in himself a gift for political oratory, must have been an intolerable prig. Irving Kristol remembers Howe from their CCNY days as "thin, gangling, intense, always a little distant, his fingers incessantly and nervously twisting a cowlick as he enunciated sharp and authoritative opinions . . . the Trotskyist leader and 'theoretician.' " Ransacking the files for his early writings, Alexander finds Howe accusing the Communist Party *Daily Worker* of the heinous sin of being "pro-American." The wartime suicide of the exiled Austrian Jewish writer Stefan Zweig is attributed by the adolescent Howe to Zweig's cowardliness as a petit bourgeois. An ideological opponent, Louis Fischer, is attacked as "king of the philistines" and "prince of liars."

The first large issue on which Howe, barely out of his teens, weighed in was World War II. He did so as the editor of a four-page sheet called *Labor Action*, and the line he took was that this was a war "between two great imperialist camps"—Nazi Germany on the one side, Britain and America on the other—"to decide which shall dominate the world." It was a war, in other words, "conceived and bred by world capitalism," and therefore neither side deserved the support of socialists. Although he was not alone in this view—Dwight Macdonald took it, and the philosopher Sidney Hook once told me that he had to argue Philip Rahv and William Phillips out of adopting it as the position of *Partisan Review*—one is inevitably reminded here of George Orwell's famous remark that there are certain things one has to be an intellectual to believe, since no ordinary man could be so stupid.

Howe was drafted and served in the army in Anchorage, Alaska. But throughout the war he continued, under a pseudonym, to attack America's participation in the conflict—this despite the fact that Hitler's systematic massacre of the Jews of Europe was becoming widely known. Anyone who did not support the so-called third-camp position (neither pro-Allied nor pro-Nazi) was dismissed by him as villainous at worst, a boob at best. As late as 1947 Howe felt it a mistake for the United States to have entered the war; in a piece discussing the Nuremberg Trials he claimed that the "real victims of Nazism" were the German working classes. Although he would later admit to the obtuseness of his views on World War II, he remained touchy, according to Alexander, about who had the right to remind him of them.

Edward Alexander understands the historical forces behind Irving Howe's turn to socialism, and he recognizes too what kept the socialist myth alive in Howe's mind and spirit up until the day of his death. Socialism apart, Alexander gives his subject high marks for acting with honor in his work as an anthologist and high cicerone to Yiddish literature in America, for his opposition to the student radicals and New Left intellectuals of the '60s and '70s, for his attacks on those who attempted to politicize the teaching of literature in universities in the early 1970s, and for his later

Irving Howe,
City College of New
York graduation, 1939

Howe in the army,
stationed in Alaska,
probably 1944

With Nina and Nicholas, 1954

With Nina and Nicholas, c. 1958–59

With Nina, c. 1958–59

Howe at Stanford University, c. 1962

With his first grandchild, Anna Bukowski, 1993

stand against deconstructionists and other practitioners of literary theory. Alexander esteems Howe's worth as a literary critic, and he seems genuinely to have liked him as a person. He strains to treat him fairly; and in my view he succeeds.

But this hardly means that he forgives all the misbegotten ideas that socialism led Howe to adopt. Politically and intellectually Alexander holds Howe's feet to the fire. He declines to allow, as softer people often do, that Howe was somehow right even when he was wrong or was right precisely for being wrong—that his putative idealism canceled his mistakes, from his neutrality during the war to his on-again, off-again feelings for Israel to his willfully blind refusal to credit the reality of the success of American democratic capitalism. Throughout, Alexander stays on Howe's case, nailing him for errors both of commission and of omission. In this exercise too I believe he treats Howe fairly.

Still, taking up Howe's political positions one by one, demonstrating how many of these positions look foolish in the light of history or in the light of one's own (inevitably) more sensible positions, has its limitations. This is a method of judgment, after all, by which few people can hope to escape whipping, history being more cunning than the human beings who make it and opinions—especially intellectual opinions—being as volatile as biotechnology stocks. A more interesting question is one that Sidney Hook put to Howe after a brutal exchange in the '40s, in the course of which Howe actually called Hook a tool of the Vatican (now there's a notion to make one smile on a gray day): "I do not know whether it is your politics or your character which makes it constitutionally impossible for you to do elementary justice to people with whom you disagree."

Elementary justice is not easy to achieve with an opponent, particularly in politics. But what about in literature? Did Howe's politics also get in the way of his literary judgments?

Howe did not come to literature through advanced academic training, for he had no Ph.D. and he was never aligned with any particular school of criticism. Beginning with his war years in Alaska, he did a vast amount of reading; he seems to have gained his education in public (as many critics do), learning as he wrote. In 1953 he was given a position at Brandeis, where Philip Rahv also taught, and he remained a university teacher—a very good one, it is said—for the rest of his days, later moving to the Graduate Center of the City University of New York.

As a literary and cultural critic, Howe had a genuine talent for dramatizing ideas. He was much aided in this by his penchant for heightened phrasings. In his prose militancy is "clenched," youth is "tensed with conviction," Faulkner's characters are "chafed" by the "clamp of family," and

Debsian socialism is invaded by "the *dybbuk* of sectarianism." These rhetorical flourishes, which do not always bear too close scrutiny, can give Howe's prose an impressive tension and luster.

Howe was a perceptive, even a penetrating reader—which is all that one can ask a critic to be—but his efforts were oddly unconcentrated. He wrote often about the phenomenon of modernism in the arts, but he came too late, as a critic, to add much to the enshrinement of the great modernist writers—Joyce, Proust, Kafka, Eliot—in the canon of Western literature. His three books on individual writers (Sherwood Anderson, William Faulkner, and Thomas Hardy) are respectable but not memorable. He could, however, write the good general essay (on Edith Wharton), the stirring essay (on T. E. Lawrence), or the surprisingly well-informed essay (on the nineteenth-century story writer Nikolai Leskov). And he was excellent on Yiddish literature; if I had to bet which of Howe's literary works has the best chance of surviving, my money would be on the 1953 anthology *A Treasury of Yiddish Stories*, which he edited with Eliezer Greenberg and to which the two men supplied a lengthy and brilliant introductory essay that put the subject of Yiddish literature on the American intellectual map.

Unlike Edmund Wilson, Howe was never able to direct the literary traffic when it came to the reputations of his contemporaries. He never wrote at serious length about Norman Mailer, whose wretched essay "The White Negro" originally appeared in *Dissent*. (Howe later apologized for it.) He left Saul Bellow pretty much alone. He once advised Ralph Ellison to align himself more strongly with the protest tradition in black writing and got absolutely scorched by Ellison in a brilliant reply. But he did resoundingly put down the early feminist writer Kate Millett, at a time when it was useful to do so. And in a 1972 essay in *Commentary* he crushed Philip Roth, who was so rattled that he composed an entire novel, *The Anatomy Lesson*, to dispatch a critic undeniably modeled after Irving Howe.

"Politics in a work of literature," wrote Stendhal, "is like a pistol-shot in the middle of a concert, something loud and vulgar, and yet a thing to which it is not possible to refuse one's attention." Howe quotes this famous sentence at the outset of his own book of essays, *Politics and the Novel* (1957). Although he has been praised by his admirers for keeping politics out of his literary criticism, and for his capacity to judge works of art on their own terms, the truth is rather more complicated.

Not that Howe's literary criticism had an entirely polemical intent. But when it came to the crunch, he could not do what, in his essay on Leskov, he remarked that all great writers do—namely, write "in opposition to his own preconceptions." In *Politics and the Novel*, which he published while still in his thirties, Howe's politics forced him, in effect, to deny the gifts of two of the greatest writers in the history of the novel: Henry James and Joseph Conrad.

That Howe was not an all-out admirer of James is less than shocking. James is, after all, not everyone's cup of caviar, and Howe's taste generally ran to more strongly patterned, less finely textured, more conflict-laden, less subtly nuanced fiction. In *Politics and the Novel* the text for Howe's anti-James sermon is *The Princess Casamassima* (1887), James's coruscating psychological study of the radical temperament. In considering the novel Howe gives out little grades—this character is strong, that one wanting in credibility—but then finally dismisses it altogether, largely on the grounds that James's cultural position renders him ill-equipped for his subject. "James's conservatism," Howe writes, "was peculiarly the conservatism of an artist who has measured all the effort and agony that has gone into the achievements of the past and is not yet ready to skimp their value in the name of the unborn and untested future."

This is hardly the only place in his criticism where Howe reveals his own preference for the ideal over the real; that "unborn and untested future" he alludes to is, of course, the possibility of utopian socialism, while "conservatism," for a New York intellectual of that day, was a word that had the status of a profanity. But he is mistaken about James. What Howe identifies as political conservatism is really something else—a disbelief in the centrality of politics itself. In a key passage in *The Princess Casamassima* James writes: "The figures on the chessboard were still the passions and the jealousies and superstitions and stupidities of man, and thus positioned in regard to each other at any given moment could be of interest only to the grim fates who played the game—who sat, through the ages, bow-backed over the table." This is a passage that Howe neglects to quote, and little wonder: the tragic view of life it encapsulates is entirely at odds with his own, politics-ridden mentality.

The case against Conrad is made even more vehemently in *Politics and the Novel*. Conrad wrote two of the great political novels in the English language—*The Secret Agent* (1907) and *Under Western Eyes* (1910)—and both are devastatingly antirevolutionary. Both, that is, come out strongly for the real over the ideal. In considering these novels Howe begins by maintaining that all of Conrad's views were formed by his father's experience in Poland, where, as a fighter for Polish freedom, he was seized by the Russians, along with Conrad's mother, subsequently dying in exile, and by Conrad's own guilt not merely over his failure to continue his father's struggle but over his need, his "conservative" need, for personal order.

A good bit of critical heavy breathing, of backing-and-filling, accompanies Howe's attempt to defuse the power of Conrad's two novels. Only at chapter's end does he allow that "in our fiercely partisan age it is difficult to read books like *Under Western Eyes* and *The Secret Agent* without fiercely partisan emotions." Imagine the emotions of Howe himself—who actually brings Trotsky in at one point to refute Conrad—when he came upon the following passage from *Under Western Eyes*:

> In a real revolution—not a simple dynastic change or a reform of institutions—in a real revolution the best characters do not come to the front. A violent revolution falls into the hands of narrow-minded fanatics and of tyrannical hypocrites at first. Afterwards comes the turn of all the pretentious intellectual failures of the time. Such are the chiefs and leaders. You will notice that I have left out the mere rogues. The scrupulous and the just, the noble, humane, and devoted natures; the unselfish and the intelligent may begin a movement—but it passes away from them. They are not the leaders of a revolution. They are its victims: the victims of disgust, of disenchantment—often of remorse.
>
> Hopes grotesquely betrayed, ideals caricatured—that is the definition of revolutionary success.

Joseph Conrad wrote that in 1910, calling every shot in the Russian Revolution that was still seven years away. You might think that he would win a point or two for political prophecy; instead the passage, which Howe quotes in part, is answered by him with a rather pathetic retort in the form of a well-worn quotation from Orwell: "All revolutions are failures, but they are not all the same failure." (In the modern age, truth to tell, they just about all are the same failure.)

George Orwell, like Irving Howe, had a little socialism problem of his own; he too could not quite let go of the subject. But Orwell, who died a relatively young man in 1950, was also a more honest writer. Irving Howe could never have written *The Road to Wigan Pier* (1937), Orwell's excruciatingly truthful account of the squalor of the working class and the kookiness of those attracted to socialist remedies for its problems. Going to Spain to observe the revolution in progress and join the fight against fascism, Orwell looked the Communist devil in the eye, and when he returned home, he once again told the truth in *Homage to Catalonia* (1938).

Hilton Kramer has written about Irving Howe that "whenever the mystique of radical politics in general and the myth of socialism in particular have been allowed to dominate in his work, the result is all but worthless." This is a hard judgment but, I believe, a correct one—correct as applied to his literary criticism and much more correct as applied to his writing on politics, which tends to be turgid, divorced from reality, and nearly unreadable.

Why did Howe invest so much intellectual and spiritual capital in so desiccating an idea? Socialism was, of course, the great compulsion of his youth, and it gave him both a social life and a way out of the immigrant Jewish milieu in which he was born. Socialism also provided the one political tradition in which intellectuals seemed to be able to exercise leadership and attain status. Nor is the power of displaced religious belief to be ignored. The last word in Howe's *Selected Writings, 1950–1990*, his final collection of essays, is given over to the conviction that the fall of the Soviet Union has in no way disqualified the socialist idea but that, to the contrary, once "the shadow of Stalinism recedes," socialism will emerge in its purer, uncontaminated form. Talk about waiting for the messiah.

From an early age Howe had locked himself into a strict definition of the role of the intellectual. In his view the intellectual was always the outsider, and intellectual life was really only valid when one lived it as a member of a minority. This minority was to be in permanent opposition, in a state of perpetual dissatisfaction with the world as it is. Only thus could one's radicalism be preserved intact. "I am dissatisfied, profoundly so, with the world as it is," said the late Alfred Kazin, who took an even greater pride than Howe in his own brand of self-righteous radicalism. "But I would be dissatisfied with any world. And I'd hate to lose my dissatisfaction."

The irony is that for Howe (as for Kazin) precisely this posture of alienation should have proved a winning ticket to the kind of worldly success he was forever claiming to deprecate. Unlike Orwell, who suffered material damage for his brave dissent from the party line on Spain, Howe never suffered at all for his radicalism. It helped land him a distinguished professorship, lectureships at Harvard and Princeton, a major commercial publisher, a MacArthur fellowship, and now posthumous beatification as a "warrior-saint" of our age.

Did Howe ever sense that the heavy bag of largely false ideas he had chosen to carry through life had marred much of his literary criticism and guaranteed the irrelevance of his politics? One wonders. To judge the real against an imaginary ideal and always find the real wanting; to refuse to repudiate one's youthful positions, no matter how callow, lest one be thought to have grown cynical; to consider oneself in permanent opposition to the life of one's time; to dramatize the fear of selling out, even as the world makes a comedy of the drama by continually showering one with rewards; to live out one's days hostage to so many wrong ideas, notions, and biases—did Irving Howe ever say to himself, how do I put this bag down and take life as it and for what it is? I suppose it would be merciful to think that he never did.

Critic

8

Robert Boyers

Politics and the Critic

Robert Boyers is Tisch Professor of Arts and Letters at Skidmore College, founder and editor of the quarterly *Salmagundi* [1965–present], and Director of The New York State Summer Writers Institute. He is the author of seven critical books, including *Atrocity and Amnesia: The Political Novel Since 1945*, *After The Avant Garde*, and *The Book of Common Praise* (July 2002). He frequently reviews books for *The New Republic*, and contributes essays to such publications as *Granta*, *The American Scholar*, *TLS*, *Dissent*, and other magazines.

Early in *Politics and the Novel* Irving Howe writes of "the vast respect which the great novelist is ready to offer to the whole idea of *opposition*, the opposition he needs to allow for in his book against his own predispositions and yearnings and fantasies." Though he was not a novelist, and did not fancy himself an artist, Irving respected, even loved "the whole idea of opposition," and he once proposed "a rule of thumb" whereby intellectuals were encouraged to "criticize whichever outlook is dominant at the moment, whether in the sphere of cultural opinion or public decision." Challenged on this, he conceded that the oppositional posture—when not directed against one's own predispositions— might well become an empty reflex, a parody of genuine oppositional criticism. But it seemed to him that the risk was well worth assuming. The habit of trimming or accommodation was potentially more damaging by far to the critical spirit than the disposition to oppose.

I met Irving in 1967. As Editor of *Dissent* magazine he had published a few of my early pieces, and he seemed to me at once the very perfect model of the intellectual as man of letters. Even his editorial letters of acceptance were, in their way, oppositional documents, taking issue with one or more of my principal contentions without in any way suggesting that I take back or revise them. Was I so very certain, he wanted to know, that Peter Weiss's play *Marat/Sade*, which was then causing a stir in New York, did not in fact reflect attitudes more and more prominent in the new Euro-American youth culture? In the polemic he had accepted for *Dissent*, Irving wrote, I had seemed rather more certain than was warranted that Weiss's play was by no means an ideological document. It was one thing, Irving wrote, to argue that a play was conceived exclusively to promote a fixed position, as Weiss's play clearly was not. But it was something else entirely to suggest—was I perhaps unwilling seriously to entertain this idea?— that such a play might nonetheless get behind a fashionably radical idea for which its author had some genuine sympathy, though as yet he had for that idea no formal name. I would do well, Irving wrote, to give this possibility "a little more thought" before I let the piece I had written go forward.

In subsequent correspondence regarding other pieces I wrote for *Dissent* Irving would urge upon me a more consistently robust, assertive manner, what he nicely called "just a bit less anxious circumspection." He admired, he said, my reluctance to fight my way out of doubts I expressed about the seriousness of so-called "revolutionary" ideas as they had lately been taken up and blithely espoused by several younger writers. But, he cautioned, I was to be careful not to allow judiciousness itself to become in my writing a motive. The state of doubt was, much of the time, a good thing, an expression of a very human tendency, but it could become—I'm not certain that this was in fact the word Irving used, though it seems to me what he intended—incapacitating.

What was worse, Irving said—and here I recall exactly what he wrote— the habit of perpetual, anxious circumspection in a "fastidiously earnest" literary mind could become more than a little tiresome. It could lead to an appetite for posturing and a style that might be a caricature of refined, mea- sured circumspection. He heard, already, in a number of my sentences—I was, was I not, a very young man, but I would know what he meant, he was sure I would not take this the wrong way—what he could only call "the Trilling sublime," a straining for an accent of high seriousness that could seem "mincing" and "genteel." He could tell that there was something in me that inclined to that accent, and though that was not, surely, a fatal inclination, it was necessary, he believed, to resist it.

When, years later, we talked about that letter, especially about Irving's reference to "the Trilling sublime," Irving assured me that he did not often find that accent in the work submitted for publication to *Dissent*. Mostly the prose of *Dissent* pieces was blunt and serviceable, often more than a little rough or crude. But I was a literary man obviously struggling to create a prose that might allow me to do the variety of things I supposed a literary essay might do. Trilling was, at his best, we agreed, a first-rate writer, whatever reservations Irving then still maintained about some of Trilling's political ideas. But his style represented a danger. It was, quite clearly, always moving at the edge of self-parody. Its circumspections were, much of the time, impressive, salutary, but they did threaten to congeal into a manner. One was not surprised to learn that careless or impatient readers found Trilling exasperating, believed that he could never quite make up his mind about anything. Irving understood, quite as I did, even at my then tender age, that Trilling's willingness to subject everything to doubt, that his "negative capability" and poise, did not in fact prevent him from making judgments and standing by them. But it was also clear that a writer less gifted than he, more susceptible to putting on a borrowed style, might well write sentences that seemed finicky and timid when he'd wanted simply— simply!—to achieve an accent of quiet conviction and proportion.

In spite of his oppositional tendencies, Irving could be, often was, a companionable and generous man. It occurred to me, very early in a relationship that was never quite intimate, that the attention he paid to the work I'd sent him for *Dissent* was remarkable. To how many other young writers did Irving write at length about the weaknesses of the articles and reviews they'd submitted for publication? Surely there were a great many others whose work required at least as much careful editorial scrutiny as my own fledgling efforts. And surely there were many who seemed to him, at least at first, more promising than I, more invested in the varieties of political and social organization that seemed to me uncongenial or hopelessly ineffectual. Yet he gave to many of us his attention and advice, husbanding his energies as best he could for his own literary work, but never shutting himself off from the steady interactions that made of *Dissent* a small community held together by an unmistakably *interested* presiding presence.

The first time I ever saw Irving in his element, saw what I'd only dimly imagined before, was in the winter of 1966. Of course Irving had been for some time a university professor, more or less at ease in the classroom and at academic meetings. But his favored element was—so it always seemed to me—the meeting hall or community center, an off-campus site where a mixed audience would congregate to listen and emote and argue and raise voices. A flyer on a bulletin board at The New School for Social Research on eleventh street, where I was then teaching evening classes, had announced that Irving was to deliver a lecture on "New Styles in Leftism." The location was a socialist meeting hall on sixth avenue just above fourteenth street. When I got there the large room, not quite an auditorium, was packed, though I managed to drag in a chair from a nearby room and to squeeze myself in along the rear wall. I recognized in the room a handful of graduate student acquaintances from New York University, and others I knew from the staff of a radical paper published at Columbia University. Familiar too were the faces of several people on the *Dissent* staff, including Henry Pachter and Lewis Coser. But the audience also included persons who did not belong to the university world, chess players who hung out on the benches in Washington Square Park, union people with affiliations emblazoned on their shirt fronts, counsellors I worked with at the War Resisters League, and more than two or three handfuls of youthful "new left" radicals who scowled at their elders and looked pissed off whenever Irving uttered something they didn't like. The room was over-heated and uncomfortable, the slatted folding chairs hard, the atmosphere anything but cozy or genteel. But the sound sytem was good, and it is probably safe to say that no one came away from the evening disappointed.

Irving was a man in his forties in 1966, but he was, as editor of *Dissent* and author of books and essays on socialism, the American Communist party, and the labor movement, a leader of what had then recently become known as "the old left." He was, as he'd often said, a democratic socialist, an opponent of "middlebrow feeling," "cautious routine," "the bureaucratization of opinion and taste," but also an opponent of Stalinist Communism and of the "new left" disposition to associate everything bad in the world with the pernicious influence of the United States. He knew that the socialist idea did not always provide a reliable way to get at social problems, that "in many countries it [had] declined into little more than an agency of liberal reform." Yet he clung to it as perhaps "the one way of escaping the insufferable choice between capitalism and Communism." That Irving's views did not seem altogether inspiring to many younger left radicals was as clear to him as to the rest of us who read *Dissent* in 1966. And it was equally clear that he would do nothing, say nothing, to blunt the criticism of those who were impatient with the equivocations of his comrades in the old left. Those who felt that a socialism no longer able to speak "in the name of a major historical transformation" was already dead would have to look elsewhere for inspiration and guidance. Irving would continue to speak as truthfully, as soberly as he could, and he would not pretend that there was "an assured connection" between the "animating sentiments" of the socialist idea and any "formulated program" to which socialists might now at any moment lend their often lukewarm support.

No doubt many of those who had come to witness Irving's speech on that winter evening in lower New York were prepared to revile what they would hear. Irving had already spoken out against the species of moral absolutism that had disfigured the new left discourse coming out of unversity campuses. He detested what he took to be the idiotic suggestion that there was no important difference between the Communist dictatorships and the western democracies. Radical intellectuals committed to sustaining this pretense were, he believed, fundamentally dishonest, attracted as they were to an abstract idea of historical process which prevented them from closely observing the actual lives of people in the societies they observed. No wonder, Irving often said, that young American radicals were so often unwilling to pay attention to the testimony of dissident intellectuals living in Eastern Europe or in the Soviet Union itself. "My instinctive solidarity," Irving wrote, "went out to those intellectuals in Poland who, whatever their enforced vocabulary, were really liberals and socialists at heart." But the new left radicals were dis-missive of "liberals," and felt no instinctive solidarity with those for whom the difference between east and west was palpable and fundamental to any reasonable sense of a plausible and decent future.

"New Styles in Leftism" took a good two hours to deliver, and it was followed by a heated though not intemperate discussion. If it was warmly greeted even by some in the audience who had come to jeer, that had everything to do with Irving's convincing assurance that he did not "desire that younger generations of radicals should repeat" the thoughts and words of his generation. More, he conceded from the first that his "composite portrait" obviously lumped together problems and ideas not all of which would belong to any one person or fragmentary constituency on the new left. If some young radicals were moved to protest that much of his lecture did not "pertain to them," he would be "delighted by such a response," quite as he was delighted by the fact that "a new radical mood" had begun to appear "in limited sectors of American society." Excesses and wrong directions were, perhaps, unavoidable, but it was necessary for those who cared about these recent developments to notice what was promising and what, precisely, was not. Those who were impatient with the exhortations of their elders on the left might at least be willing to consider the views of those who sympathized deeply with aspects of their disaffection and mistrust.

Though I have, still, after thirty-seven years, the notes I took at Irving's lecture, and soon after that event reviewed for *The New Leader* Irving's book, *Steady Work*, which includes his lecture among its miscellaneous essays, I had not gone back to the text of the lecture for many years. Obviously it now seems dated, as any front-line dispatch from a culture-war would be. It spoke of the civil rights movement as a work in progress. Marxism-Leninism was described as a theory in which a small but substantial number of intelligent people continued to believe. The idea that "authoritarianism is inherent or necessary in the so-called socialist countries" continued, so it then seemed, to be popular with many on the left. The shock tactics once associated with the slogan "epater le bourgeois" and newly adopted by sixties radicals seemed to Irving to cry out for analysis and response.

Oddly, though, the lecture seems in many ways as fresh and new today as it seemed when first it was delivered. In no small measure this has to do with the extraordinary verve of Irving's writing, its color and polemical force, its analytic shrewdness and command of historical perspective. In a lecture citing recent *Village Voice* columns and newly fashionable "pop art guerrilla warrior[s]" like Leroi Jones, Irving casually brings to bear on his material the history of the American labor movement, the writings of T.S. Eliot, Tocqueville and Karl Marx, and the history of key terms like *alienation, establishment, participation,* and *nationalism.* The text is punctuated by memorable, deliberately provocative formulations: "The stress has been," Irving writes, "upon moral self-regeneration, a kind of Emersonianism with shock treatment"; "For the Negroes in [Malcolm's] audience," Irving asserts, "he offered the relief of articulating subterranean feelings of hatred, contempt, defiance, feelings that did not have to be held in check because there was a tacit compact that the talk about violence would remain talk . . . The formidable sterility of his speech, so impressive in its relation to a deep personal suffering, touched something in their hearts"; "The sophisticated middle class" played to by the more radical sectors of the new left, after responding with predictable "outrage, resistance, and anger," soon comes around, as expected, "rolls over like a happy puppy on its back, moaning 'Oh baby, *epater* me again, harder this time, tell me what a sterile impotent louse I am and how you are so tough and virile, how you're planning to murder me, *epater* me again."

All of this seems still an extraordinarily skillful, effective performative display of the critical intelligence, at once engaged and serious, informed at every point by the interplay of idea and emotion, unwilling to give up on politics yet alert to the distortion of political thinking by fixed philosophical and ideological dualities. Elsewhere Irving had demanded of the imaginative writer "that calm surrender to the rhythms of an imagined situation which is indispensable to the true novelist," and it is clear that, for all of the polemic urgency and occasional satirical subversiveness of Irving's portraiture, "New Styles in Leftism" is marked by just that "calm surrender" Irving valued. Moved as he was by many of the instincts and demands set out by sixties radicals, he yet wished to look somewhat less feverishly at the evolving spectacle, to calmly imagine what might be possible even within the given terms and limitations of "established" order. "I think it is a gross error, " he writes, "the kind of deep-seated conservatism [!] that often alloys ultraradicalism— to say that everything in the major sectors of American society is static, sated, 'Establishment.' Who, twenty-five or thirty years ago, could have foreseen that Catholic priests and nuns would be marching into Montgomery? Who could have foreseen the more thoroughgoing ferment in the American churches of which this incident is merely a symptom? Instead of scoffing at such people as civil rights 'tourists,' we ought to be seeking them out and trying to get them to move a little further, up North, too."

But what made Irving's lecture so especially effective was its obvious sympathy with the grounds of radical revolt. Much that he said about the murderous rhetoric of black nationalists and the "sheer irresponsibility" of those who sneered at Dr. King or talked about " 'the west' as if it were some indivisible whole" seemed persuasive for the standard, unimpeachable reason, namely, that Irving came across as a reasonable, candid man who had thought a good deal about the issues he engaged. This went almost without saying. But Irving's sentences were animated by something else, by a shared sense of the relevant "background" for radical politics at that present time. For all of his aversion to the acting-out and personalizing that marked the politics of the new left, for all of his conviction that one needed always to distinguish between gesture and act, between genuine politics and the radicalism of "moral rectitude," he understood perfectly that "the society we live in fails to elicit the idealism of the more rebellious and generous young." Others of Irving's generation would resort to psychoanalytic categories to account for the rebelliousness of sixties radicals, and even go so far as to explain opposition to the Vietnam war as "reaction formation" and neurotic disorder. But Irving felt that in 1966 it was often the best and most generous of the young who were full of passionate intensity, and it was more than strategy that led him to concede, in the opening minutes of his lecture, that "the widespread disenchantment" of the young was not merely comprehensible but rational. "The intelligent young know," he argued, "that if they keep out of trouble, accept academic drudgery, and preserve a respectable 'image,' they can hope for successful careers, even if not personal gratification. But the price they must pay for this choice is a considerable quantity of inner adaptation to the prevalent norms."

Under these circumstances, which Irving was at great pains to anatomize, it was essential to acknowledge that American society especially was seductive in the blandishments it offered to its more conformist citizens, for whom "duplicity" and "accommodation" often seemed not a heavy price to pay for comfort and social status. Irving drew upon a wide range of sources for his view of alienation and what Czeslaw Milosz had called "The Captive Mind," and though he knew that the captive mind was one thing in totalitarian countries and quite another in the west, he was sensitive to the difficulty of sustained resistance in countries like the United States, where a large proportion of the population had reason to suppose that their lot would steadily improve. The "generous young" were rightly impatient with the pace of change, and skeptical about the goals of liberal reformers whose outlook was practical, who were satisfied to work within a system geared to repudiate any fundamental revaluation of values.

In these terms, Irving also understood that the system in the United States made "very difficult" a coherent political opposition. The politics of personal style and inflammatory gesture was a response to a situation in which idealism often felt hopeless or inexpressible, and "real politics" could seem pitifully inadequate, a thin substitute for conviction. The sixties radicals who enacted in more and more extravagant ways their disaffiliation from politics as usual were expressing simultaneously their "nausea" at the sterile, accommodationist behavior of their "decent" elders and "a tacit recognition of impotence." The hope everywhere apparent in Irving's lecture, as in so much else he wrote in those years, was that radicals and liberals, the old left and the new, might "properly and fraternally disagree" yet also work together to create a politics that was more than the expression of a felt impotence.

In fact Irving was drawn, some would say inordinately drawn, to ask again and again the questions *what constitutes a genuine politics?* and *what are the forms available to the best and the brightest at a time when a coherent political opposition is not viable?* Though he addressed these questions often in the pages of *Dissent* and in pieces published elsewhere, it may well be that he addressed them most cogently in his literary criticism. The first book of Irving's I read was *Politics and the Novel*, a book published originally in 1957 and recommended to me by another *Dissent* colleague named Henry Pachter in a lunch at The New School cafeteria in the fall of 1963. Pachter, a 57-year old German refugee intellectual who had served as Dean of the New School, held court at the same table in that cafeteria two afternoons each week in those days, and he was always eager to recommend to the occasional literary types who made their way to his table one or another means of acquiring "a serious political education." It was Pachter who alerted me to the public meetings occasionally sponsored by *Dissent*, and only a year later persuaded me to start a new magazine of my own—we called it *Salmagundi*—which would attract literary intellectuals and, at the same time, introduce them to material that combined literary and political analysis—"exactly," Henry said, "the way I wish I could do it, and exactly the way Irving does it in *Politics and the Novel*."

Though Irving's book did take on what he called—with more than a little misgiving—"political novels," and did acknowledge the variety of motives informing works so different as Dostoyevski's *The Possessed* and

Conrad's *Nostromo*, the book did come around more or less insistently to the troubling idea that politics will often seem impossible, or irrelevant, or incoherent where it also seems most necessary, in circumstances where political opposition would seem self-evidently desireable. Re-reading the book in the late sixties, one had to think about its bearing on the political excesses and fanaticisms of that time. The new left, whatever the unfamiliar guises it sometimes assumed, was more than a little familiar in the sense of futility it often reflected. Even university radicals at Berkeley, who had managed to bring a major university almost to its knees and, in the process, to confront it with important questions, must have had to ask themselves—at least in the later stages of their uprising - the kinds of questions confronting characters in the novels Irving studied, questions like *what permanent gains might be expected from our success?* So Irving suggested in many of the essays written ten years after publication of *Politics and the Novel.* "After all the excitement," he wrote, and with no trace of *schadenfreude* or dire pessimism, would not the students have to ask themselves "Did it really matter?" Was their revolt, truly, "the beginning of a sustained inquiry by American students into the nature and purpose of the education they receive," a prelude to a redirection of the university informed by "a true vision of what a university is supposed to be"? Political struggle had made it seem for a while that issues raised in novels like *The Princess Casamassima* or *Fathers and Sons* would inevitably be engaged, that political action would generate a concern with long-term objectives, in the universities and in other social institutions, but rapidly that prospect diminished.

Just so, in many of the political novels Irving studied, even the least cynical characters rapidly succumbed to despair or diverted their energies away from politics. All too often characters behaved as if they were *not* moved principally by comprehensive visions of a world more attractive, did *not* wish to join with others in fraternal movements designed to improve their common condition. Often their behavior seemed irrational, or at least resistant to ordinary explanation, and it was not an evasion of responsibility for a first rate writer to suggest that the political behavior of individuals and of groups is more often "enigmatic" than our fondness for social science categories would lead us to expect.

Of course Irving was never content to stop with suggestions. He did not accept that words like "enigma" or "mystery" or "irrational" could satisfy our desire to understand social and political life. Neither could moral reflection begin and end with the simple notion that human beings were disappointing, that they inevitably betrayed the political ideas to which they intermittently rallied, so that politics itself would seem suited only to those—"the worst," as Yeats once had it—with a lust for power. It was acceptable to say, as Irving did, that "social classes have . . . an appetite for power," or that often "even aspects of private experience supposedly inviolable" may be shown "to be . . . infected with ideology" or susceptible to corruption. But it was not therefore reasonable to conclude that all political ideas were equally suspect, equally irrelevant, or that politics itself as a species of human activity could never be ennobling, never challenge "the stabilized hypocrisy of society."

And yet Irving did compulsively return to the political novel in which political action seemed almost impossible and political hope seemed largely the province of fools or the terminally delusional. Again and again he was drawn to the example of those who confronted "the feeling of hopelessness" and yet "circle[d] about the world of politics," as if they might discover a way to act effectually without abandoning altogether their finer ideas and sentiments. Turgenev's *Smoke*, Irving writes, "is a reflex of frustration, an impotent lashing out . . . ," and his mostly ineffectual liberalism in general "now seems closer to us, closer to our indecisions and hesitations." Turgenev's more robust and abrasive protagonist Bazarov, in *Fathers and Sons*, "would like to throw stones," Irving writes, "but no one pays attention, no one is disturbed." The man who proposes to "smash other people," who has nothing but disdain for "sugary liberal" types, suspects that he is, in reality," a harmless person." The Bazarov who believes he might make a difference in the Russia of the nineteenth century, whose sense of politics is confrontational and unforgiving and maximalist in its ambitions, sees that really he "wasn't needed," that he stands as yet merely "on the threshold" of a future he cannot envision or summon into being. Bazarov's vision, somewhat like Turgenev's, is at once—so Irving insists—"political and not political," and those most prepared for struggle in a society not quite susceptible to a radical re-fashioning may find that they are, alas, "too strong to survive," reduced proudly to declaring, as if anyone were listening, as if some political consequence might conceivably be involved, that they consulted no one else's ideas but their own. However heartfelt, so spurious an assertion could not but seem to Irving to bespeak a total alienation from any conceivable politics.

In several respects the most challenging of the novels Irving studied was Stendhal's *The Charterhouse of Parma*. Stendhal was, as Irving wrote, "a dubious character," and *The Charterhouse* was a book teeming with con-tradictions and resistant to solemnity. Set Stendhal alongside other major writers with an interest in politics and the contrasts are unmistakable. Not for Stendhal the spiritualist mystifications of Dostoyevski, the "stable and respectable morality toward which Conrad strives," or "the tone of massive solemnity James assumes." For Irving Stendhal is a writer only mildly interested in the fate of ordinary people and not generally hopeful about their capacities. He is, as well, a writer with a limited patience for theories and ideas, though he entertains them and uses them up *as if* he sought in them some sustenance they consistently refused to furnish. *The Charterhouse* was, not surprisingly, the work one might have expected of a fellow who was at once "a rebel and a *bon vivant*," a work neither "respectable" nor moral, whose favorite characters seem "impervious, like some majestic natural force, to moral argument."

To read Irving on *The Charterhouse* is not at all to feel that one is in the hands of a "radical" critic with a commitment to socialism or liberalism or a humane view of ordinary working people. His achieved sympathy with Stendhal's novel is consummate, the grasp of political circumstance and cultural moment scrupulously communicated in a way that perfectly serves an imaginative engagement with the novelistic project. Occasionally one notes what were surely features of Irving's attachment to radicalism, though here those features are mostly cast as human, not specifically po- litical, characteristics. The Duchess, or Sanseverina, of Stendhal's novel, whom Irving seems to love almost as much as does Stendhal, is "one of the least snobbish figures in literature," Irving writes. She admires "generosity, impetuousness, gaiety, passion"— though also, as Irving gladly concedes, "a certain ruthlessness in reaching for them."

Irving also clearly approves Stendhal's judgment of his beloved Count Mosca, who is made to fail when "he lives too closely by his own pre- cepts, by his inured political habits." Irving would seem also to understand, sympathetically, if not entirely to approve, the idea, so compelling to the Sanseverina, that the young deserve our love precisely "because they are less respectful" and "more ferocious." All of these sentiments, ideas, enthusi- asms, Irving anatomizes and celebrates not in the spirit of a critic with a program to advance or a position to defend, but with the conviction that Stendhal's novel, "forever vivacious and subversive," is a work indispensable to us, a work that will not "allow us the luxury of becoming dull." He loves it, and would have us love it, not for its correct ideas, or its politics, not because he agrees with it or would wish anyone to emulate its characters, but because it represents a challenge to our generally fixed, impeccably decent ideas of the good, the true and the acceptable.

Given Irving's work in *Politics and the Novel*, not to mention the dozens of reviews he wrote for the *New York Times Book Review* and other periodi- cals often extolling the virtues of "dissident" anti-communist or "conserva- tive" writers like Aleksandr Solzhenitsyn, George Konrad, Milan Kundera, Joseph Skvorecky, Saul Bellow and V. S. Naipaul, it was astonishing to many of us that, in the 1970's and '80's, he became the favorite target of neo-conservative culture critics. Of course Irving had always been an embattled figure, and he had long fought to prevent the flight of American intellectuals from the left. But that effort had seemed, in the '50's, very much a minority affair, and not even a cold warrior in that decade would have argued that Irving represented a significant threat to "the American way of life." In the '60's, with his attacks on infantile leftism and his resistance to the counter culture, he might well have seemed a useful, if unreliable, ally to neo-conservatives who soon regarded him as the man they loved to hate. Even in the '70's, when he attacked the feminism of Kate Millett and lamented the fact that "good causes"—especially those in which he believed—seemed often to "attract poor advocates," he routinely adopted positions not especially popular with his own left constituency, and though he remained very much a man of the left, it was not easy to think of him in categorical terms.

Obviously, Irving embodied a view of the world and of the intellectual enterprise that seemed to his antagonists repulsive. Midge Decter chiefly held against him what she called "a will to remain utopian." His magazine, she said, is dull, "clotted with old thoughts devoid of any serious reference to reality and merely concerned with the purity of its appearance." Hilton Kramer, noting Irving's stature among liberal intellectuals and his access to the pages of *The New York Times Book Review*, complained that Howe was a representative of "established power" and thus had no right to be "wrapping himself in the tattered mantle of rebellion." Joseph Epstein noted that "If one reads through a book like Irving Howe's *Politics and the Novel* [the neo-conservatives made the same case about other works by Irving], we discover that Howe does not quite approve any novelist . . . whose politics do not mesh with his own anti-capitalist, waiting-for-Elijah, socialist utopianism."

Never mind, for the moment, that Irving typically celebrated writers whose politics in no way resembled his own. Ignore the personal animus do deeply inscribed in the various neo-conservative essays devoted to Howe. Consider, for the moment, simply the electric charge contained in the word *utopian* as it is wielded by Howe's critics. No doubt utopianism requires a capacity for hope or faith that most of us cannot summon. Typically we say of a utopian thinker that he is foolish in the degree that he refuses to acknowledge the facts of life. But Irving Howe did not believe that the dictatorship of the proletariat would inevitably produce a humane society. He did not contend that socialism inevitably produced noble citizens and great works of art. He never said that capitalism inevitably dehumanized its constituents and tended to bring about the revolution it most wished to forestall. If he was utopian, he was so only in the modest sense of believing that political, social and cultural conditions might be better than they were and that it was worth reminding people that what they had was not good enough. Far from striking empty postures, he had concrete proposals to make on everything from American race relations to the military-industrial complex. His proposals were animated, all of them, by a conviction that realism and accommodation are different things, and that only a realism that sets itself against the facts can become a virtue.

But the word *utopian* obviously meant more to the neo-conservatives that I've yet suggested. It meant a willingness to sacrifice the present on behalf of a future that was patently incredible. In this sense, Howe was the arch enemy because he consistently attacked the present order in the name of a dispensation that didn't exist. His example seemed dangerous because he sapped the strength of those who might otherwise have taken arms against liberationist types and others who promoted cultural disorder. Critics like Decter lectured Howe to the effect that "politics in the twentieth century has a way of presenting people with stark choices," so that "the pretense of commitment to a third alternative is itself always choice—on the wrong side." Never mind that Howe styled himself an anti-Communist and a supporter of democratic institutions. Never mind that he was as often critical of people on the left as of people on the right. He refused to subscribe to the neo-conservative view—so nicely described by Gore Vidal—that "all's right with America if you're not in a gas chamber, and making money." Clearly, therefore, he was a moral incompetent, his attack on American foreign and economic policy in the Reagan years ungrateful, insensitive, anti-American.

In fact, the neo-conservative critique of the so-called utopian impulse was fundamentally, and deliberately, misleading. Anyone who had read Irving's political criticism knew that it was in no way neutral or evasive or coy. It was a committed criticism if ever there was one. Irving favored revolution when there seemed no other way to overthrow dictators. Sometimes he was committed to avoiding unnecessary violence in places that had known too much violence, and with little to show for it. He was always committed to finding ways to promote democracy. To say that such a perspective is utopian is to dismiss it simply because it cannot be relied upon to take the same side—"our side"—in every dispute. But of course "our side" is not so easy to define as some wish us to believe. Was it is American interests to supportr a friendly though deeply repressive regime in Latin America when one supposed that ten years hence a revolutionary regime in the same country would likely hold us accountable for that support? It was not utopian to think ahead or to imagine that American-supported tyrannies might be overthrown by their own people.

But the neo-conservative critique of utopianism was deeply flawed in another way. It failed to acknowledge that the utopian impulse is itself a constitutive element in every serious act of criticism. We refer to it implicitly when we demand that criticism be disinterested, or when we say that the business of art is to put us in mind of questions rather than answers. The editor of *The New Criterion* liked to lecture audiences about the decline of standards, but he had no capacity to imagine an ideal standard from which all valid judgments may be said to issue. We don't judge the desirability of a political order by comparing it only with the obvious brutalities of another system. Neither do we evaluate a new novel only by considering how well it is paced, or how amusing are its locutions. We operate from what we take to be an adequate standard, which we apply in good faith, not expecting that the objects passing before us will measure up in every way, but determined that failure or insufficiency be identified and, where possible, accounted for. The standard, we acknowledge, has something to with what we like, but we try to differentiate between what we like and what we feel we are entitled to admire and recommend. There is, we say, no standard worth defending which does not require struggle.

In *Politics and the Novel*, when Irving spoke of "the vast respect which the great novelist is ready to offer to the whole idea of opposition," he had in mind something entirely antithetical to the demands leveled by his neo-conservative critics. When Midge Decter insisted that Irving take sides in her sense, she was insisting, in effect, that he offer no resistance to his own predispositions, that he settle his ambivalences and determine to see things in "the right way. To be political, to be "serious," in Decter's terms, was to take up a position and do nothing that might conceivably compromise it. To promote high culture, in this sense, was to celebrate paintings or books that could not be used for the "wrong" political purposes by our enemies. Criticism was, then, the act of "correcting" or dismissing works that might prove to be ideologically contaminating. Those, like Irving, who cultivated "oppositional" tendencies were by definition unhealthy, ambivalent in a way that suggested a failure of nerve. The business of right-thinking persons— so we were often instructed by the neo-conservatives—was not to engage works of art but to learn how to use them or to avoid being used by them. Power, not insight, was the name of the neo-conservative game, here as in every other transaction they pursued.

And so, if Irving seemed to them dangerously unreliable, that impression had everything to do with his willingness to embrace the example offered by the great novelists he adored. "If we ask ourselves," he had written, "what is the source of Dostoyevski's greatness, there can of course be no single answer. But surely part of the answer is that no character is allowed undisputed domination of the novel, all are checked and broken when they become too eager in the assertion of their truths." And what does it mean, precisely, to *check* and *break* in the way Irving proposes to us? In a novel the procedure may have more to do with a juxtaposition of voices or perspectives than with a contest or dialectic of contrary assertions. In *The Possessed*, Irving argues, opposing characters as yet unprepared for reconciliation are nonetheless made "ready for each other," so that a reader might actually see ahead to some future possible reconciliation never to be realized novelistically but *thinkable* all the same. The Conrad who hated Dostoyevski's unrepentant "confusion and insanity" nonetheless absorbed him and allowed his influence "everywhere to be seen" in *Under Western Eyes* and *The Secret Agent*, so that his own inclination to detachment, sanity and order might be *checked*.

As a critic Irving was resolute in self-opposition and in breaking and checking those many others "too eager in the assertion of their truths." On occasion he repeated too insistently an idea of his own, but in the main, and especially when he was moved to anger or rebuke, he tried to check the impulse by looking briefly at his own failings or recounting a fragment of his personal experience. Such was the case when he took on Kate Millett's *Sexual Politics* and pronounced its author "a figment of the zeitgeist, bearing the rough and careless marks of what is called higher education and exhibiting a talent for the delivery of gross simplicities in tones of leaden complexity." What angered Irving were the sweeping pronouncements of Millett's book, her relentless, reckless disregard of historical detail and cultural nuance. "About the experience of working-class women," Irving wrote, "she knows next to nothing, as in this comic-pathetic remark: 'The invention of labor-saving devices has had no appreciable effect on the duration, even if it has affected the quality, of their drudgery.' Only a Columbia Ph.D. who has never had to learn the difference between scrubbing the family laundry on a washboard and putting it into an electric washing machine can write such nonsense. As with most New Left ideologues, male or female, Miss Millett suffers from middle-class parochialism."

One might have supposed, on the basis of those sentences alone, that Irving was himself descended from a family in which the washboard was a household presence. The pitch of the rebuke is too sharp to seem a reflection of scholarly research alone. And though Irving resorts now and again in his essay to a more familiar species of academic one-upmanship ("Had Miss Millett read carefully the scholarly authorities she cites" or "we must recognize that fifty or sixty years ago people could not possibly see things as they are seen today: that is known as historical perspective."), his corrections are here most effective, and not altogether characteristic, when they draw upon experiences so deeply rooted that they seem to him unanswerable. "Was my mother a drudge," he asks at the close of his essay, "in subordination to the 'master group'? No more a drudge than my father who used to come home with hands and feet blistered from his job as presser. Was she a 'sexual object'? I would never have thought to ask, but now, in the shadow of decades, I should like to think that at least sometimes she was."

No doubt the passage will seem to some readers not at all unanswerable, but it does, after all, come at the end of an essay in which substantial concessions are made. Often, in a piece notable for the steady heat it generates, Irving briefly checks his anger, recalling that, yes, in fact, the women of his acquaintance *do* "have it harder than men," "do suffer disadvantages." There are, surely, he understands, "blunter and cruder variants of male bossdom and female subordination" than he himself has known. And yes, there will be important differences in gender relations as we move from one group or class to another. It is essential, surely, to speak of these matters with the authority of intimate acquaintance and observation, though it is equally obvious that no one observer can have experience of all classes and all varieties of gender relations.

And yet, and yet, Irving would seem again and again to repeat, correcting for his own instinct to check the forward momentum of his angry disapproval: Those who are "driven by some ideological demon" cannot manage the work of analysis. "It is an outrage," he writes, "to reduce [men and women] to mere categories of ideology," and cultural critics "caught up in a masochistic tremor of overdetermination" will see "only butterflies broken by brutes" and will, in consequence, have no patience or love for small differences, "will have nothing to do with the small struggles and little victories" of ordinary people. Instead, they will find in their hearts mainly "contempt for those who find some gratification in family life, contempt for 'the usual.' "

The movement in Irving's prose, in Irving's thought, is often of this kind, an alternation of hard thrusts, checks and corrections, modulated arguments and fierce polemic ripostes. Of course he was never cautious about the targets he chose. Those who were most influential, most celebrated, were often those he countered most aggressively. And yet he never forgot that there was something *on behalf of which* he contended. Ideas were not merely his stock-in-trade. They mattered, and those who abused them or handled them clumsily made it harder for the rest of us to distinguish between a viable or noble idea and a merely provocative or "interesting" idea. In the American intellectual community, Irving came more and more to believe, the very status of ideas or theories was no longer properly understood. "A cry of woe is not a theory," he wrote, "and neither is a description." Elsewhere he wrote that "a theory that can't be refuted can't be demonstrated," and he was not at all averse to demanding of new ideas that they "make sense" and seem at least marginally "plausible." And though, again, he surely continued to appreciate the need for checks and corrections, he often scorned the "equanimity" that could treat radically different ideas and events in the same "creamy" or "detached" tone, as if the critic were not at all implicated in what he was writing about or disturbed by the incongruities he had, perhaps unwittingly, set before his reader.

In person Irving could seem, at least occasionally, brusque, not because he was cold or detached but because he had, like most of us, work to do. In our phone conversations over many years he always seemed to me attentive and efficient, eager to make an appointment for dinner but determined not to give more than five or ten minutes to our preliminary contact. Though we exchanged a fair number of letters—perhaps thirty or forty—he often sent me postcards initiating an exchange or responding to my queries. When we had several days together, at *Salmagundi*-sponsored conferences especially, he was genial and solicitous, talkative and contentious, eager to draw me out and to have his own extended say. When we strolled together in Manhattan or in Saratoga Springs, he came out with things that clearly were not for the ears of those he criticized, but he never seemed anxious about my discretion, or bothered to swear me to silence. He had an opinion on just about everything, but was modest about his grasp even of subjects he knew quite well, and once, when tried to persuade him to write for *Salmagundi* about a Balanchine ballet—he had written one memorable essay on his infatuation with Balanchine's work—, he said that, until he knew as much about the dance as Robert Garis he'd be embarrassed to pronounce on any particular ballet. He could study Balanchine dances night after night at The New York State Theatre, but he would never master the thing well enough. Other amateurs might do well writing about things they'd come to late in life, but he was not such an amateur. He was pleased when others praised his versatility and breadth, his capacity to move easily from politics to literature. But he knew the difference between trading opinions with friends over the dinner table and publishing one's views in books or magazines.

In addition to the many enemies Irving made in the course of a long career, there were many who envied him. A brilliant young man who had done undergraduate work with me at Skidmore College and moved on to do a Ph.D. at Buffalo reported that, at his doctoral orals in the late seventies, he was practically laughed out of the room when he said that Howe was the literary man he most admired. Those who laughed knew that Irving had little use for most of the academic literary theorists who had come to preside at most doctoral orals, and at least one in the Buffalo examination room had been taken apart by Irving in a biting review. It seemed easy for these people to dismiss Irving as a "journalist," to suggest to my young friend that he would do better to adopt as his model someone who wrote principally for other academics and whose idea of politics never went further than putting tendentious formulations in brackets. They were equally dismissive of Orwell, and Edmund Wilson.

But in spite of the enemies and the theorists, not to mention the irritation he provoked in a good part of his own left-liberal constituency, Irving was never reluctant to take on his own allies, including those who published in *Dissent*, and no doubt his scruple and his courage were galling to those whose commitment to one or another party line never permitted them to criticize one of their own. Irving was not a mild man, but I never saw him consumed with the disfiguring hatred, or hauteur, or dismissive contempt that one finds so often in the pages of magazines that attacked him. He earned his reputation as a fierce polemicist, but he gave his opponents their due, and in conversation he was as apt to complain about the self-righteous cruelty of an ostensibly liberal *New Republic* journalist as about the gifted and judicious critic who, alas, had no stomach for battle.

Irving published essays and reviews in dozens of journals over the years, and of course literary intellectuals will be familiar with at least some of his books, among which *Politics and the Novel* and the Modern Masters *Trotsky* seem to me the most brilliant and important; *A World More Attractive* his most original collection of miscellaneous essays; *The Critical Point* the most stirring example of his polemical wit and his sometimes adversarial relation to contemporary culture; and *World of our Fathers* the most sustained and ambitious product of his always searching historical imagination.

But I can't help feeling that Irving was most himself in the immediate give-and-take of argument and discussion, where his ability to listen and consider was ever tested by his instinct to challenge and contest. Never have I known anyone at once so civil and courteous and yet so forthright and probing. In a conference on "Kitsch," for example, I observed him challenging other participants, asking questions, offering examples, now and again resisting the very terms of the discussion, but throughout having a good time—as he was usually bound to do, so long as he had around him lively minds who could take the heat and radiate some in his direction. Near the conclusion of the three-day, nearly fifteen- hour kitsch meeting conducted at Skidmore, he attempted, in a way extraordinary for its generosity, to evoke and pull together some of the many things that had been said about our subject, concluding that the word "kitsch" was simply unsatisfactory. It was too vague. It could mean or suggest too many different things. It might well obscure more than it illuminated. The entire business reminded him, he said,

> Of an experience I had last year when I was ill. I was in Mt. Sinai Hospital, and I asked a doctor what my problem was. He spouted, 'myocardial infarctation,' or something like that. I turned almost pale as if he had accused me of kitsch. I said, 'what does that mean?' The old doctors refused to say, because they thought it an insult to their dignity. A young doctor took a piece of paper, made a drawing of the arteries around the heart, and showed me exactly what the problem was, and it was a very simple problem.

Irving had been disappointed—so he told us—by developments in the American academy, by the flight from what he called "ordinary language," by the increasing resort to "terminology, apparatus, methodology," not only among scientists but among literary people. It seemed to him most often possible "to see what one says" and to "say what one sees" without making readers feel "puzzled" or "inferior," without trying "to inflame or mislead response." He accepted that it might be necessary now and then to resort to special terms, but only as a last resort, after he had made every effort "to specify in concrete description" what had brought him to use a word like "kitsch." And he accepted, too, that in the end his reluctance to use certain kinds of language might have had more to do with personal temperament than with the principles he espoused. "The differences between us," he conceded, "really involve a traditional difference of intellectual style (which will continue, I suppose, as long as human beings try to think). A difference between, roughly speaking, the Anglo-Saxon, of which I'm a familiar representative, and the Continental." He wouldn't hope to persuade anyone inclined to speak of "kitsch" not to use the word, but he would insist that a word that might suggest a great many different things ought to be resisted.

"To define kitsch," he argued, "as the utopia of communism, fascism, and liberal democracy seems to me an example of the wide-ranging imprecision that I object to." In the end he agreed that it was "fun" to debate the uses of such a term, and to work around something that furnished few opportunities for consensus, and he was content at last to ask only that the thirty colleagues seated with him around the conference table send him a postcard whenever they were tempted to use the word "kitsch." In the months following our meeting, I received three such postcards from Irving himself.

9

Nathan Glick

The Socialist Who Loved Keats

Nathan Glick has been an editor and writer on political and cultural matters.
He was an early denizen of Alcove One at CCNY (City College of New York)
which served as a hangout for budding Trotskyites and socialists in the late
1930s. (Alcove Two was home to a much larger cohort of official Young
Communists.)

Glick recalls: "I remember the Irving Howe of those days as moody and
embattled. But on at least one occasion he relented and asked if he could
try my violin, which I had parked in Alcove One after orchestra rehearsal.
He then proceeded to play the 'Internationale' a bit scratchy but in tune."
(Early violin lessons seem to have been a familiar experience for future
Jewish literary critics: Alfred Kazin wrote affectionately about his duets
with Isaac Rosenfeld, who played the flute.)

After a stint at teaching history in high school, Glick became a frequent
contributor and part-time editor at the *New Leader*. In 1949 he became New
York editor of the U.S.-sponsored journal *Der Monat*, edited by Melvin
Lasky in Berlin, with the task of finding American contributors who could
hold their own against Europeans like Arthur Koestler, Ignazio Silone, Gun-
ther Grass and George Orwell. Lasky went on to edit *Encounter* in London.
In Washington, Glick founded and edited the quarterly *Dialogue*, which
was distributed abroad by the U.S. Information Agency in ten languages.

Irving Howe, who died in 1993, holds a unique and still oddly influential
place in American intellectual life. Undaunted by normal constraints on
time and energy, he pursued two consuming careers simultaneously, as
literary critic and as political gadfly. Remarkably, he also taught English,
wrote a monumental work of social history (*World of Our Fathers*, winner
of the 1977 National Book Award), and helped to salvage a rich but dying

language. In none of these realms did he make any concessions to political correctness or literary fashion.

In a period that saw a steady decline of socialist movements and an almost unanimous acceptance of market capitalism, he persisted in calling himself a democratic socialist, not because he expected socialism to revive and succeed but because he wanted to reiterate the urgent moral need for a fairer, more fraternal, more egalitarian society. Howe attracted a youthful following drawn to his tough-minded idealism, itself traceable to such incorruptible forebears as Eugene V. Debs and Norman Thomas, socialist leaders of a more innocent and hopeful age.

Beyond politics, Howe had been immersed since adolescence in the art and ambiguities of literature. During a bout of scarlet fever he read the collected poems of Milton, Keats, and Wordsworth. By age nineteen he was lecturing the comrades on the loss of faith in Matthew Arnold's "Dover Beach" and the clash between Western reason and Eastern mysticism in Thomas Mann's *The Magic Mountain*. He left a sizable body of literary criticism that faithfully conveyed in each case the essence of a work and the quality of the author's mind. Such a legacy may not produce a school of disciples—his voice was too idiosyncratic for easy emulation—but it may well sustain its beneficent influence on emerging younger critics. It is symptomatic of Howe's resilient double nature that he wrote books about the union leader Walter Reuther and the novelist William Faulkner, about Leon Trotsky and Thomas Hardy, about socialist doctrine and literary modernism.

Irving Howe may have been the last of a special breed of wide-ranging literary-political New York intellectuals who were grouped around the *Partisan Review*. Although its fees were pathetic and its circulation rarely over 10,000, by the late 1940s the *Partisan Review* was recognized as the country's most prestigious and influential voice of high culture. Its special flavor was provided by a small group of regular contributors who came to be known as "the New York intellectuals." No one has more relentlessly analyzed, criticized, and celebrated this group than Irving Howe, a latecomer and troublemaker but one of their own. The New York intellectuals, he wrote in a magisterial essay so titled, "have a fondness for ideological speculation; they write literary criticism with a strong social emphasis; they revel in polemic; they strive self-consciously to be 'brilliant'. . . . [Their] social roots . . . are not hard to trace. With a few delightful exceptions—a tendril from Yale, a vine from Seattle—they stem from the world of the immigrant Jews." The sly references to Dwight Macdonald and Mary McCarthy, both of whom were among the founding editors of *PR*, could be expanded to include many more non-Jews. It is testimony to the magnetic appeal and rising reputation of *PR* that T. S. Eliot offered the journal one of his *Four Quartets* and that the critic and novelist Elizabeth Hardwick left her native Kentucky for New York because, she confessed, "I wanted to become a New York Jewish intellectual."

In recent years a deluge of memoirs, critical studies, and Ph.D. dissertations have attested to the powerful influence the New York intellectuals had on the cultural tastes of American elites and on the reading lists of university literature and sociology courses. But Howe called attention as well to the impact of the *PR* style on the emerging group of Jewish novelists that included Saul Bellow, Bernard Malamud, Philip Roth, and Norman Mailer: "I think it no exaggeration to say that since Faulkner and Hemingway the one major innovation in American prose style has been the yoking of street raciness and high-culture mandarin which we associate with American Jewish writers."

This association of apparent opposites so intrigued Howe that he returned to it often in discussing the New York intellectuals. And in a curious way it could be seen in the two conflicting impulses of his own literary career. On the one hand, he strove for a tone of high moral seriousness and an elevated language that early on legitimized his ambition to be accepted as a significant critic. On the other, he wanted to avoid academic stuffiness and to preserve elements of the blunt style of polemic—sardonic, fast-paced, at times merciless—that he had mastered in the sectarian alcoves of the City College of New York.

The dominant qualities in Howe's critical prose are its lucidity, its muscular flexibility, and its drive, all serving his gifts for vivid exposition and persuasive analysis. But there was also a lighter side to this earnest critic. When a writer charmed or impressed him, he would occasionally incorporate the author's tone and tempo into his own commentary. A particularly infectious example of this mimetic talent erupted when Howe introduced the brainy sad-sack hero of Saul Bellow's *Herzog*.

> Where shall a contemporary novel begin? Perhaps unavoidably: with the busted hero reeling from a messy divorce and moaning in a malodorous furnished room; picking at his psyche's wounds like a boy at knee scabs; rehearsing the mighty shambles of ambition ("how I rose from humble origins to complete disaster"); cursing the heart-and-ball breakers, both wives and volunteers, who have, he claims, laid him low; snarling contempt at his own self-pity with a Johnsonian epigram, "Grief, Sir, is a species of idleness"; and yet, amidst all this woe, bubbling with intellectual hope, as also with intellectual gas, and consoling himself with the truth that indeed "there were worse cripples around."

Having indulged himself with this savory imitation of Bellow's style, Howe returned to his own sober voice, delivering sweeping yet shrewdly accurate appraisals of the author.

All of Bellow's books—whether melancholy realism, moral fable, or picaresque fantasia—represent for him a new departure, a chosen risk in form and perception. Bellow has the most powerful mind among contemporary American novelists, or at least, he is the American novelist who best assimilates his intelligence to creative purpose. This might have been foreseen at the beginning of his career, for he has always been able to turn out a first-rate piece of discursive prose; what could not have been foreseen was that he would also become a virtuoso of fictional technique and language.

The essay on Bellow was written in what I would call Howe's "middle period," roughly 1960–1975, when he evolved an apolitical approach to literature, along with a style of clarity, intellectual rigor, and emotional responsiveness. In retrospect, his major work of the 1950s, *Politics and the Novel*, marked his transition from political man incidentally fascinated by literature to professional literary man (he taught English for nearly forty years, at Brandeis, Stanford, and the City University of New York) who wrote and edited political articles in his spare time. Howe found that each of eleven selected novelists, from Dostoevsky and Hawthorne to Malraux and Orwell, raised troubling questions about morality, character, and motive. The temptation to deliver judgments based on socialist convictions must have been strong. But Howe made a deliberate effort to avoid the often righteous tone of his political writing. The essays in *Politics and the Novel* display an unexpected tolerance of diverse ideologies, along with an empathy even for weakness of character and an appreciation of eccentricity and charm for their own sake.

At times, however, he went too far in his swing toward what Edmund Wilson facetiously called "liquorary quiddicism" and adopted refined mannerisms and abstract formulations borrowed from Henry James or Lionel Trilling that clearly did not suit his natural voice—for example, "the very yearning for choice reveals the power of destiny." But at his best—and most of *Politics and the Novel* sustains an impressive level of commentary—he could be passionate and pungent. Summing up Turgenev's political wisdom in *Fathers and Sons* and other novels, Howe revealed how far he himself had come from the doctrinal certainties of his youth. "He speaks to us for the right to indecision, which is almost as great a right as the right to negation. He speaks to us for a politics of hesitation, a politics that will never save the world but without which the world will never be worth saving. He speaks to us with the authority of failure."

What is most striking in *Politics and the Novel* is Howe's appetite for novels that are intellectually challenging and construct their plots against a background of crucial historical movements, even when their politics are conservative or reactionary, as is the case in Dostoevsky's *The Possessed*, Conrad's *Under Western Eyes*, and James's *The Princess Casamassima*. Yet some years later, when he confronted Theodore Dreiser's *An American Tragedy*, a novel lacking the intellectual force or historical significance of those earlier works, Howe rejected the fashionable disparagement of the author's crude style and half-baked ideas. Dreiser, he insisted, "ranks among the American giants, the very few American giants we have had. . . . What makes him so absorbing a novelist, despite all of his grave faults, is that he remains endlessly open to experience." Unlike the typically dispiriting naturalists, Dreiser "is always on the watch for a glimmer of transcendence. . . . [for] the possibility of 'a mystic something of beauty that perennially transfigures the world.'" But along with this high-flown if deeply felt sentiment, Howe recognized that Clyde Griffiths, Dreiser's ill-fated hero, embodies a very different universal quality: "He represents . . . our collective smallness, the common denominator of our foolish tastes and tawdry ambitions. He is that part of ourselves in which we take no pride, but know to be a settled resident."

As a critic, Irving Howe cast a wide net. His sympathies extended to obscure novelists and poets; he tried single-handedly to restore the reputation of Edwin Arlington Robinson. He wrote about several generations of Jewish American novelists whose roots and outlooks resonated familiarly in his own experience. And he wrote about Emerson, Hawthorne, and Whitman, whose Transcendentalist idealism he found both distant and personally affecting. Starting with an admiring book about Thomas Hardy, Howe proceeded in his later years to rediscover for an intellectual public some of the famous but at the time underestimated figures of nineteenth-century British fiction—among them Sir Walter Scott, Anthony Trollope, and George Eliot.

On separate occasions Howe's strong views about contemporary American writers infuriated Ralph Ellison and Philip Roth, and led to unusually memorable ripostes. In a long essay on black writing, Howe praised Richard Wright's novel *Native Son* (1940) for its racial ferocity and "clenched militancy." He took issue with James Baldwin's objection that Wright's "protest" fiction represented blacks only as victims. He also deplored Ralph Ellison's comment, on receiving the National Book Award for *Invisible Man* (1952), that he tried "to see America with an awareness of its rich diversity and its almost magical fluidity and freedom." With an uncharacteristic rhetorical flourish Howe laid down his private party line: "How could a Negro put pen to paper, how could he so much as think or breathe, without some impulsion to protest?"

So peremptory a pronouncement by a Jewish critic who claimed all of world literature as his terrain clearly invited attack. Ellison rose to the occasion with a searing essay ("The World and the Jug," included in his book *Shadow and Act*) that went beyond simply answering Howe to an eloquent recall of his own critical awakening and his choice of literary models. "I was freed not by propagandists or by the example of Wright . . . but by composers, novelists, and poets who spoke to me of more interesting and freer ways of life. . . . While one can do nothing about choosing one's relatives, one can, as artist, choose one's 'ancestors.' Wright was, in this sense, a 'relative'; Hemingway an 'ancestor.' " The exchanges between Howe and Ellison were sharp but civil, with Howe yielding somewhat toward the end; polemics on a coruscating level, they deserve to be reissued under one cover.

Howe's other target of provocation was Philip Roth, a literary street fighter more than capable of taking on his tormentor. A decade after writing a favorable review of Roth's first book, *Goodbye, Columbus* (1959), Howe decided that the novelist's rising reputation, with the publication of *Portnoy's Complaint* (1969), needed major surgery. In a full-scale broadside, "Philip Roth Reconsidered," Howe committed an act of what he might have called literary slum clearance. He convicted Roth of vulgarity, condescension, and moral callousness before going on to specific stylistic crimes.

Another decade later—resentment percolating over time—Roth introduced into his semi-autobiographical novel *The Anatomy Lesson* the critic Milton Appel, whose harsh reconsideration of the hero's work cut him to the quick. "You pervert my intentions, then call me perverse!" Zuckerman-Roth shouts over the phone to his accuser. "You lay hold of my comedy with your ten-ton gravity and turn it into a travesty. My coarse, vindictive fantasies, your honorable, idealistic humanist concerns." But to an interviewer Roth once held up his Irving Howe file and said wistfully, "He was a real reader."

Most of Howe's criticism was not so embattled. On the contrary, writing about novels and poems served him as an escape from the polemical strains of politics, a way of moving from the public realm to the private, from social issues to personal relations. In the last years of his life, having spent more than three decades dealing with complexity and subtlety, he turned his attention to discovering some basic secrets of fictional art. How can an author convey goodness without sentimentality or bathos? Why does the "tone" of a novel, that elusive emanation of style, often speak to us more strikingly than the solid logic of incident and character? Why do certain "gratuitous details," not essential to a novel's structure, remain most vividly in the mind and memory?

These are some of the questions Howe addressed in short pieces collected by his son Nicholas in a posthumous volume titled *A Critic's Notebook* (1994). Answering them, he displayed a side of his critical persona not prominent earlier. Here he was playful, ruminative, modest, and curious. He found a special wisdom and delight in the works of writers' late years—such as the "transparency" and "lack of complicating devices" in one of Chekhov's last stories. A comment on Leo Tolstoy opens with this touching tribute: "Reading the aged Tolstoy stirs the heart. He will not yield to time, sloth, or nature. He clings to the waist of the lifeforce. Deep into old age, he battles with the world, more often with himself, returning in his diaries, fictions, and tracts to the unanswerable questions that torment him. Blessed old magician, he is free of literary posture and the sins of eloquence." Turning in his own later writings toward a Tolstoyan plainness, Howe shared the old magician's "need for meaning" and "restlessness of mind," even as he too on occasion succumbed "to moral crankiness . . . to intemperate demands for temperance."

The journey from combative youth to contemplative old age—in politics as in literary taste—was a long and instructive one, much of it told in *A Margin of Hope* (1982), Howe's "intellectual autobiography," the most personal and engaging of his books. Howe grew up in the east Bronx during the Great Depression after his father lost the family grocery and was reduced to the hand-blistering job of presser. Radicalism was in the air, and at the age of 14 he joined the Young People's Socialist League where he found a kind of surrogate family: fraternal, argumentative and English-speaking. As Howe gravitated toward the more doctrinaire Trotskyist faction, the "movement" almost totally consumed his time and energy, giving him the illusory feeling that he and his comrades could, without too much trouble, transform the world. His description of life in a radical sect vividly evokes its heady combination of sophistication and innocence, apocalyptic pronouncements and secret doubts.

Alcove One in the City College cafeteria during the late 1930s was the ideal place to sharpen one's polemical and analytical skills. This was where the fringe radicals—those shunned by the much more numerous young Communists in Alcove Two—converged after classes to trade political gossip or deliver authoritative judgments on the civil war in Spain, the trials of Old Bolsheviks in Moscow, or the impending war in Europe. It is hardly surprising that this atmosphere of non-stop debate nurtured an unusual proportion of future intellectual stars, among them sociologists Daniel

Bell, Nathan Glazer and Seymour Martin Lipset, and political journalists Irving Kristol and Melvin J. Lasky (longtime editor of the London monthly, *Encounter*).

In a nostalgic memoir of those years, written from his changed perspective as "godfather of the neoconservatives," Kristol recalled that his involvement in Trotskyist politics was the source of his real college education by prompting him "to read and think and argue with a furious energy." Daniel Bell, a social-democratic anomaly tolerated because of his formidable intellectual range, remembers Howe as the alcove "commissar" who later changed not only his ideas but, more remarkably, his temperament, the way he held his ideas.

The 1950s saw a broad movement among the New York intellectuals away from dogmatic leftism and toward a more flexible liberalism and a more benign appraisal of American society. Even as he moved in that direction, Howe was among the last of his former comrades, and the most reluctant, to give up an intransigently radical stance. Although he spent most of the postwar decade, after a stint in the Army, building an academic and literary career, he missed the excitement of a "movement," a community of fellow believers "absorbed in ideas beyond the smallness of self."

How does one create a movement out of abandoned doctrines and uncertain hopes? Howe's answer was apologetically ironic: "When intellectuals can do nothing else they start a magazine." In 1954 he and a colleague at Brandeis University launched *Dissent*, a quarterly that advocated, and at the same time tried stumblingly to define, "democratic socialism." As might be expected, a magazine so earnest and political in its ambitions did not produce the cerebral fireworks of the old *Partisan Review*. Times had changed, and even radical intellectuals had found jobs and tenure in the universities. Much of the theoretical and analytical writing in *Dissent* bore the heavy weight of academic stolidity. The redeeming liveliness came from younger writers grappling with the more urgent problems of improving daily life—in housing, health care, welfare, and race relations—or from less ideological reporting by seasoned journalists about, for example, life among the unemployed in a Pennsylvania mining town, or the chaotic early period of the Sandinista takeover in Nicaragua.

Perhaps the most valuable function of *Dissent* and its contributors in the late 1960s and early 1970s was to keep their democratic sanity when all around them on the New Left—students, professors, and *The New York Review of Books*—were losing theirs to some apocalyptic vision of revolution inspired by Fidel Castro, Mao Zedong, and Ho Chi Minh.

But for Howe and his colleagues—Michael Harrington, whose book *The Other America* (1962) helped to launch the War on Poverty, and the political philosopher Michael Walzer—the main purpose of *Dissent* was to clarify the moral status and practical viability of socialism, vaguely defined as a more equitable, more universally democratic society. They were on strong ground in deploring the obvious inequities and injustices of capitalism. But they also recognized the far deadlier injustices of societies around the world that called themselves socialist. The position they took was that socialism could not be said to have failed; it had simply never been tried, because, in Howe's words, "there can be no socialism without democracy."

The real question for the *Dissent* circle was Can there be socialism *with* democracy? To their credit, they took this question seriously. They had seen power corrupt and absolute centralized power corrupt absolutely. Was it possible to avoid the totalitarian potential of socialism? One response argued that since all modern societies, including capitalist ones, are moving toward some form of economic collectivism, the crucial issue is whether controls will be democratic and participatory or bureaucratic and authoritarian. Another argued that power and authority should be scattered by way of autonomous industries, small private enterprises, and worker involvement in management, so as to create an economic version of checks and balances.

Howe admitted that the solutions suggested were tentative, inconclusive, and possibly unworkable. But he insisted that his utopian vision of socialism served a useful function, even if it could never be attained. Just as religious faith provides fallible humankind with a touchstone for private moral behavior, he argued, so too could faith in democratic socialism nudge people's resistant consciences toward a more decent and generous level of public behavior. The epigraph to Howe's collection of political and social essays, *Steady Work* (1966), restates this religious-secular equation in an astringently self-mocking way. "Once in Chelm, the mythical village of the East European Jews, a man was appointed to sit at the village gate and wait for the coming of the Messiah. He complained to the village elders that his pay was too low. 'You are right,' they said to him, 'the pay is low. But consider: the work is steady.' "

The Messiah, alas, never arrived in the small towns of Eastern Europe. So by the tens of thousands the inhabitants of the *shtetls* sought a more tangible salvation in America. From 1880 to 1914 approximately one third of all Eastern European Jews emigrated, a total of nearly two million, most of them to the United States. They came to escape pogroms, poverty, and restricted horizons. Irving Howe told their story in fascinating detail and sweeping historical perspective in *World of Our Fathers*. He described the shock of adapting to an entirely new, mostly urban world. He traced their gradual entry into American politics (especially the leftist variety), business (especially Hollywood), labor unions (especially in the garment trade), and cultural life. America gave the immigrants unprecedented security and opportunity, and gained in return an infusion of energy and enterprise, intellectual passion and theatrical flair.

Howe recognized the richness and historical uniqueness of the Jewish experience in the United States. But he also saw the costs of success: the dispersion of bustling city neighborhoods into bland, assimilated suburbs, the weakening of a strain of "intense moral seriousness" as Jews moved up the economic ladder. Most of all Howe regretted the inevitable loss of an entire culture centered on the Yiddish language—a colorful world of poetry, prose, theater, and ritual that the immigrants brought with them, only to find their children and grandchildren losing interest as they became Americanized.

Like most children of East European immigrants, the young Howe shunned the limited "kitchen" Yiddish of his parents, just as he reddened with embarrassment when his father called him to supper from street games with the accented name "Oiving." Until the late 1940s Howe distanced himself from his Jewish heritage, rejecting Judaism along with religion generally, showing only a passing interest in the new state of Israel.

After his discharge from the U.S. Army at the end of World War Two, Howe caught up with the devastating events of the Holocaust and lost his faith in the imminence of socialism. He began to read the great Yiddish writers: Sholom Aleichem, I. L. Peretz and Mendele M. Sforim. In 1953 he published an article about Sholom Aleichem that revealed an unexpected empathy for the life of the *shtetl* and an unreserved admiration for its most infectious chronicler, known to most Americans only as the creator of Tevya, the philosophical milkman-hero of the musical, *Fiddler on the Roof.* Tevya, Howe wrote, "talks to God as to an old friend whom one need not flatter or assuage. Tevya, as we say in America, gives him an earful . . . . That, for Tevya was what it meant to be a Jew."

Soon after his article appeared, Howe received a letter from Eliezer Greenberg, a Yiddish poet who proposed that they join forces to translate Yiddish prose and poetry into English. Over the years they turned out six volumes, with accompanying essays by Howe that are probably the most knowledgeable and inviting introductions to Yiddish literature available in English. The high point of their collaboration came when Greenberg read out loud a story by Isaac Bashevis Singer, a writer then known only to readers of the Yiddish press. Hearing it, Howe realized that he had just stumbled onto a major talent, and persuaded Saul Bellow, not yet famous, to do the translation.

The editors of *Partisan Review* made literary history when they published

"Gimpel the Fool," later the title story of Singer's first collection in English. Singer soon became a regular contributor to *The New Yorker*, Bellow turned out his cerebral, high-spirited novels, and in the 1970s both won Nobel Prizes. Such momentary victories, however, did not obviate the fact that the store of Yiddish readers and writers was steadily declining. When in low spirits Howe would ask himself: "Another lost cause?"

But the marginalization of Yiddish had a wider resonance. Howe recalls asking Jacob Glatstein, one of the most brilliant poets in that language, what it felt like to be a major poet in a minor culture. His answer was bitter: "I have to know about Auden but Auden doesn't have to know about me." The distinguished Mexican novelist, Carlos Fuentes, makes a similar complaint, although Spanish is certainly a vigorously alive language, in contrasting what he calls "central and eccentric" writing. Central cultures—like those of England, France, Germany, Russia and the United States—tend to believe, according to Fuentes, that they speak with "a direct and open line to the ear of Divinity," because of their political and economic power. In this galaxy, Mexico, Poland and Egypt, for example, are viewed as "eccentric." They suffer, like the Yiddish poets, from the humiliation of indifference, the inability of their cultures to command international attention.

Howe's attraction to lost causes was a direct consequence of his longing for the "heroic," a word that appears often and almost always with approval in his writing. But who could have imagined that Irving Howe, the prideful man of the Left, would find an empathic hero in T. E. Lawrence? The famed Lawrence of Arabia, author of *Seven Pillars of Wisdom*, was an acknowledged agent of British imperialism, using his entrée into the Arab leadership to further British military advantage in the First World War against the Turks, then allied to the Germans.

Yet Howe's long essay "T. E. Lawrence: The Problem of Heroism" is one of his finest, because it draws on feelings far deeper than political sympathy: "If we come to him admiring whatever in his life was extraordinary, we remain with him out of a sense that precisely the special, even the exotic in Lawrence may illuminate whatever in our life is ordinary." But Howe was not wholly uncritical of this limelight-seeking adventurer. He saw Lawrence's early feats of physical endurance and his later feats of military bravura as "in part symptoms of a vanity which took the form of needing always to seem original."

Like Lawrence, Howe yearned to play a heroic role in some socially transforming historical event. His own vanity took the form of needing always to seem more principled and militant than his political adversaries. Even when he expressed doubts about the nature and viability of socialism, he could not forgo a posture of self-righteous superiority to those, especially old comrades, who no longer shared his dwindling faith. Still, there is something admirable in his unwavering insistence that American society could be fairer, more fraternal, more pervasively democratic, than it is. But he could hardly have found it heroic to wind up de facto on the fringe of the left wing of the Democratic Party.

Irving Howe's real heroism was acted out less on the ideological plane of politics than in the imaginative arena of literature. Over the past several decades, as the idols of his youth—George Orwell, Edmund Wilson, and Lionel Trilling—disappeared from the scene, Howe remained, along with Alfred Kazin and Robert Alter, among our most reliable literary critics, the most open to writers old and new, the most patient and penetrating, the most accessible. He was, in Philip Roth's grudging phrase, "a real reader," for whom literature was a way of keeping the soul alive.

10

Nicholas Howe

A Lover of Stories

Nicholas Howe is the son of Irving Howe. He has been professor of English at the University of California at Berkeley since 2002. Formerly he taught at the Ohio State University, the University of Oklahoma, and Rutgers University. The following short piece appeared in the *Dissent* memorial issue devoted to Irving Howe (Fall 1993).

My father moved in a world of stories. He told his own in *World of Our Fathers* and *A Margin of Hope*; he wrote about those of Faulkner and Hardy, Anderson and Wharton, Dreiser and Sholom Aleichem, Leskov and George Eliot, T. E. Lawrence and Pirandello, Delmore Schwartz and Raymond Carver, Tolstoy and Umberto Saba—the list amazes as much for its diversity as its length. With Ilana, his wife, he collected the shortest of stories, and together they made an anthology—*Short Shorts*—unlike any ever done: one that could satisfy his belief that very few pieces would not be better if cut by 20 percent. With this love of stories he welcomed my wife, Georgina, into the family, surprised but always delighted to have a novelist for a daughter-in-law.

His love of stories, his hope that he might make some sense of the world through them, gives me a way of talking about his complexity and yet also his simplicity as a man and writer. So let me tell you a story about him, a story that helps me understand the wholeness of his life's work. In the fall of 1986 he came to visit me in Oklahoma, and we took a road trip to the Wichita Mountains, about two hours southwest of Norman, where I then lived. These mountains rise up from a prairie that matches the mind's-eye view of Oklahoma: flat, dry, windswept, treed with a scattering of cottonwood and blackjack oak. These mountains are part of a wildlife refuge that holds, among other animals, a vast herd of buffalo; in an irony my father found delicious these buffalo descend from a few that had been shipped out to Oklahoma in 1905 from the Bronx Zoo. As we sat in the November sun eating sandwiches and drinking coffee, my father talked of the landscape and the way its hard vastness evoked fundamental qualities of American life. If he seemed out of place there, with his city clothes and his New York quickness, the place itself was not alien to him; it had for years been part of his imaginative landscape. After lunch we drove deeper into the Wichitas and visited Holy City, a stage set made from native red granite where the locals put on a passion play each Easter. For the rest of the year the Stations of the Cross stand gaunt and eerie against the blue Oklahoma sky. The story of the place tells of an émigré Austrian pastor who was sent out to tend the souls of Indians and who came to feel, in a moment of hallucinatory loneliness, that the landscape of the Wichitas bore an exact resemblance to that of Judea. Gazing at the scene, savoring its story, smiling at our being together there of all places in the world, my father turned to me and said with wonder: "It's straight out of Flannery O'Connor." I never felt closer to him than at that moment, for with that one sentence he gave me the story that would help me live in that alien landscape. It was his way of telling me he understood.

As we drove back to Norman that afternoon, we passed through a series of small towns that seemed to be losing their place in the landscape. My father asked the same question as we passed through each of them; it was the question he asked wherever he traveled: "How do people make a living here?" I tried to answer as best as I could: they worked in the feed mill or the grain elevator; they were roughnecks in the oil fields; they raised wheat or cattle. Some ran stores that served the outlying district. And many, I said, had no work. Oklahoma was then in a bust; the price of oil had dropped by more than 50 percent a few years before, and these towns were deep in depression. One glance down empty main streets told him as much; he had grown up in the East Bronx of the '30s and knew the smell of poverty wherever he encountered it. The story he wanted to hear was about those without work; he was haunted by it in Oklahoma or New York, Italy or Israel. He wanted always to know how people in a place managed to escape the humiliation of being without a job, of being without the simple but sustaining dignity that comes with work and the ability to provide food and shelter and perhaps a bit more to those we love.

And yes, there were writers who told this story, who knew it as well as he did. He wrote about them with a comrade's voice that you can hear most beautifully in the sentences about Ignazio Silone that run like a bright thread through many of his books. But I think that each of the many thousands of pages he wrote during his long life as a socialist—a life of writing that ran for more than fifty years and included not just the big books but also numberless op-ed pieces, reviews, bits for *Dissent*, forgotten dispatches from the front—drew on this same story. My father was a socialist—and make no mistake about his allegiance—because he understood the humiliation that comes to those without work, to those without the bare security of a decent living. He did not always write about these humiliations; he knew that pleasure mattered, and he found it most deeply in listening to music; he reserved as his favorite word of praise *delicious*. But he also knew that his life was sustained, in a phrase he took from a Hasidic story, by the steady work of waiting. In the tale, of course, the watchman of Chelm waits for the Messiah and complains to the village elders that his pay is too low. To which they respond, "Yes, the pay is low. But consider, the work is steady." My father knew that any messiah who was likely to appear this late in the twentieth century would only betray those who followed him. He knew that he could only wait and write and hope for something much more modest—for a world more attractive.

The final words should be my father's. Let me read to you the closing paragraph of an essay he wrote in 1955 about Walt Whitman, a poet he loved for his egalitarian sympathies and his New York stories.

And a final unorthodox note: It is generally said that Whitman declined in poetic power after the Civil War. This is true in a way, the poems of the later years being obviously more fragmentary and short-breathed than those of the earlier ones. But among the later pieces there are some with the most subtle refinement and humor. In his very old age he wrote a twelve-line poem called *After the Supper and Talk* in which he describes his reluctance to leave—we need hardly be told what it is that he must leave:

After the supper and talk—after the day is done,
As a friend from friends his final withdrawal prolonging,
Good-bye and Good-bye with emotional lips repeating,
(So hard for his hand to release those hands—no more will they meet,
No more for communion of sorrow and joy, of old and young,
A far-stretching journey awaits him, to return no more.)
Shunning, postponing severance—seeking to ward off the last word ever
    so little,
E'en at the exit-door turning—charges superfluous calling back—e'en
    as he descends the steps,
Something to eke out a minute additional—shadows of nightfall deep-
    ening,
Farewells, messages lessening—dimmer the forthgoer's visage and form,

Soon to be lost for aye in the darkness—loth, O so loth to depart!
Garrulous to the very last.

"No praise is needed," my father ends, "nor could any be sufficient for the frank pathos and relaxed gaiety of that final line. This is the way a man, and a poet, should end."

11

Brian Morton

The Literary Craftsman

For biographical information on Brian Morton see chapter 1, "A Man of the Left," by Mark Levinson and Brian Morton.

Writers sometimes write a little differently after their reputations are made. Some become mandarins in their old age—wise, all too wise. Some let the belt out a few notches and settle into verbosity.

A few, at the height of their fame, struggle to reinvent themselves or to refine their craft. These writers win our admiration and our love.

Irving found his style very quickly. His earliest work displays the tense lucidity that marked his prose for the rest of his life. His voice on the page was so confident that you might have thought it came easily, but he said that it didn't: he once said that he put almost everything he wrote through nine or ten drafts. In an essay on Orwell he wrote that the "discipline of the plain style—and that fierce control of self that forms its foundation—comes hard."

In the last few years he subtly remade his writing style. His earlier voice, though lucid before all else, had been bravura, self-consciously dazzling. As he said of the prose of the "New York intellectuals," it was "the style of brilliance." Now his work became even more spare, less adorned.

He left hints about this change in two pieces he wrote for the *New Republic*. In an article about the late works of Leo Tolstoy he described him, "deep into old age," as a writer who had worked his way "free of literary posture and the sins of eloquence." And in a review of a book by Yitzhak Zuckerman, a survivor of the Warsaw Ghetto uprising, published less than a month before he died, he said that Zuckerman "speaks plainly, without verbal flourish or the wanton rhetoric that has disfigured some writings about the Holocaust. . . . The dryness of his voice as he recalls terrible events comes to seem a sign of moral strength."

I don't know why Irving's voice grew more austere. It may be that after he had made his reputation, the claims of the self grew less insistent, and he no longer felt the need to dazzle. But I don't really believe it can be put down to personal reasons alone. I think it had something to do with his lifelong meditation on the nature of our time—the century of Auschwitz and the gulag, a time, as he wrote in *A Margin of Hope*, that "has been marked by a special terribleness." I think he belongs to the small fraternity of writers who took the experience of our century into the way they saw the world, into the weather of their prose. Orwell, Silone, Primo Levi . . . a few others.

In the end there was winter in his prose, but not because he was an old man. The chaste late voice was something like a voice of witness.

I miss his curiosity, his wit, the demands of his restlessness. The sheer pressure of his intensity turned the most casual encounter—a quick lunch at the coffee shop near his house—into something electric, charged.

Everyone knows he was a steady worker, but the word *steady* doesn't say nearly enough. He devoted himself to his calling with a matchless intensity; he gave of himself as deeply as anyone can. When he'd hang up the phone without saying good-bye—his famous habit—I often found myself smiling. I took pleasure in the thought of him turning quickly back to his desk, his task, his passion.

12

Paul Roazen

How Irving Howe Shaped My Thinking Life

Paul Roazen was born in Boston in 1936 and educated as a political theorist, first at Harvard (B.A., 1958), then at the University of Chicago, and also at Magdalen College, Oxford. He received his Ph.D. at Harvard in 1965 and taught in the government department from 1961 to 1971. Afterward he was a professor of social and political science at York University in Toronto until becoming a professor emeritus in 1995. He has published seventeen books and edited several more.

Looking over everything that Howe published, I have to feel a bit shame-faced about how comparatively little of his work I have read. My personal library does still contain marked-up copies of his critical study of Faulkner, along with his short books *Leon Trotsky* and *American Newness*, as well as collections like *A World More Attractive* and *Selected Writings*. But his *Politics and the Novel* had the most outstanding impact on me. I first bought it in early 1960, while I was doing graduate work in political theory at Oxford; it was a period when I was becoming disenchanted with the academic study of politics, and I would shortly return to Harvard to complete my Ph.D. When I first read *Politics and the Novel*, I was increasingly aware of political science's many inadequacies. Howe's book helped support my inclination to believe that political thinking was to be found not just in the texts considered canonical among academic political philosophers; all the great imaginative writers of the past had something of their own to contribute. As a matter of fact, I began to think that what had partly attracted me to the study of political theory in the first place was the degree to which the greatest social philosophers in history had been able to express artistic visions that perhaps literary critics were best able to help me understand.

I know that around the time I first read *Politics and the Novel* I pre-pared a tutorial essay on Dostoevsky's *The Possessed*. The study of politics at

Oxford could be so old-fashioned as a discussion of the merits of proportional representation, and my tutorials had become dispiriting; I ended up spending my time reading every great novel I could lay my hands on. So when I finally got my supervisor, Sir Isaiah Berlin, as my tutor, I specifically asked to concentrate on reading some political novels. Was I implying, he skeptically asked, that Trollope was worth studying? When I countered with Dostoevsky's name, he seemed unable to turn me down. At the time I suspected that Berlin felt that somehow one ought to be self-educated on such subjects, but he fell in with my proposed line of study. In any event I had already decided that I would be returning to the United States, and Berlin probably believed that there was little point in failing to comply with my request.

There was nothing specific to Howe's interpretation of Dostoevsky that I recall being decisive for me. Rather, I think it was the range of the writers Howe tried to understand in *Politics and the Novel* that was so inspiring. I soon came to think that the humane liberalism of Howe's outlook infused everything he sought to understand. I have had occasion at various times to reread *Politics and the Novel* and even think that Howe was capable of being fallible in his judgments. For example, Howe had difficulties, I suppose on ideological grounds, in appreciating just how much of a giant Conrad could be. Conrad's conservatism and his indictment of radicals in *The Secret Agent* were, I think, rather harsher than Howe felt capable of swallowing. But Howe showed such an admirable range of political catholicity of taste, and such a lack of doctrinaire convictions, that I felt he had helped legitimize my own inclination always to try to include great literature within my object of study. So even at the outset of my academic career, Howe helped encourage me to believe that one should not allow formal professional objectives to hinder one's pursuit of trying to become an educated person.

I am pretty sure I first registered Howe's name in the course of hearing an enthusiastic endorsement of him from a left-wing, non-Stalinist friend I had met at the University of Chicago in 1958–59. It would have been Howe's essays that seemed most memorable then, as well as his editing of *Dissent*. Hannah Arendt's "Reflections on Little Rock" appeared in *Dissent* in 1959, and the outrageousness of her argument set my small circle of acquaintances agog. It continues to strike me that Arendt's admirers today appear to be relatively unaware of her defense of Governor Orval Faubus in what was the greatest challenge to federal authority since the Civil War. Howe's *Dissent* had been willing to publish her piece, but accompanied by the critiques of some who seriously objected to her reasoning.

I sent Howe a piece entitled "Psychoanalysis and Moral Values" that

I thought he might like, and *Dissent* brought it out in 1971. I felt that Irving's editorial suggestions were altogether admirable. In 1986 *Dissent* also published a particularly outspoken review of mine about a book on the fate of psychotherapeutic training in Nazi Germany.

The only time Irving and I actually met was during the early 1970s, at York University in Toronto, where I then taught and where he had two children who were undergraduates. We spent a splendid couple of hours in my office, talking about everything under the sun. I remember him being impressed by my dating back to Lyndon Johnson's ill-fated presidency the series of steps by which the happy record of having liberal justices appointed to the Supreme Court was decisively reversed. (The frustration of Johnson's attempt to move his crony Abe Fortas up to becoming Chief Justice left, after Fortas's resignation, two seats for Richard Nixon to fill.) I found Howe to be wholly natural and completely without officiousness, his manner so unlike the disappointing self-importance of someone a bit older, like Lionel Trilling. One of the York deans, with a particular interest in Jewish studies, was afterward outraged, not at me but just in principle, to think that Howe had been on campus without his having been invited to give some public presentation.

Howe tried to encourage me to contribute to *Dissent*, but I begged off on the grounds that I was no kind of socialist, at which he seemed to want to indicate that he too felt most closely allied with the American tradition of liberalism. The only other memorable aspect of my contact with him comes from our occasional correspondence, revealing that we shared a distaste for the high-handedness of Arendt's official biographer. I hope that there is still time for me to fulfill the inspiration of *Politics and the Novel*, although how to put together in a book-length study my own interest in literature and politics remains a challenge. People are sometimes inclined to think that the influence teachers have is primarily personal, underestimating thereby the impact of the written word. My own contact with Howe came primarily from his books, especially the essays, and as I contemplate rereading once again *Politics and the Novel*, I feel confident that he would not be at all offended by my coming to some different judgments than he expressed earlier.

13

John Rodden

"My Intellectual Hero":

Irving Howe's "Partisan" Orwell

John Rodden has taught at the University of Virginia and the University of Texas at Austin. He is the author of *The Politics of Literary Reputation: The Making and Claiming of "St. George" Orwell* (1989) and *Scenes from an Afterlife: The Legacy of George Orwell* (2003) and the editor of *Lionel Trilling and the Critics* (1999), among other books.

I

George Orwell was a major influence and near-constant presence in Irving Howe's life for almost a half century. But Howe's intellectual relationship to Orwell deepened over time and was strongly conditioned by Howe's ideological evolution and by contemporary political and social events. His history of reception of Orwell can be roughly demarcated into four phases.

Howe first met Orwell in his quarterly "London Letter" (1941–46) in the pages of *Partisan Review*. An antiwar Trotskyist, an editor of a Trotskyist weekly, and a contributor to the theoretical organ of Max Shachtman's Independent Socialist League (ISL), *The New International*, Howe castigated Orwell in its pages as "pro-imperialist." Orwell's wartime support for the Allies and his insistence in *PR* in 1942 that pacifism was "objectively pro-fascist" outraged the twenty-two-year-old Howe.

By 1949, however, when he read *Nineteen Eighty-Four*, Howe was drifting away from Trotskyism. Nevertheless, though the *Partisan* and ISL circles moved in overlapping orbits (already by 1947 Howe was writing for *Partisan*), Howe still saw himself chiefly as a political man, and his primary reference group was the Shachtmanite sect. Howe was "half in . . . and half out" of "our little group" of dissident Trotskyists—ISL membership in the mid-1940s hovered around five hundred, a tiny faction within a faction of the American Left—and his primary reference group in the late 1940s was not the *Partisan* writers but the Shachtmanite sect, which had split with the mainline Trotskyists in 1940 over whether Stalin's betrayal of the Russian Revolution deprived the Soviet Union of its status as the workers' fatherland. Trotsky said no, blaming Stalin alone for its Stalinism; the Shachtmanites insisted yes, arguing that the real revolution had not yet happened.[1]

It was in the context of these intramural Marxist disputes and practical problems of revolutionary action that Howe responded to *Nineteen Eighty-Four*, unlike Orwell's other vocal *Partisan* admirers (e.g., Lionel and Diana Trilling, Philip Rahv, Alfred Kazin, Daniel Bell, Dwight Macdonald, Arthur Schlesinger).[2] Although many of the older *Partisan* writers were Trotskyists in the 1930s (and Macdonald and Isaac Rosenfeld were Shachtmanites in the early 1940s), they had already shed their revolutionary socialism and Marxist scholasticism for social-democratic politics; Howe was responding to Orwell from a stance the *Partisan* writers no longer shared.

Howe's essay-review of *Nineteen Eighty-Four*—published in *New International* in November–December 1950—was largely a meditation on whether, deliberately or inadvertently, socialism could be "twisted into something as horrible as '1984,' " even by "we, the good people, the good socialists." Howe concluded that Orwell had answered, somberly, in the affirmative. Howe emphatically agreed. *Nineteen Eighty-Four* was a ghastly picture of what socialism could become, "not merely from Stalinism" but even from "genuine socialist efforts." The lesson of *Nineteen Eighty-Four*, said Howe, concerned precisely how to conduct the transition to socialism. Orwell's valuable warning was that democratic practices could not automatically be taken for granted after a revolution. Democracy would more likely be preserved during the transition to socialism if workers shared political and social power with other classes.[3] Still, Howe also noted his "numerous disagreements" with Orwell's democratic socialism and approved Lenin's criticisms of gradualist Eduard Bernstein.[4]

Yet even in 1950 Howe was moving toward his conclusion of a few years later that workers had much more to fear from Leninism than from social democracy. Already he was a wearied veteran of a dozen years of Marxist infighting, feeling a sense of exhaustion and frustration about the political irrelevance and impotence of the Shachtmanites. A socialist at the age of fourteen, an editor at twenty of the Trotskyist paper *Labor Action*, and one of the original organizers of the ISL in 1942, Howe had felt his commitment to revolutionary socialism waning ever since his return to New York after four years of military service in Alaska. Capitalism was not crumbling, he realized, and America was not Nazi Germany.

The break eventually came, without fanfare, when Howe submitted his resignation letter to the Shachtmanites in October 1952. As his involvement gradually lessened, Howe concluded that his real calling was that of a writer and literary critic. Already by 1949 he had coauthored (with B. J. Widick) a highly praised prolabor study on the rise of the industrial unions, *The UAW and Walter Reuther*. It was soon followed by two books of literary-biographical criticism, *Sherwood Anderson* (1951) and *William Faulkner* (1952).

And as he began to see himself less as an activist and political journalist and more as a literary man, Howe began to exchange his old reference group of the Trotskyists for the larger, cultivated world of the *Partisan* writers.

II

During the war years Orwell had been one of the very few writers whom most first-generation members of the PR circle—including *Partisan*'s pacifist, revolutionary wing (Macdonald, Clement Greenberg) and its more moderate, culturally oriented wing (Rahv, William Phillips, Trilling)—admired.[5] Their estimations grew enormously after *Animal Farm* (1945), *Dickens, Dali, and Others* (1946), *Nineteen Eighty-Four* (1949), and the posthumous essay collections. Now, with his full entry into the *Partisan* circle and his transition to "writer," Howe's own admiration for Orwell intensified, and the range of questions that he brought to his thinking about Orwell broadened and diversified.

From the mid-1950s to the early '60s Howe came increasingly to identify with Orwell, and this second stage of his reception (circa 1955–63) is marked less by ideological and more by historical, literary, and personal concerns, some of which he shared with other *Partisan* writers. Chief among the former was the nature and development of totalitarianism. *The Origins of Totalitarianism* (1951), that brilliant and controversial masterpiece of Hannah Arendt, an "elder" member of the New York intellectuals, had an enormous impact on the thinking of the *Partisan* writers and the intellectual world generally. Especially during the period of "de-Stalinization" in the mid-1950s, when debate raged about the possibility that the Soviet system was altering fundamentally, Arendt's book sparked numerous historical and theoretical discussions as to whether totalitarianism was the form of authoritarian government characteristic of the modern bureaucratic, collectivist age.

Howe's major contribution to Orwell's critical reputation in the 1950s was to help lift *Nineteen Eighty-Four* above mere Cold War polemics and place it within the context of these discussions. Partly as a result of Howe's widely reprinted *American Scholar* essay, "Orwell: History as Nightmare" (1956), *Nineteen Eighty-Four* was soon being treated by journalists and political scientists alike as a work of political theory, an abstract model of the totalitarian state (or, in Howe's phrase, "the post-totalitarian" state).[6] Following Howe's declaration that "no other book has succeeded so completely in rendering the essential quality of totalitarianism," and his detailed examination of Orwell's "view of the dynamics of power in a totalitarian state," critics treated *Nineteen Eighty-Four* as the fictional counterpart to theoretical studies on totalitarianism by Arendt, Richard Lowenthal, Carl Friedrich, and Zbigniew Brzezinski.[7] Indeed, because *Nineteen Eighty-Four* antedated *The Origins of Totalitarianism* and similar political treatises, some critics saw it as inaugurating this emergent tradition and suggested that it had inspired Arendt and later theorists.

Howe contributed to this tendency in his *Nineteen Eighty-Four: Text, Sources, Criticism* (1963). His edition includes a supplemental section on "the politics of totalitarianism" that features extracts from the work of Arendt and Lowenthal designed to present *Nineteen Eighty-Four* as a "typology" of a totalitarian world.[8] By 1983, when Howe edited *1984 Revisited: Totalitarianism in Our Century*, he could fairly write that Orwell's book "occupies a central place" in "the vast literature concerning totalitarianism." It was a place that Howe himself, with his praise of Orwell's "theoretical grasp" of totalitarianism, had done much to establish.[9] "Orwell: History as Nightmare" was published in 1957 as the closing chapter of Howe's *Politics and the Novel*, probably his best-known work of literary criticism. Howe placed *Nineteen Eighty-Four* last in a distinguished line of political novels—following works by recognized masters including Stendhal, Dostoevsky, Conrad, James, Turgenev, Malraux, Silone, and Koestler—and grandly pronounced that *Nineteen Eighty-Four* "brings us to the end of the line. Beyond this—one feels or hopes—it is impossible to go. In Orwell's book the political themes of the novels that we have been discussing in earlier chapters reach their final and terrible flowering."[10]

"Orwell: History as Nightmare" also had an even more direct—though inadvertent—influence on *Nineteen Eighty-Four*: the essay was the germ of the "nightmare" interpretation of *Nineteen Eighty-Four*. Howe argued against critics like Anthony West who viewed *Nineteen Eighty-Four* "primarily as a symptom of Orwell's psychological condition." The key word here is *primarily*; Howe was advancing a subtle, syncretistic, psychosocial interpretation of *Nineteen Eighty-Four*. The work referred not only to Orwell's personal history, insisted Howe, but also to the history of the twentieth century; it was not just a private nightmare but part of "the social reality of our time."[11] Howe was not the first to discuss *Nineteen Eighty-Four* as a "nightmare," but earlier characterizations were made in passing and were narrowly political.

Howe called *Nineteen Eighty-Four* "the nightmare of the future." Writing amid growing psychobiographical interest in Orwell—three critical/biographical studies and numerous essays on Orwell had already appeared in the six years since his death in January 1950—Howe tried to fuse psychology and politics in discussing Orwell's "nightmare." But the unintended effect of his essay was to give hostile psychological critics of *Nineteen Eighty-Four* another catchword to sling. Following unsympathetic Marxist and psychoanalytic critics, journalists and reviewers began to describe *Nineteen Eighty-Four* as a "nightmarish" projection of a dying prophet's childhood terrors, rather than as a satiric political novel. Likewise, unexpectedly, admirers used Howe's "nightmare" characterization to bolster their psychological argument that Orwell "died" for *Nineteen Eighty-Four* and that the "nightmare" of tubercular agony he endured to complete his gift to the world testified all the more to his nobility of spirit and love of humanity.[12] Howe closed "Orwell: History as Nightmare" on a benedictory note: "There are some writers who live most significantly for their own age; they are writers who help redeem their time by forcing it to accept the truth about itself, and therefore saving it, perhaps, from the truth about itself. Such writers, it is possible, will not survive their time, for what makes them so valuable and so endearing to their contemporaries—that mixture of desperate topicality and desperate tenderness—is not likely to be a quality conducive to the greatest art. Perhaps it shouldn't matter to us. We know what they do for us, and we know that no other writers, including the greater ones, can do it."[13]

One notices the adroitly elastic use of first-person pronouns; Howe "knows" what books like *Nineteen Eighty-Four* do for "us" and what should and should not matter to "us." But the concerns here and throughout this essay are Howe's: Orwell and *Nineteen Eighty-Four* are significant and valuable and endearing because they speak to Irving Howe as a writer and radical—and, as we shall see, because they had helped redeem and force him to accept "the truth" about his political self and about the little intellectual groups in New York in whose identities lay part of his own.

For the "we" of this essay's close is Howe's own. By 1954 Howe had founded (with Lewis Coser) the bimonthly *Dissent* and had "part[ed] company with most of the New York intellectuals I had admired."[14] "The *Dissent* group"—a cluster of unaffiliated radicals dedicated to democratic socialism—was but "a tiny minority within the intellectual world," Howe admitted, but its members took it upon themselves to keep the idea—and ideal—of socialism alive in midcentury America.[15]

Howe's relationships with several of the early *Dissent* writers (including Meyer Schapiro, Michael Harrington, C. Wright Mills, and Paul Goodman) are profiled in his autobiography, *A Margin of Hope* (1982). The "Dissenters" still considered themselves Socialists (with a capital *s*) throughout the '50s.[16] Howe was the intellectual leader of this small yet influential group. Taking stock of his verbal resources, he searched at this early moment of his writing career for suitable literary models—and settled on Orwell: "I decided to work hard to write like Orwell—not, heaven knows, that I succeeded, but it made sense to try, since whatever strength of style I had lay in a certain incisiveness." Orwell and Edmund Wilson became Howe's chief literary benchmarks.[17]

And yet, even before his *Dissent* years, Howe had felt himself growing far apart from the *Partisan* writers on political matters. This became especially evident to him in *Partisan*'s 1952 symposium, "Our Country and Our Culture," in which Howe dissented from the *Partisan* near-consensus that American intellectuals should disavow their "alienation" and become "part of American life." The *Partisan* writers were to Howe "intellectuals in retreat," espousing "a liberalism increasingly conservatized."[18]

All this lay behind Howe's "we"—and behind his insistence on the quality of "desperation" in Orwell's work—at the close of "Orwell: History as Nightmare." The resonances were already clear from Howe's 1955 *Partisan* article on Orwell, "A Moderate Hero." Howe rejected the view of most liberals that Orwell should be seen as a "good" man, a "conscience," or a "saint." Such characterizations, Howe thought, softened or spiritualized Orwell's angry radicalism. Too "cozy" with the conservative spirit of the mid-'50s, liberal critics like Lionel Trilling, V. S. Pritchett, and John Atkins were unnerved by the gritty, irascible, even ill-tempered side of Orwell, claimed Howe. Unable to fathom Orwell's "desperation," they sought to remake him into "a moderate hero," "a down-at-the-heels Boy Scout who voted Labour." Likewise, lacking Orwell's own "fiery" imagination, they were incapable of understanding his passion for justice and decency, so they recast it in moral terms as a species of "sainthood."[19]

Chafing at what struck him, accurately, as the overcautious neoliberalism of the *Partisan* crowd and clearly speaking for the embattled radicalism of his new group around *Dissent*, Howe scorned the liberals' "modified" Orwell, averring that Orwell was no moderate and no saint. Trilling had memorialized Orwell as a "virtuous man" in his introduction to the first American edition of *Homage to Catalonia* (1952). But such a figure was too soft for Howe, nothing like his image of a combative Orwell, his refreshingly immoderate hero, his "revolutionary personality." So Trilling's "man of truth" became Howe's "truculent" man, befitting Howe's own more aggressive, less guardedly urbane personality:

The more one learns about Orwell, the more one begins to doubt that he was unusually virtuous or good. . . . Neither the selflessness nor the patience of the saint, certainly not the indifference to temporal passion that would seem a goal of sainthood, can be found in Orwell. As a "saint" Orwell would not trouble us, for by now we have learned how to put up with saints: we canonize them and thus are rid of them. In fact, one sometimes suspects that, behind the persistent liberal effort to raise Orwell from the mire of polemic to the clear heavens of sainthood, there is an unconscious desire to render him harmless. It is as a man and a writer that Orwell makes his challenge to the writers who follow him. He stirs us by his example, by his all-too-human and truculent example. For he stood in basic opposition to the modes and assumptions that have since come to dominate American and English literary life. He was a writer who rejected the middle-class pattern. . . . He knew how empty, and often how filled with immoderate aggression, the praise of moderation could be. . . . He wasn't a Marxist or a political revolutionary. He was something better and more dangerous: a revolutionary personality.[20]

"One must choose between God and Man," Orwell had maintained in his 1949 essay on Gandhi, "and all 'radicals' and 'progressives' . . . have in effect chosen Man."[21] Orwell rejected belief in "sainthood" because he had resolutely chosen "Man"; Howe, also an atheist, repudiated literary and spiritual canonization in Orwell's name. One must, Orwell insisted, choose: to wait for Sugarcandy Mountain above or work for a socialist utopia below. Howe drew the necessary conclusion as to the corollary choice: "the clear heavens of sainthood" or "the all-too-human" political "mire."

For Howe, as for Orwell, sanctity meant nonattachment; sainthood and communitarianism were mutually exclusive. Yet Howe's main reservation actually concerned the likely political consequences flowing from use of the term *saint*: moderation, gradualism, quietism. His Orwell, Howe insisted, was no "man of truth"—he was a political figure: an honest radical. Not a "political revolutionary"—but, at this nadir of American socialism, an image of a "revolutionary personality" who could help radicals keep the spirit of revolution alive was "something better." "Saint" and "virtuous man," however, would not do. They evoked in Howe not Atkins's and Trilling's inspiring images of the fully committed, extraordinary ordinary man (Atkins's "social saint") but the figure canonized by British conservative Richard Rees as a "self-mortifying saint." It is the latter image that seemed to Howe almost inhuman and indifferent to temporal passion, that could not serve as the model for those who would launch a political movement, that appeared so far from human capacity that it ceased to "challenge" "us."

Here again we see Howe speaking with plural pronouns. And once again it is Irving Howe who was not "stirred" by a "virtuous," "saintly" Orwell—as Trilling, Atkins, Pritchett, and Rees had been. One could well ask Howe, as Richard Rovere, another liberal, soon did in *The Orwell Reader* (1956): "But what is [a 'revolutionary personality'] except another term, one with secular and socialist overtones, for a saint? A 'revolutionary personality' is what the Ethical Culturalist calls Jesus Christ."[22]

Yet what Howe needed in the mid-1950s was not just a literary model but a model of the radical writer. Orwell's personal importance for Howe was couched in the closing lines of "Orwell: History as Nightmare," in which Orwell seems inspiring not only to "us" but also to Irving Howe at a "desperate" moment in American radicalism, in the mid-'50s. For Orwell reaffirmed Howe's conviction that "some writers" are indeed "valuable" precisely because they "live for their own age," "help redeem their time," acquiesce to an ephemeral and "desperate topicality," and compel their generation "to accept the truth about itself"—whether or not their work "survives" or is "great art." And Orwell reminded Howe that his own fate and vocation might be to join the ranks of such writers, the ranks of Orwell and Ignazio Silone. Socialism might one day reemerge as a viable movement in America if dissenting intellectuals preserved a sense of their calling, preserved "a margin of hope."

"I bridled at the notion that the literary life was inherently more noble than the life of politics," Howe recalls. "I bridled because acknowledging this could have been politically disabling at a time when politics remained essential, but also because I knew that it held a portion of obvious truth—otherwise, how explain my inner divisions?" Striving for literary excellence and yet to keep alive socialism's "animating ethic," Howe found in Orwell the political self that he believed, fairly, Trilling and the *Partisan* ex-radicals had forsaken. Howe wanted "instances of that poise which enables a writer to engage with the passions of the moment yet keep a distancing skepticism." Trilling "spoke for part of what I wanted, yet another, perhaps larger, part of me had to speak against him."[23] Trilling spoke for the skeptical Howe, Orwell for the passionate Howe. "I saw Orwell," Howe recalls, "as a fellow spirit—a radical and engaged writer."[24]

Trilling would not have described Orwell this way. Nor as a "revolutionary" personality. Nor, given his valuation of Orwell's respect for "the familial commonplace" and the "stupidity of things," as a rebel against middle-class life.[25] But Howe needed a more unbridled, more iconoclastic figure. For Howe an Orwell hemmed in by the conventional bourgeois pattern was "empty," politically "harmless." "Dangerous" was "better": only a recognizably radical image could truly "challenge" and "trouble us."

III

In the mid-'60s, partly in strong reaction to the authoritarian radicalism of the New Left, Howe felt impelled "toward a liberalizing of radicalism"—and toward the hesitant renewal of his relationship with Trilling.[26] But Howe's respect and admiration for Orwell remained constant—as did his dissatisfaction with American liberalism, which had merely emerged from "a contagion of repressiveness" in order to enter "a time of structured deceit": the illusion of a Great Society, the tragedy of the war in Vietnam.[27] Looking back in 1969 on Orwell's reception during the Cold War, Howe felt vindicated in his 1955 judgment that the liberals' moderate image of Orwell "tells us a great deal more about the historical moment than about Orwell."[28] The same might be said for Howe's revised image of Orwell in the late '60s.

But what changed in this third stage of his reception (circa 1965–73) was not Howe's esteem but the content and context of his image of Orwell. By this time, after the 1963 publication of *Nineteen Eighty-Four: Text, Sources, Criticism*, Howe was coming to be regarded as Orwell's main American defender and radical champion. Now, however, Howe was defending Orwell not from appropriation by liberals but from denigration by radicals. Fascist, flag waver, war hawk—the diatribes against Orwell from the American New Left poured forth, variously based on random passages from *Burmese Days*, *The Road to Wigan Pier*, *Animal Farm*, *Nineteen Eighty-Four*, or a *Tribune* column.

In *Mr. Sammler's Planet* (1970), Saul Bellow, a friend of Howe and a fringe member of the *Partisan* circle, imagined the hostile response to Orwell from some of Mark Rudd's SDS followers at Columbia. Sammler, the Old Left guest lecturer brought in to talk about the 1930s, could well have been Irving Howe:

"Old Man! You quoted Orwell before."
  "Yes?"
  "You quoted him to say that British radicals were all protected by the British navy. . . ."
  "Yes, I believe he did say that."
  "That's a lot of shit."
  Sammler could not speak.
  "Orwell was a sick counterrevolutionary. It's good he died when he did."[29]

But Howe could speak, and did: "Something within me—sentimentality, conscience, stubbornness—kept murmuring that I had an obligation to speak."[30] Writing in January 1969, in the wake of the Columbia student uprisings and near the height of the Movement's influence, Howe declared acridly that, when it came to sharing and understanding the experience of workers, the student Left and its older enthusiasts like Murray Kempton had much to learn from Orwell:

> He saw them and liked them as they were, not as he or a political party felt they should be. He didn't twist them into Marxist abstractions, nor did he coddle them in the fashion of the New Left populism. He saw the workers neither as potential revolutionaries nor savage innocents nor stupid clods. He saw them as ordinary suffering human beings; quite like you and me, yet because of their circumstances radically different from you and me. When one thinks of the falseness that runs through so much current writing of this kind—consider only the "literary" posturings of Murray Kempton—it becomes clear that Orwell was a master of the art of exposition. . . . Orwell's deepest view of life [was] his faith in the value and strength of common existence: "The fact to which we have got to cling, as to a life-belt, is that it is possible to be a normal decent person and yet to be fully alive." Let that be inscribed on every blackboard in the land![31]

Whereas in the '50s he had felt caught between *Partisan's* neoliberalism and his own liberal radicalism, Howe now felt boxed in between the New Left's "kamikaze radicalism" and his own Left-liberalism. What the "larger part" of Howe had sought and found in Orwell during the moderate '50s was passion; but the larger part of him, frustrated and outraged with the excesses of the young radicals, needed Trilling's "distancing skepticism" by the close of the '60s.[32]

This too Howe eventually came to find in Orwell: "I came to appreciate more deeply the side of Orwell that wanted and needed to get away from politics."[33] This "outsider" stance was the one that Orwell had arrived at too, and one notices that in his 1969 essay Howe now spotlights those qualities in his model that he had previously downplayed. Howe now stresses the nonpolitical dimension—the moral, literary, and even spiritual aspects—of Orwell, though he rails once more against those who call Orwell a "saint." Howe emphasizes the nonpolitical in Orwell not by tempering Orwell's radicalism, however, but by proclaiming Orwell's rugged virtuousness: "He is the greatest moral force in English letters during the last several decades: craggy, fiercely polemical, sometimes mistaken, but an utterly free man."

Orwell achieved a "state of grace" in his prose by "sloughing off the usual vanities of composition," which enabled him to speak "as a voice of moral urgency."[34]

As he had in the '50s, Howe responds to the political climate and his personal situation of 1969, remolding Orwell as he assimilates him, bending him into the figure he needs, not without a touch of exaggeration and sentimentality. Howe imagines that, as a writer living with workers and speaking to readers, Orwell "solved the problem of narrative distance" involved in sharing and communicating his experience. In "Hop Picking" and *The Road to Wigan Pier*, Orwell understood the necessary balance between proximity and distance: he neither "coddled" the workers nor "twisted" them into "Marxist abstractions." He was "driven to plunge into every vortex of misery or injustice that he saw," but he retained sufficient perspective to "see what looms in front of his nose."[35] Howe's Orwell of 1969 is the figure Howe wished he might have been in the '60s. To plunge in without getting sucked into the vortex: this is what both the young leftists and Howe had not done, why they and he needed a distancing skepticism to check centripetal passions.

Generational distance prevailed instead. To the New Left, Orwell and Howe belonged to an Old Left "scarred by the past," bearing "marks of corrosion and distrust," "skeptical of Marxism," "rigidly anticommunist," in Howe's words.[36] And "middle-aged Socialists" like himself, Howe admitted, though respectful of the early achievements of the New Left (e.g., the civil rights campaigns, the SDS community-action projects) resented the young for repeating their elders' procommunist follies of the 1930s—and for depriving them of "the role of mentor to the young."[37] Orwell had performed that role for Howe in the early postwar years, the role Howe himself might have inherited in the 1960s. But in an anguished, heartfelt tribute Howe insisted, as if he were Bellow's Sammler giving the student Left a history lesson of a forgotten era, that Orwell was and remained "a model for every writer of our age."[38] And Howe allowed himself, in closing, to imagine that "if he had lived," Orwell would have steered a course similar to his own, lambasting both Establishment politicians and apocalyptic populists:

> For a whole generation—mine—Orwell was an intellectual hero. He stormed against those English writers who were ready to yield to Hitler; he fought almost single-handed against those who blinded themselves to the evils of Stalin. More than any other English intellectual of our age, he embodied the values of personal independence and a fiercely democratic radicalism. Yet, just because for years I have intensely admired him, I

hesitated to return to him. One learns to fear the disappointment of fallen heroes and lapsed enthusiasms. I was wrong to hesitate. . . .

It is depressing to think that, if he had lived, he would today be no more than sixty-five years old. How much we have missed in those two decades! Imagine Orwell ripping into one of Harold Wilson's mealy speeches, imagine him examining the thought of Spiro Agnew, imagine him dissecting the ideology of Tom Hayden, imagine him casting a frosty eye on the current wave of irrationalism in Western culture!

The loss seems enormous. . . . He was one of the few heroes of our younger years who remains untarnished. Having to live in a rotten time was made just a little more bearable by his presence.[39]

IV

By the 1980s Howe had become publicly identified with his "intellectual hero." In this fourth stage of his reception (circa 1974–93) Howe came to be admired by many Left-liberals as the American Orwell of his generation. For instance, Sanford Pinsker saw Howe as a "moral conscience," a tribute that echoed V. S. Pritchett's famous declaration of Orwell as "the conscience of his generation": "The passion of his argument, by turns fiercely moral and scrupulously fair, the clarity of his prose, a voice that speaks with authority and power and the unmistakability of a thumbprint: Howe is a case study in powers that grew more refined, more subtle, even as they retained a kinship with the sheer exuberance of those times, those places. In this regard, Howe retains a position as a moral conscience, almost unparalleled in contemporary letters." Or as Josephine Woll recalled after his death, in a comparison that many of his *Dissent* friends would have endorsed, "For Irving, Orwell was the model of a writer; for me, Irving was."[40]

The "countdown to 1984," which pushed Orwell into the incessant glare of the international media, also solidified the perception of Howe as Orwell's American spokesman and successor. Campus speeches on Orwell, conference talks and radio interviews about Orwell, a *New Republic* cover story, a new and expanded edition of *Nineteen Eighty-Four: Text, Sources, Criticism*, the edited volume *1984 Revisited: Totalitarianism in Our Century*: in 1983–84 Howe seemed to be the designated American keeper of the Orwell flame. Howe became increasingly identified with Orwell during these years, even as he himself gained a reputation beyond intellectual and academic circles as a result of his widely acclaimed bestseller *World of Our Fathers* (1976).

Moreover, with the neoconservative embrace of Orwell in 1983–84, Howe assumed, once again, the role of defender of the radical Orwell. "Kidnapping Our Hero": that was how an indignant Irving Howe characterized Norman Podhoretz's claim to Orwell as a forerunner of neoconservatism, insisting that "to the end of his life Orwell remained a writer of the Left."[41] As in the '50s Howe was guarding Orwell on his right flank, but by the 1980s Howe's own radicalism had attenuated to "radical humanism."[42] Nonetheless, though he now put more emphasis on the "conservatism of feeling" in *Nineteen Eighty-Four,* Howe strongly affirmed Orwell's own socialism, branding Podhoretz's claim to Orwell "vulgar":[43] "Neither Trilling nor I ever said that Orwell 'is me' or 'is like' me. My construction of Orwell is just that—a construction—and of an admittedly self-serving kind. But it is a clearer and more openly acknowledged image than Trilling's in the '50s, and I make no claims about a 'posthumous' Orwell as Podhoretz does."[44]

I would claim that Irving Howe also had his "partisan" Orwell. Still, one does sense that, as much as any Anglo-American intellectual prominently identified with Orwell, Howe was quite "like" him. Even his convictions about prose style, voiced in the preface to the third edition of *Politics and the Novel*—reissued just months before his death in 1993—directly echo Orwell's famous aspiration to write "prose like a window pane": "Now, especially at a time when critical writing is marked by jargon and obscurantism, my inclination is to care most about lucidity. The writer of expository prose, I now feel, should strive for that most difficult of styles: a prose so direct, so clear, so transparent, that the act of reading comes to seem like looking through a glass."[45]

Orwell is one of "the writers who have meant most to me," one of "the crucial witnesses," Howe says at the close of his autobiography. "It is with their witness that, along the margin, I want to identify," a witness to witnesses.[46]

If, in the end, one affirms with Howe that Orwell died a "democratic socialist," it is in no small part, I think, also to pay witness—and final respect—to a perception of Orwell's integrity, intelligence, and self-knowledge.

Notes

1. See Irving Howe, "The Dilemma of *Partisan Review*," *New International* (February 1942): 24; "*Partisan Review* Goes to War," *New International* (April 1942); Howe, *A Margin of Hope*, 114.

2. See the reviews of Orwell's work by Diana Trilling, Rahv, and Bell in Jeffrey Meyers, ed., *George Orwell: The Critical Heritage* (London: Routledge, 1975). Kazin boosted *Nineteen Eighty-Four* in the July 1949 *Book-of-the-Month Club News*; Schlesinger reviewed *Animal Farm* enthusiastically on page 1 of the *New York Times Book Review* on August 25, 1946.

3. Irving Howe, *"Nineteen Eighty-Four*—Utopia Reversed," *New International* (November–December 1950): 366–68.

4. Howe, *"Nineteen Eighty-Four*—Utopia Reversed," 366.

5. On the wartime rifts among the *Partisan* editors, see S. A. Longstaff, *"Partisan Review* and the Second World War," *Salmagundi* (Winter 1979): 108–29.

6. Irving Howe, "Orwell: History as Nightmare," *American Scholar* (Spring 1956): 193–207. In addition to its appearance in *Politics and the Novel*, the essay was reprinted under the title *"1984*: History as Nightmare" in *Nineteen Eighty-Four: Text, Sources, Criticism*, ed. Irving Howe (New York: Harcourt Brace, 1963), 188–96.

7. Howe, *"1984*: History as Nightmare," 190, 194.

8. Howe, *"1984*: History as Nightmare," 194.

9. Howe, preface to *1984 Revisited: Totalitarianism in Our Century* (New York: Harper Collins, 1983), ix.

10. Howe, *"1984*: History as Nightmare," 196.

11. Howe, *"1984*: History as Nightmare," 190.

12. For an example of the latter see George Steiner, "True to Life," *New Yorker*, March 29, 1969; reprinted in Meyers, *George Orwell*, 363–73.

13. Howe, *"1984*: History as Nightmare," 196.

14. Howe, *A Margin of Hope*, 211, 213–14, 229.

15. Howe, *A Margin of Hope*, 242, 217–18, 238.

16. Howe, *A Margin of Hope*, 293.

17. Howe, *A Margin of Hope*, 146. In *Decline of the New* Howe says that his culture heroes include Silone, Orwell, Sholom Aleichem, and Edmund Wilson.

18. Howe, *A Margin of Hope*, 237, 227–28.

19. Irving Howe, "Orwell as a Moderate Hero," *Partisan Review* (Winter 1954–55): 105–6.

20. Howe, "Orwell as a Moderate Hero," 106–7.

21. *The Collected Essays, Journalism and Letters of George Orwell*, ed. Sonia Orwell and Ian Angus (London: Secker and Warburg, 1968), 4, 449.

22. Richard Rovere, introduction to *The Orwell Reader* (New York: Harcourt Brace, 1956), xx.

23. Howe, *A Margin of Hope*, 232, 321–22.

24. Irving Howe, interview with the author, October 8, 1983.

25. Lionel Trilling, introduction to George Orwell, *Homage to Catalonia* (New York: Harcourt Brace, 1952), xvi, xviii.

26. Howe, *A Margin of Hope*, 324.

27. Howe, *A Margin of Hope*, 295.

28. Irving Howe, "As the Bones Know," in *Decline of the New*, 102.

29. Saul Bellow, *Mr. Sammler's Planet* (New York: Viking, 1970), 35.

30. Howe, *A Margin of Hope*, 314.

31. Howe, "As the Bones Know," 102.

32. Howe, *A Margin of Hope*, 324.

33. Howe, interview with the author, October 8, 1983.

34. Howe, "As the Bones Know," 103.

35. Howe, "As the Bones Know," 98–99.

36. Howe, *A Margin of Hope*, 291–92.

37. Howe, *A Margin of Hope*, 315.

38. Howe, "As the Bones Know," 97.

39. Howe, "As the Bones Know," 97, 103.

40. Sanford Pinsker, *Georgia Review* 45 (Winter 1991): 802–3; Josephine Woll, *Dissent* (Fall 1993): 541.

41. "Kidnapping Our Hero" is the subtitle of an address delivered by Howe at West Chester University, October 8, 1983.

42. Howe, *A Margin of Hope*, 345. Or, as he wrote in the preface to the 1992 edition of *Politics and the Novel* (New York: Horizon Press, 1957): "This work [of 1957] bears distinct signs of a Marxist outlook. [Today] I still hold firmly to the socialist ethos which partly inspired this book. But the ideology to which these essays occasionally return no longer has for me the power it once had. . . . A pedantic title for this book might have been *Revolutionary Politics and the Modern Novel*. For it pays little attention to the kind of novel written by George Eliot, George Meredith, and Trollope."

43. Howe, interview with the author, October 8, 1983.

44. Howe, interview with the author, October 8, 1983; Howe, *A Margin of Hope*, 350.

45. Howe, *Politics and the Novel* (1992), xi.

46. Howe, *A Margin of Hope*, 350.

14

William E. Cain

Howe on Emerson:

The Politics of Literary Criticism

William E. Cain is Mary Jewett Gaiser Professor of English and American Studies at Wellesley College, where he teaches courses in American literature, American studies, Shakespeare, and composition.

Cain received his B.A. degree, summa cum laude, in 1974 from Tufts University and both the M.A. (1976) and the Ph.D. (1978) from Johns Hopkins University. He became a member of the Wellesley faculty in 1978 and has taught in the American studies program as well as in the English department.

The author of *The Crisis in Criticism* (1984) and *F. O. Matthiessen and the Politics of Criticism* (1988), Cain has edited many books, including *William Lloyd Garrison and the Fight against Slavery: Selections from* The Liberator (1995), *The Blithedale Romance: A Cultural and Critical Edition* (1996), and *A Historical Guide to Henry David Thoreau* (2000). He is also the author of a study of American literary criticism, included in *The Cambridge History of American Literature*, vol. 5, *1900–1950* (2003).

Cain met and began to exchange letters with Irving Howe in the late 1980s. His interview with Howe appears in *American Literary History* 1, no. 3 (Fall 1989): 554–64.

Is Emerson to blame? In two important books, *Socialism and America* (1985) and *The American Newness: Culture and Politics in the Age of Emerson* (1986), Irving Howe suggests that the answer is "yes": to Emerson must be assigned the burden of responsibility for the failure of socialism—or even for a socialist *movement*—to establish itself in the United States. Howe makes his case with intelligence and insight and with an authority earned from decades of keen reflection and literary and political experience. But it is puzzling that Howe should identify Emerson as the figure whose work has prevented the United States from achieving a lot or a little socialism, as though he has led Americans astray from a path they might otherwise have taken. As much as I admire Howe, and as much as I have learned from him, in my view to say this about Emerson amounts to failing to read this writer with full attentiveness: it is to equate Emerson with a position that his work itself, his actual *writing*, does not sustain.

In *Socialism in America*, with a backward glance toward Werner Sombart's *Why Is There No Socialism in the United States?* (1906), Howe surveys the "objective" factors that historians have identified to explain the lack of success of socialism in this country: the absence of a feudal past; the prosperity enjoyed by America's workers—or at least, Howe adds, the *perception* that workers here benefit from a higher standard of living and greater social mobility; the availability of land; the complex organizational challenges posed by immigration (i.e., many languages and diverse traditions); and the American political system and the two-party centrism that it has fostered. But in Howe's judgment the compelling explanation is cultural, not political or economic or sociological, and to characterize it Howe employs the term *Emersonianism*.

For Howe, Emersonianism is the abiding American myth, the ideology that saturates—that *is*—the culture. "What I mean to suggest," he says, "is that Emerson, in a restatement of an old Christian heresy, raised the *I* to semidivine status, thereby providing a religious sanction for the American cult of individualism. Traditional Christianity had seen man as a being like a God, but now he was to be seen as one sharing, through osmosis with the oversoul, directly in the substance of divinity."

"This provided," Howe continues,

> a new vision of man for a culture proposing to define itself as his new home—provided that vision by insisting that man be regarded as a self-creating and self-sufficient being fulfilled through his unmediated relation to nature and God. The traditional European view that human beings are in good measure defined or described through social characteristics and conditions was, at least theoretically, discounted; the new American, singing songs of himself, would create himself through spontaneous assertions, which might at best graze sublimity and at worst drop to egoism. The American, generically considered, could make his fate through will and intuition, a self-induced grace.[1]

There are a number of passages in Emerson that one could cite to support Howe's summary. In "The Divinity School Address" (1838), for example, Emerson states: "Jesus Christ belonged to the true race of prophets. He saw with open eye the mystery of the soul. Drawn by its severe harmony, ravished with its beauty, he lived in it, and had his being there. Alone in all history, he estimated the greatness of man. One man was true to what is in you and me. He saw that God incarnates himself in man, and evermore goes forth anew to take possession of his world. He said, in this jubilee of sublime emotion, 'I am divine. Through me, God acts; through me, speaks. Would you see God, see me; or, see thee, when thou also thinkest as I now think.' "[2]

According to Emerson's daring account, Jesus is important for the insights into human possibility he reveals. Jesus is not a divine being essentially different from you and me; his glory comes from his sublime success in achieving the potential for divinity embodied in everyone. He became divine—God incarnated—because he perceived and was faithful to human greatness. More precisely: Jesus became godly through the affirmation about himself he made, through the sheer words that declared his astounding intuition: "I am divine." Jesus tells us—that is, Emerson tells us that Jesus tells us—that when we see and think as he does, we spring into godliness ourselves.

Emerson's contemporaries felt the thrill of vivid affirmations like this one, responding, as Howe observes, to the highly individualized, self-creating, and self-renewing appeals that Emerson made. Henry David Thoreau, for example, writing in his journal in the mid-1840s, praised the intensity of Emerson's life and art: "There is no such general critic of men and things, no such trustworthy and faithful man. More of the divine realized in him than in any." Abraham Lincoln's law partner William Herndon, in a May 12, 1857, letter to the abolitionist Wendell Phillips, lauded Emerson as "a pretty great man. In his way he is a transcendent genius. I hardly know as great a man." The scholar-minister Octavius Brooks Frothingham stated in his *Recollections* (1891) that Emerson "led the dance of the hours. He was our poet, our philosopher, our sage, our priest. He was the eternal man." The radical minister Theodore Parker also paid tribute to Emerson, calling him in March 1850 "the most American of our writers," the one who embodied "the idea of America," "the idea of personal freedom": "On earth only one thing he finds which is thoroughly venerable, and that is the nature of man; not the accidents, which make a man rich or famous, but the substance, which makes him a man. . . . The traditions of the churches are no hindrances to his thought; Jesus or Judas were the same to him, if either stood in his way and hindered the proportionate development of his individual life." In December 1857 Parker celebrated "the triumph of Emerson, who has a more glorious history than any American of this generation!"[3]

The poet Walt Whitman, the biographer and essayist Moncure Conway, the essayist and poet Oliver Wendell Holmes Jr., the poet-critic James Russell Lowell, and countless others made similar statements about the power of Emerson's personality and writing. His impact on American culture was immense, as Howe maintains. And Emerson's work continues to inspire and energize critics today. In the words of Denis Donoghue, "Emerson is not merely a poet and a sage: he is the founding father of nearly everything we think of as American in the modern world. To the extent to which the sentiments of power, self-reliance, subjectivity, and independence attract to themselves a distinctly American nuance, its source is Emerson." Harold Bloom makes the point with breathtaking succinctness: "Emerson is God."[4]

I am in awe of Emerson as well and so tend to agree with these claims from Thoreau to Bloom. (Well, maybe saying that Emerson *is* God overstates the point a bit.) But I am not sure that in truth these claims reflect the moment-to-moment experience of Emerson's writing. These critics and intellectuals through the ages are describing and celebrating Emersonianism, just as Howe is criticizing Emersonianism—that is, Emerson as a sociopolitical force and cultural influence. But I think that Emerson's writing ultimately resists this kind of appropriation. His pages are indeed filled with phrases and sentences that summon up luminous prospect and creative possibility, which is why he has proven inspiring to writers, artists, and musicians. There's lots of Emersonianism in Emerson, no doubt about that—tributes to individual prowess, celebrations of persons intrepid enough to express their divinity, and so forth. But to me the striking thing about Emerson is the constant action that his language takes against the individualism he promotes.

There's the Emerson of "The Divinity School Address" and "Self-Reliance" (1841), but also the Emerson of passages like this one, from the essay "Fate":

Nature is no sentimentalist,—does not cosset or pamper us. We must see that the world is rough and surly, and will not mind drowning a man or a woman; but swallows your ship like a grain of dust. The cold, inconsiderate of persons, tingles your blood, benumbs your feet, freezes a man like an apple. The diseases, the elements, fortune, gravity, lightning, respect no persons. The way of Providence is a little rude. The habit of snake and spider, the snap of the tiger and other leapers and bloody jumpers, the crackle of the bones of his prey in the coil of the anaconda,—these are in the system, and our habits are like theirs. You have just dined, and, however scrupulously the slaughter-house is concealed in the graceful distance of miles, there is complicity,—expensive races,—race living at the expense of race. The planet is liable to shocks from comets, perturbations from planets, rendings from earthquake and volcano, alterations of climate, precessions of equinoxes. Rivers dry up by opening of the forest. The sea changes its bed. Towns and counties fall into it. At Lisbon, an earthquake killed men like flies. At Naples, three years ago, ten thousand persons were crushed in a few minutes. The scurvy at sea; the sword of the climate in the west of Africa, at Cayenne, at Panama, at New Orleans, cut off men like a massacre.[5]

Emerson then turns his attention for a moment to the United States, only to leap from there to the horror of disease and the frightfulness of predators:

Our western prairie shakes with fever and ague. The cholera, the small-pox, have proved as mortal to some tribes, as a frost to the crickets, which, having filled the summer with noise, are silenced by a fall of the temperature of one night. Without uncovering what does not concern us, or counting how many species of parasites hang on a bombyx; or groping after intestinal parasites, or infusory biters, or the obscurities of alternate generation;—the forms of the shark, the labrus, the jaw of the sea-wolf paved with crushing teeth, the weapons of the grampus, and other warriors hidden in the sea,—are hints of ferocity in the interiors of nature. Let us not deny it up and down. Providence has a wild, rough, incalculable road to its end, and it is of no use to try to whitewash its huge, mixed instrumentalities, or to dress up that terrific benefactor in a clean shirt and white neckcloth of a student in divinity. (945–46)

Emerson relishes these reminders of death and destruction on both an intimately personal and a massively panoramic scale. What he's describing is terrible and terrifying yet also fascinating, even invigorating to him, as he knows it will also prove to us. There is a method to nature's apparent madness: Providence exists and is a benefactor, rendering aid and kindly service. But it is a rough and rude Providence, wild and incalculable, simultaneously in and beyond any and all social contexts. Perhaps, as "The Divinity School Address" proposes, you and I, seeing and thinking like Jesus, can become divine. But the mocking humor of Emerson's final image in this excerpt from "Fate" exposes the clash and conflict and subversion that Providence places with unaccountable fierceness in the individual's way.

But I do not want to give the impression that later in his career Emerson qualified the fervent individualism that he espoused earlier and that Howe's judgment is mistaken for that reason. Such an argument could be made, but the qualifications and resistances are there in Emerson from the beginning, overlooked and underattended to, but present nonetheless.

Consider this passage from "The American Scholar" (1836), a passage on "the offices" of the scholar that both does and does not lend itself to Howe's generalizations: "They [i.e., these offices] are such as become Man Thinking. They may all be comprised in self-trust. The office of the scholar is to cheer, to raise, and to guide men by showing them facts amidst appearances. He plies the slow, unhonored, and unpaid task of observation."[6] No sooner does Emerson assign significant work to the scholar—cheering, raising, and guiding men—than he deglamorizes it as slow, unhonored, and unpaid. It is no longer active work (doing something) but observation (watching).

He next seems to grant a reward to the scholar after all: "Flamsteed and Herschel, in their glazed observatories, may catalogue the stars with the praise of all men, and, the results being splendid and useful, honor is sure" (63). Emerson's point, however, turns out to be that the observing scholar will not receive the acclaim that men such as Flamsteed and Herschel enjoy:

> But he, in his private observatory, cataloguing obscure and nebulous stars of the human mind, which as yet no man has thought of as such,—watching days and months, sometimes, for a few facts; correcting still his old records;—must relinquish display and immediate fame. In the long period of his preparation, he must betray often an ignorance and shiftlessness in popular arts, incurring the disdain of the able who shoulder him aside. Long he must stammer in his speech; often forego the living for the dead. Worse yet, he must accept,—how often! poverty and solitude. For the ease and pleasure of treading the old road, accepting the fashions, the education, the religion of society, he takes the cross of making his own, and, of course, the self-accusation, the faint heart, the frequent uncertainty and loss of time, which are the nettles and tangling vines in the way of the self-relying and self-directed; and the state of virtual hostility in which he seems to stand to society, and especially to educated society. (63)

Here Emerson makes the scholar seem not only solitary but pedantic, even somewhat foolish, waiting for a few facts and correcting old records. Expect rough treatment and dishearteningly slow return on one's investment—that's Emerson's lesson. Expect to be poor and to feel lost and lonely, self-hating and hated by others.

But Emerson then shifts course, to the heady compensation that ultimately the scholar will receive for his sacrifices:

For all this loss and scorn, what offset? He is to find consolation in exercising the highest functions of human nature. He is one, who raises himself from private considerations, and breathes and lives on public and illustrious thoughts. He is the world's eye. He is the world's heart. He is to resist the vulgar prosperity that retrogrades ever to barbarism, by preserving and communicating heroic sentiments, noble biographies, melodious verse, and the conclusions of history. Whatsoever oracles the human heart, in all emergencies, in all solemn hours, has uttered as its commentary on the world of actions,—these he shall receive and impart. And whatsoever new verdict Reason from her inviolable seat pronounces on the passing men and events of to-day,—this he shall hear and promulgate. (63–64)

It is a wonderful passage, filled with honorific images and bracing injunctions. But I think Emerson means his words to be soul stirring and yet disconcerting, troublingly vague and mysterious. At one moment in our reading we are told that the scholar stands in "virtual hostility" to society, and then, a moment later, we are told that the scholar, at the height of human nature, lives on public, illustrious thoughts. How does Emerson—how do we—get from there to here? It sounds majestic until one begins to put some pressure on the language, which is what we should do if we aspire to be the "man thinking" whom Emerson is urging us to become. An alert, engaged, critical responsiveness to Emerson's language is in keeping with the "thinking" he describes, and such thinking makes it impossible to take away neatly from his writing the ideas about "individualism" that Howe foregrounds. Emersonianism, of course, derives from Emerson, but Emerson is as much antagonistic toward Emersonianism as he is expressive of it. His writing yields the doctrines that Howe describes, but only if one leaves out of account the particulars in the writing that challenge, undercut, and destabilize them.

Part of what I am getting at here is Howe's limitations as a reader of Emerson. But I am also interested in the limitations of his practice as a critic more generally, limitations that I now see as connected with the strengths that long ago drew me to his work in the first place. In *Socialism and America* and *The American Newness* Howe draws upon Emerson to comment on and judge American social and political history. No New Critic he, Howe always believed that literary criticism invariably leads to (is bound up with) social, cultural, and political commentary and critique. In this respect he is very much in tune with the views of the other New York intellectuals and contributors to *Partisan Review*.[7] Reading the text closely is important, Howe often notes, but that's not enough for him, and it's his movements outward from the text, into politics, ideas, and social history, that have made him for me (and for many others) so provocative, so stimulating. I have always valued him because he wrote as more than a literary critic. The problem I find—all the more so today, when genuinely literary criticism is so rare—is that when Howe writes that way, he is not really a literary critic but something else instead.

On one level I agree with the praise that has been given to Howe for the kind of critic—the more than literary critic—he was. His friend and *Dissent* colleague Michael Walzer has said: "The art of the literary intellectual is to read the novel as a novel, the poem as a poem, and still reach for a judgment that isn't narrowly literary—to hear the moral or political resonance of plot and character, verse and image. Howe provides a model of how this is done." Similarly the British critic Frank Kermode, commenting on Howe's *A Critic's Notebook* (1994), remarks, "Howe shows what it is like for a man interested in politics to read great literature with a developed literary sensibility."[8]

But again one wonders: is it possible to be a literary critic and at one and the same time to make social and political judgments? My increasing suspicion is that if we read with an acute literary sensibility we will at best regard social and political judgments as tentative, as provisional. Where Howe, and Walzer and Kermode, are wrong is, I think, in taking for granted that one can move from literature to morality and politics. One can, but then one has become no longer a literary critic but a critic of morality and politics.

Reading Emerson as a literary critic means exactly that—reading as a literary critic, concerned to respond to and describe the operations and organizations of this writer's language. Reading Emerson for ideas about politics, American society, the failure of socialism—that is another, different kind of task and activity. The point is not that Howe shows how we can do both things but, rather, that Howe's practice reveals we cannot do both things, not at once. Once Howe starts to describe and criticize Emersonianism, he has left literary criticism behind, because a literary-critical engagement with Emerson does not produce such simplifying generalizations. Emerson is very different from Emersonianism, and a literary critic should take pains to articulate this difference.

The disjunction between literary and political criticism is evident in another of Howe's judgments on the "individualism" of Emerson's essays: "Once we turn to the politics available in the American system and to the structures and relationships of American society, especially in the age of multinational corporations, that individualism turns out to be sadly inadequate. It often becomes 'mythified' in ways that hinder thought and obstruct radical, even liberal reforms."

Howe continues: "To speak out against the Vietnam War, as Thoreau spoke against the Mexican War, even if almost everyone else remains mute: that is a splendid part of the native heritage. But it's delusional to suppose that the Emersonian categories, even the best of them, are sufficient for understanding or correcting the deep injustices and appalling imbalances of power and wealth characteristic of American capitalism."[9]

But as a writer Emerson does not give us "categories" to think with; he is far more complicatedly testing of our thought and feeling than such a term suggests. Once we start referring to "categories," we have shed ourselves of Emerson and are talking about Emersonianism. That's a category that we have extracted from essays that are intended to subvert categorical thinking and dramatize that such thinking is not authentic thinking at all. This is where the radicalism of Emerson is found, in the activity and experience of his writing.

Consider this final example, Howe's assessment in *The American Newness* of Emerson's "conflict" over the slavery crisis:

> How painful this inner conflict was can be seen in the contrast between two passages from his journals, written about a year apart during the early 1850s. The first is a stirring denunciation of the Fugitive Slave Law: "And this filthy enactment was made in the 19th century, by people who could read and write. I will not obey it, by God" (July 1851).
>
> The second is notorious: "I waked at night, and bemoaned myself, because I had not thrown myself into this deplorable question of Slavery. . . . But then, in hours of sanity, I recover myself and say, God must govern his own world . . . without my desertion of my post which has none to guard it but me. I have quite other slaves to free than those negroes, to wit, imprisoned spirits, imprisoned thoughts, far back in the brain of man" (August 1852).
>
> If there is one place where Emerson is open to a sharp moral judgment, it is here. It may be, as some admirers suggest, that he is rehearsing the familiar conflict, experienced by many writers, between personal interest and social conscience. But there is something sadly disingenuous—the writhing of a man who suspects he is in the wrong—when he uses language to suggest an equivalence, or even similarity, between "slave" meaning shackled men and women and "slave" referring to undeveloped thoughts and spirits.[10]

The ease with which such a judgment on Emerson can be made should give us pause. Rather than criticize Emerson for failing to throw himself into abolitionism, we should ask what the writing in this passage might or might not say about us. Responding to Emerson's language here means taking his claims and distinctions seriously, an exercise of intellect we will miss if we content ourselves with judging him. Maybe, for himself, Emerson is exactly right: the best work for him is remaining faithful to his post, keenly aware as he does so of both the case of the slaves and the judgments that others will pass on him, judgments that he has anticipated and felt the force of himself. The passage is painful for us, painful because it demands that we consider—as Emerson has himself—why imprisoned thoughts and spirits exact a higher claim than imprisoned persons. Emerson doesn't "suspect he is in the wrong"—Howe has it backwards. Emerson suspects, he believes, he is in the right.

Moral and political generalizations are inevitably part of our response to and discussion of literature. These give criticism a range and degree of social relevance and testify to one kind of effect from our experience of books we feel passionately about. Howe's criticism shows this commitment to the social and political ideas and insights that literature provides. But even as I respect and honor Howe for his critical example, I want to say that his example is not that of a literary critic as I understand the term. A literary critic is literary, and for me this means recognizing how the language of literature resists the kinds of formulations and categories about Emerson that Howe proposes.

I am not saying that what Howe does cannot be done: he demonstrates that it can be, and he does it very well. But, as his treatment of Emerson reveals, such criticism comes at the expense of literary criticism, of the writing itself. A writer's organizations of language are inevitably simplified when we take from them (or bring to them) social, political, and moral agendas of our own. Howe turns Emerson's writing into a body of thought called Emersonianism, and in the process he makes judgments that Emerson's language contends against and disallows. Emerson is greater than that, greater because of the intense challenges and hard pleasures that his writing offers.

Notes

1. Irving Howe, *Socialism and America* (1985; repr., San Diego: Harcourt Brace Jovanovich, 1986), 135. For background and bibliography on the themes of American individualism and socialism see, among many discussions, Michael Kammen, "The Problem of American Exceptionalism: A Reconsideration," *American Quarterly* 45, no. 1 (1993): 1–43; and Michael Denning, " 'The Special American Conditions': Marxism and American Studies," *American Quarterly* 38, no. 3 (1986): 356–80.

2. Ralph Waldo Emerson, *Essays and Lectures* (New York: Library of America, 1983), 80. Unless otherwise noted, all quotations are taken from this edition.

3. Henry David Thoreau, *Journals*, 14 vols. (Boston: Houghton Mifflin, 1906), 1: 431–32; Irving Bartlett, *Wendell and Ann Phillips: The Community of Reform, 1840–1880* (New York: Norton: 1979), 158; Octavius Brooks Frothingham, *Recollections and Impressions, 1822–1890* (New York: Putnam's, 1891), 48; Robert E. Collins, *Theodore Parker, American Transcendentalist: A Critical Essay and a Collection of His Writings* (Metuchen NJ: Scarecrow, 1973), 176–77; and Octavius Brooks Frothingham, *Theodore Parker: A Biography* (Boston: James R. Osgood, 1874), 441.

4. Denis Donoghue, *Reading America: Essays on American Literature* (New York: Knopf, 1987), 37; and Harold Bloom, "An Interview," in *Wild Orchids and Trotsky: Messages from American Universities*, ed. Mark Edmundson (New York: Penguin, 1993), 201.

5. Ralph Waldo Emerson, "Fate" (1851), in *Essays and Lectures*, 945. Subsequent references will appear in the text.

6. Ralph Waldo Emerson, "The American Scholar" (1836), in *Essays and Lectures*, 63. Subsequent references will appear in the text.

7. See, for example, Alexander Bloom, *Prodigal Sons: The New York Intellectuals and Their World* (New York: Oxford University Press, 1986); Neil Jumonville, *Critical Crossings: The New York Intellectuals in Postwar America* (Berkeley : University of California Press, 1991); and Harvey M.Teres, *Renewing the Left: Politics, Imagination, and the New York Intellectuals* (New York: Oxford University Press, 1996).

8. Michael Walzer, foreword to Irving Howe, *Selected Writings, 1950–1990*, (San Diego: Harcourt Brace Jovanovich, 1990), xiv; Frank Kermode, "World of Our Father," review of *A Critic's Notebook* (1994), *New Republic*, October 17, 1994, 57. The same point is stated by Nathan Glick in "The Socialist Who Loved Keats," *Atlantic Monthly* (January 1998): 99–105.

9. Irving Howe and Leo Marx, "Emerson and Socialism: An Exchange," *New York Review of Books*, May 28, 1987, 48–49. For Marx's review of *The American Newness* see *New York Review of Books*, March 12, 1987, 36–38. It is reprinted in Marx's *The Pilot and the Passenger: Essays on Literature, Technology, and Culture in the United States* (New York: Oxford University Press, 1988), 337–47.

10. Irving Howe, *The American Newness: Culture and Politics in the Age of Emerson* (Cambridge: Harvard University Press, 1986), 59–60.

15

George Scialabba

Howe Inside My Head

George Scialabba lives in Cambridge, Massachusetts, and has written about politics and culture in *Dissent*, the *American Prospect*, the *Nation*, the *Boston Review*, the *Boston Globe*, the *Washington Post*, and many other publications.

I met Irving Howe only once. We shook hands, spoke a few cordial words, nothing more. Before that we had exchanged a couple of brief, friendly notes about book reviews I'd written for his quarterly, *Dissent*. Nevertheless, I had a fairly intense relationship with Howe. I can best characterize it by quoting from an essay by a friend of Howe's, the editor and critic Theodore Solotaroff. A young writer asks Solotaroff whom he writes for. Solotaroff reflects a bit and answers, "I guess I write for a few good voices inside my head."

I wrote—still write, will always write—for Irving Howe and a few other people. Not all these people agree with or even like each other—sometimes the conversation inside my head gets a bit rowdy. But each is, for my purposes, indispensable. Howe is there for a number of reasons, chief among them, perhaps, his cosmopolitanism. Ever since I came across the phrase—by Henry James, I think—"one of those on whom nothing is lost," it has been my ignis fatuus, my will-o'-the-wisp. (A similar ideal, *Vielseitigkeit*, or "many-sidedness," descends from Goethe through Marx to the classical socialist tradition.) In the modern and especially the postmodern world this aspiration to comprehensiveness has become problematic. To put it all together, always heartbreakingly difficult, is now just about impossible. There's too much to know, too much to care about, too much available information, too much possible experience.

But in the generation preceding mine, perhaps for the last time in this cycle of European civilization, it was not an absurd hope. And as well as, maybe better than, anyone else in his generation, Howe succeeded in negotiating a dual allegiance to literature and to politics, the claims of beauty and the claims of justice. No one can fully live up to either set of claims, much less both; and Howe failed now and then, in one or another respect, at least in my opinion. But very few other people in this century have been as informed and discriminating, as passionate and illuminating, about literature and politics and above all about the relation between them.

Contemporary criticism is, alas, all but overgrown by theories about the relation between literature and politics. Howe had no theory, as far as I can make out. He didn't even have a method, unless, as T. S. Eliot said, the only method is to be very intelligent. Here are a few specimens of that sharp, wry, rueful intelligence.

First, from "The Culture of Modernism," a paragraph that probably says as much as any paragraph could about the most vexed question of twentieth-century literary criticism:

We read the late novels of D. H. Lawrence or the cantos of Ezra Pound, aware that these are works of enormously gifted writers yet steadily troubled by the outpouring of authoritarian and Fascist ideas. We read Bertolt Brecht's "To Posterity," in which he offers an incomparable evocation of the travail of Europe in the period between the wars yet also weaves in a justification of the Stalin dictatorship. How are we to respond to all this? The question is crucial in our experience of modernist literature. We may say that the doctrine is irrelevant, as many critics do say, and that would lead us to the impossible position that the commanding thought of a poem need not be seriously considered in forming a judgment of its value. Or we may say that the doctrine, being obnoxious, destroys our pleasure in the poem, as some critics do say, and that would lead us to the impossible position that our judgment of the work is determined by our opinion concerning the author's ideology. There is, I think, no satisfactory solution in the abstract, and we must learn to accept the fact that modernist literature is often—not in this way alone!—"unacceptable." It forces us into distance and dissociation; it denies us wholeness of response; it alienates us from its own powers of statement even when we feel that it is imaginatively transcending the malaise of alienation.

In *Politics and the Novel* Howe draws a masterly contrast between Hemingway and Silone in a passage that includes a phrase, "the heroism of tiredness," that has since been applied often to Howe himself:

If we compare Silone's view of heroism with that of Hemingway, we see the difference between the feelings of a mature European and, if I may say so, an inexperienced American. For Hemingway heroism is always a visible trial, a test limited in time, symbolized in dramatic confrontations. For Silone heroism is a condition of readiness, a talent for waiting, a gift for stubbornness; his is the heroism of tiredness. Hemingway's heroic virtues are realized in situations increasingly distant from the social world, among bullfighters and hunters and fishermen; Silone's heroic virtues pertain to people who live, as Bertolt Brecht has put it, in the "dark ages" of modern Europe, at the heart of our debacle.

Howe concludes with a wistful but clear-eyed comment that, though of universal application, taught me something unexpected about the moral resources of my own heritage: "Silone is not at all sentimental about the peasants, for the sardonic humor that twists through his books is often turned against their coarseness and gullibility. But they are his, by adoption or blood, and he remains hopeful, with a hopefulness that has nothing to do with optimism, that from the hidden inarticulate resources of the poor, which consist neither of intelligence nor nobility, but rather of a training in endurance and an education in ruse—that from all this something worthy of the human may yet emerge."

Finally, from a review of Orwell's *Collected Essays*, a passage that is keenly, poignantly satisfying because, consciously or not, Howe is describing not only Orwell but himself as well, especially in his marvelous final sentence:

My sense of Orwell, as it emerges from reading him in bulk, is rather different from that which became prevalent in the conservative fifties: the "social saint" one of his biographers called him, the "conscience of his generation" V. S. Pritchett declared him to be, or the notably good man Lionel Trilling saw in him. The more I read of Orwell, the more I doubt that he was particularly virtuous or good. Neither the selflessness nor the patience of the saint, certainly not the indifference to temporal passion that would seem to be a goal of sainthood, can be found in Orwell. He himself wrote in an essay on Gandhi: "No doubt alcohol, tobacco, and so forth are things a saint must avoid, but sainthood is a thing that human beings must avoid."

As a "saint" Orwell would not trouble us, for by now we have learned how to put up with saints: we canonize them and are rid of them. Orwell, however, stirs us by his all too human, his truculent example. . . . If he was a good man, it was mainly in the sense that he had measured his desperation and come to accept it as a mode of honor.

As these examples suggest, Howe has written his own epitaph, and far better than I, at any rate, could hope to—not only in his autobiography, *A Margin of Hope*, which is immensely wise, generous, and entertaining, but above all in "The New York Intellectuals," probably his best-known essay, and deservedly so, for its density, velocity, and lucidity are astonishing. "The radicalism of the thirties," Howe wrote,

> gave the New York intellectuals their distinctive style: a flair for polemic, a taste for the grand generalization, an impatience with what they re-garded (often parochially) as parochial scholarship, an internationalist perspective, and a tacit belief in the unity—even if a unity beyond im-mediate reach—of intellectual work. . . . [This style] reflected a certain view of intellectual life . . . one which, for better or worse, differed radi-cally from the accepted modes of scholarly publishing and middle-brow journalism; which celebrated the idea of the intellectual as antispecialist, or as a writer whose specialty was the lack of a specialty: the writer as dilettante-connoisseur, *Luftmensch* of the mind, roamer among theories.

Not all readers have a taste for that style, and not many writers have a talent for it. But Howe had the talent and I had the taste, so into my head he went and has lodged there ever since.

Jew

16

Morris Dickstein

World of Our Grandparents

Morris Dickstein belongs to a younger generation of New York intellectuals that came of age in the 1960s. At Columbia he studied with Lionel Trilling, F. W. Dupee, Steven Marcus, and Daniel Bell, and he published his first piece in *Partisan Review* at the age of twenty-two. He worked with Raymond Williams and F. R. Leavis as a Kellett Fellow at Cambridge and completed his academic training in English Romantic literature with Harold Bloom at Yale, which led to his first book, *Keats and His Poetry* (1971). He began writing about contemporary culture for the *New Republic, Commentary*, and the *New York Times Book Review* in the late 1960s and found himself teaching at Columbia during the 1968 student uprising. His encounters with the turbulent upheavals of the period culminated in *Gates of Eden* (1977), a study of the sixties that combines criticism with cultural history, politics, and personal experience. The book was nominated for a National Book Critics Circle Award in criticism and was republished in new editions in 1989 and 1997. *Newsweek* described it as "a vivacious, highly original work" that "stands a very good chance of remaining a permanent book of reference on the period." His other books include a study of the public intellectual tradition in criticism, *Double Agent* (1992); an edited collection of essays, *The Revival of Pragmatism* (1998); and a history of postwar American fiction, *Leopards in the Temple* (2002). Since the 1980s he has also written numerous essays on film and on Jewish writing and culture, as well as several autobiographical pieces, among them a brief memoir for the fiftieth-anniversary issue of *Partisan Review* in 1984. He has taught English and film at the City University of New York since 1971 and founded the Center for the Humanities at the CUNY Graduate Center in 1993. He served as a contributing editor of *Partisan Review* from 1972 to 2003, when the magazine ceased publication, and has written on film and the visual arts for *Dissent*.

Books that last, books that still matter, change from generation to generation. Two decades after it first appeared, *World of Our Fathers*, Irving Howe's
stirring history of Jewish immigrant life on New York's Lower East Side,
is at once the same book and subtly different. Its world is more remote,
with few survivors still among us, yet also more immediate, because of the
bustling new immigration today. This is a paradox worth exploring. What
kind of book was it, and how did Irving Howe of all people come to write
it? How has the book changed, especially for young people encountering
it for the first time?

As history *World of Our Fathers* remains a fresh and invigorating book,
exhaustively researched, wonderfully readable, unfailingly humane, even
tender in its sympathies. It's an elegy for a lost world, executed with a
faultless eye for detail and a dispassionate critical intelligence. Where others
have waxed lyrical about our immigrant past, Howe's book is measured,
searching, and evocative. It lives up to the credo found on the last page:
"We need not overvalue the immigrant Jewish experience to feel a lasting
gratitude for having been part of it. A sense of natural piety toward one's
origins can live side by side with a spirit of critical detachment."

Howe's blend of empathy and detachment enabled him to write a cultural
anthropology of every facet of the Jewish immigrant experience: the *shtetl*
itself; the difficult voyage; the shock of arrival and resettlement; the crowded
tenements and long working hours; the terrible poverty and homesickness;
the marriage and funeral customs; the social movements, especially the
struggle to build labor unions; the settlement houses and synagogues; the
matchmakers, dance halls, and Catskill retreats; the politics of Tammany
Hall; the war of ideas in the cafés and newspapers; and especially the culture
of Yiddish—from poets, novelists, and intellectuals to theatrical divas and
popular entertainers. If this was not exactly the world of *all* our fathers, it
was a broad prototype of what they experienced. It was also an exemplary
version of the immigrant experience in general, from the wretched living
conditions and the loss of language to the painful clash between old folkways
and new realities, leading to conflicts between the generations.

Howe was an unlikely yet inevitable person to write this book. Like most
second-generation immigrants, he worked hard to put the ghetto behind
him. He was a political activist and literary critic, not a historian. The
New York intellectuals of his generation rarely wrote books, concentrating
mainly on essays, but he was possessed by the historical imagination as it
touched the world that had formed and nurtured him. Born in 1920, only
a few years before the flow of immigration was cut off, he grew up on the
proletarian streets of the East Bronx, not on the Lower East Side. When
his father's grocery business failed in 1930, the family was forced to move

to a poorer neighborhood, and he learned a lesson about class he never forgot.

Like other New York intellectuals who came of age in the thirties, he set sail as a committed internationalist, not a Jewish writer. His conversion to socialism at the age of fourteen, he thought, had liberated him from merely tribal solidarity. "In the years before the war," he once wrote, "people like me tended to subordinate our sense of Jewishness to cosmopolitan culture and socialist politics." He cut his teeth politically in a radical Marxist sect, but after the war he evolved into a broad-gauged essayist steeped in modern literature and twentieth-century politics—a contributor to *Partisan Review*, founder of *Dissent*, and an incisive literary critic.

The social and literary issues that agitated him had no special ethnic accent; they owed far more to Marxism, modernism, and the European social novel. But history, in the shape of the war and the Holocaust, conspired to remind him of his Jewish origins, and he turned to Yiddish literature, then virtually unknown among American readers, as a way of coming home. Beginning in the early 1950s, in an endless stream of critical essays and finely conceived anthologies, he helped bring this literature into the cultural mainstream just as its creative power was waning. For Howe *World of Our Fathers* was the culmination of a circuitous journey that brought him back to Judaism, not as a religion but as a secular culture that was fast going under, a dying world. Was it "another lost cause added to my collection"? he wondered much later.

Since the 1890s many articulate Jews and fascinated outsiders had written about the Lower East Side; it was the social crucible of a new "transnational" America, as Randolph Bourne called it. But they often wrote in a parochial spirit, either as muckrakers exposing urban blight, as ideologues debating issues within the community, as social tourists exploring the Lower Depths, or as lyrical celebrants gilding the lily of their own humble beginnings. Unlike Jacob Riis or Michael Gold, Howe had little interest in the social pathologies of the Lower East Side as a "culture of poverty." Compared to the Harry Goldens and Sam Levinsons of the 1950s, he was immune to the sentimental tug of Borscht Belt nostalgia. The historians' overworked metaphor of the "epic" of immigration was not his glass of tea. Instead his arresting vignettes and deftly sketched profiles recapture the tumultuous, not always attractive humanity of the Lower East Side. Stressing the traumas of acculturation and the dream of a better life, Howe offered both suburbanites and intellectuals of his own generation a more complex sense of where they came from.

The book was Howe's real autobiography—evoking the world of his actual father, to whom he had been "a son with a chilled heart" (as he said ruefully in *A Margin of Hope*), and the Jewish world and language he had once truculently scorned. When I first met him in the early 1970s, he himself had become the angry father doing battle with the writers and young activists of the sixties generation. He had always been a biting polemicist, but in collections like *Steady Work* (1966), *Decline of the New* (1970), and *The Critical Point* (1973) he launched some especially blistering attacks on the New Left and the counterculture, whose values he largely shared, and on late-sixties writers like Kate Millett and Philip Roth, whose sexual iconoclasm might once have delighted him. But in other essays (on the New York intellectuals, for example, and on literary modernism) a different Howe emerged, softer and more retrospective, a writer reintegrating himself with a past he had once taken for granted, summing up an epoch that was rapidly disappearing into history. Above all Howe mellowed in his work on Yiddish literature, taking refuge from cultural polemics without losing his critical voice—striking a nice balance between filial piety and keen discrimination.

This mellower Howe is the voice we hear in *World of Our Fathers*, fair to a fault about everyone from nativist critics of immigration and snobbish uptown Jews to the cartoonish figure of the Jewish mother. He takes a special pleasure in noting the discomfiture of radicals and anarchists whenever their worldliness is undercut by a wave of Jewish fellow feeling. This shock of recognition was, after all, his own story. Still, his socialism, now far less doctrinaire, remains central to the book. A few critics accused him of leaving out religion—the synagogue and yeshiva world of the Lower East Side—others of ignoring the "world of our mothers." (The book provoked a raft of studies of women's role in Jewish immigrant culture.)

Neither charge is quite fair, but it can be said that religion figures in the book largely as "secular messianism," the secular translation of religious vision into social hope. "Traditional faith still formed the foundation of this culture," he writes, "if only by providing norms from which deviation had to be measured." And the most vivid women included are social activists like the labor firebrand Rose Schneiderman; Lillian Wald of the Henry Street Settlement; and Belle Moskowitz, the brains behind New York's progressive governor Alfred E. Smith. Howe's emphasis on socialism, organized labor, and Yiddish, if slightly disproportionate, feeds the autobiographical power of the book. He had lived the world he was writing about, and, like so many good historians, he projected his deepest loyalties onto a reading of the past.

This is one reason why the book reads differently today from twenty years ago. Younger readers might be more disconcerted by their fathers' impassioned socialism and unionism than by their threadbare poverty. Taking the safety net of the welfare state for granted (just when it has been shredded), they may not understand, first, how working-class socialism emerged from the actual experience of poverty, nourished by notions of social justice ingrained in the Jewish tradition, and, second, that its egalitarian idealism had little in common with the discredited bureaucratic socialism that collapsed in the 1980s.

Despite the recent decades' waves of renewed immigration, which included many Russian Jews, a historical rift has opened up between us and the players in Howe's story. Howe's initial readers, who made the book a surprise bestseller, were the second-generation Jews whose lives were somewhat neglected in his pages. They were the strivers who had not become intellectuals, socialists, or union activists but had made it in America in business or the professions. They had migrated to the suburbs after the war, only to see their well-educated offspring turn against their values. They had tried to forget the bruising poverty, fractured speech, moral inhibitions, and naive idealism of the ghetto. But despite their lavish temples and generous philanthropy, they came to feel a void in their sense of Jewish identity. In Howe's book they were able to reconnect historically, with few sentimental illusions, to a world they had long repressed, as Howe himself had done. *World of Our Fathers* found its way into virtually every literate Jewish home; it provided an emotional catharsis for a generation of aging sons and daughters.

The immigrant experience meant less to their children and grandchildren, who were more likely to turn to Israel, to religion, or to searing testimonies about the Holocaust as a way of finding their identity and forging links with Jewish traditions. Irving Howe knew very well that he was writing at the end of something—the end of socialism; the end of Yiddish; the end of what he called "Jewish secularism," a rich but transitional culture that had developed at the end of the eighteenth century almost as a substitute religion. Even before the Holocaust incinerated most of Europe's Yiddish-speaking Jews, Yiddishists in America understood that they were pursuing something that would soon be effaced by assimilation, a culture that might never achieve the power and endurance of religious belief. Like a blazing comet, this made its efflorescence seem all the more brilliant.

In a lecture at Hunter College in March 1993, just six weeks before he died, Howe, depleted by a long, draining illness, recited a Kaddish for the world whose history he had written: "The immigrant experience, which until recently has been the major substance of American Jewish life, is receding into memory. . . . Nostalgia grips us all, yet cannot provide the bread or wine of a common future. For what is fading is not just the sweatshops and tenements—we are well rid of them. . . . What is also fading is the pale bloom of Yiddish. . . . The effort to maintain a distinctive Jewish way of life in the diaspora apart from religious institutions and beliefs was indissolubly bound up with a distinctive Yiddish culture. Such a culture clearly will not play a major role in the lives of American Jews." But he reminded his audience that this was merely a long-term trend, a historical probability: "the long term is . . . long. In the short run, the mixture of shared experience and common memory may be enough."

Howe also quotes from the conclusion of *World of Our Fathers*: "Cultures are slow to die; when they do, they bequeath large deposits of custom and value to their successors; and sometimes they survive long after their more self-conscious members suppose them to have vanished." From ethnic humor to liberal politics, from cuisine to scholarship, the immigrant experience left a sediment of manners, morals, and values that still sharply affects Jewish (and American) life today. It seems clear that Yiddish and socialism were only temporary vehicles of Jewish secular identity, which has always reshaped itself from contemporary sources, from the Enlightenment and Zionism to American pluralism and the counterculture.

In his inimitable style of serious joking Howe once remarked that Israel had become the religion of American Jews, with the Holocaust as its liturgy. Yet both Israel and the Holocaust engaged him deeply in his last years. And when I saw him in synagogue at the end of Yom Kippur, just before the gates of judgment were said to swing shut, I imagined I was witnessing the death of socialism, or at least of socialism as a self-sufficient secular faith. (His wife, Ilana, tells me he was simply accompanying her in place of a friend who could not make it.) Irving Howe's scrupulous book, written with the assistance of Kenneth Libo, is a collage of texts and memories that almost restore a half-forgotten time, now no longer the world of our fathers but of our grandparents and great-grandparents. But it also exposes our braided link to the larger ethnic mix of contemporary life.

Today's multicultural America, with its new immigrants, its babel of languages, its resurgent nativism, its terrible pockets of poverty, its Darwinian faith in the free market, and its ruthlessly concentrated corporate power, bears a striking resemblance to American society before World War I. Many of the positions staked out in today's cultural debates—pluralism, universalism, bilingualism, cultural nationalism, identity politics—were rehearsed during the first decades of the twentieth century. The outcry against immigrants in the 1990s is as familiar as the uncritical celebration of ethnic ties. The tension between identity politics and universal values—between the ghetto and the polis—is endemic to modern American life. Younger Jews, intermarrying in large numbers, caught between tribalism and assimilation yet often finding themselves excluded from the rainbow coalition of today's minorities, could do far worse than to study the historical forces that helped shape their present lives. In *World of Our Fathers* Irving Howe turned his own reckoning with the past into a richly textured lesson for posterity.

17

Leonard Kriegel

Father Figures

Leonard Kriegel is a Bronx-born literary critic and has spent his entire life in New York City, having attended Hunter College, Columbia University, and New York University, and then teaching at City College of the City University of New York beginning in 1961.

A socialist and Jew, Kriegel shares many of Howe's political and literary interests as well. He has authored a critical study of Edmund Wilson and two volumes of fiction, along with *Working Through: An Autobiographical Journey in the Urban University* (1973).

When it arrives at the point at which its achievements are summed up and a reckoning presented, a culture has gotten as far beyond the tragedies of its own history as is humanly possible. To understand this is to understand the tough integrity of Irving Howe's *World of Our Fathers*, a great work of the historical imagination and a painful elegy in which the author's own sense of loss is matched by his insistence on seeing a dying culture as it was, its limitations as well as its attractions carefully placed before the reader. Working from within the crucible of his own past, Howe evokes the world of the Eastern European Jews in America almost as if he were writing memoirs rather than history. It is a remarkably personal book. And it demands a personal response. If we are still close enough to a world that the writer can force us to trace our own lives from its not-yet-hidden swirls, then history, like fiction, is inevitably *personal* and *intimate*. And if, like Jacob wrestling with the angel, you have struggled with your own duality, *your* American matched against *your* Jew, then *World of Our Fathers* is your history because the hand lies heavy on your back.

But if the legacy is ours, the story Howe tells belongs to the fathers: "We need not overvalue the immigrant Jewish experience in order to feel a lasting gratitude for having been part of it." The peculiar nature of the immigrants' response to America, this *goldneh medinah* that was both blessed and cursed (often in the same breath), formed the basis for the ways in which their children and grandchildren would deal with America. To claim for the Jewish experience of America an uncontested singularity would be false. But it would be equally false to subsume that experience within the general context of immigrant history. The Jews were similar to and yet unlike other peoples who come to these shores. They possessed the culture of Yiddishkeit, and because of that they brought to the immigrant's tribulations something new. Carrying within itself the seeds of its own dissolution, Yiddishkeit succeeded in creating a particular tone for urban America, a tone that, as the culture that gave it life recedes into memory and myth, continues to exert its hold on those who have inherited the voice while no longer understanding the language. The true subject of *World of Our Fathers* is the dissolution of the world of Yiddishkeit, a dissolution that today seems irremediable, inevitable, even self-willed.

The culture of Yiddishkeit was a folk culture given powerful literary expression at exactly that moment in history when its death throes had been set in motion. The Enlightenment had already doomed Yiddish as a language—although Hitler and his minions hurried the process of destruction by a century—and there cannot be a culture without a language. It is difficult to believe that Yiddish could have withstood the impact of modernism. Its strength was residual, strongly tied to tradition and parochialism as well as to its need to insulate itself from a world it at once envied and regarded with long-conditioned hostility. Perhaps its chief glory in America must be seen as its willingness to sacrifice itself. Was there, among other immigrant peoples, a verbal construction similar to *tsu oysgrinen zikh*—"to cease being a greenhorn"? Ignorant of the ways of America, the *grine* was, by definition, a barrier to children determined to live what "acculturation" meant even before they had heard the word. Yiddish journalists might sigh in print for "the old country," but they rarely failed to exhort their fellow immigrants to learn English, to Americanize themselves as quickly as possible, to let the *shtetl* dissolve in its own bones while their children came to terms with the menace and promise of urban America. Yiddish socialists and trade unionists employed their rich language to satisfy the Jewish craving for universal brotherhood, which, like Christianity, possessed its greatest appeal for those who were homeless and uprooted and poor, dreadfully poor, poorer than it is possible for their Scarsdale-reared grandchildren and great-grandchildren to believe.

One reads the familiar details of that poverty in *World of Our Fathers*. And one wonders whether it is of any use to remember that the population density of the Yiddish Lower East Side at the turn of the century was probably greater than that found in any other place at any other time. The fact is that the Yiddish Lower East Side is finished. And the poverty has itself been banked as a platitude. Success creates its own illusions. For the well-fed young, poverty may even be attractive. But for those reared in the culture of poverty, it is simply the inevitable accent of the collective voice. In the Yiddish world the poor were a mirror of the collective strivings as well as the collective fate. The poor constituted both audience and material. It is not by accident that the writer and his audience were cemented together here as they have never really been in the American world. The Scarsdale grandchildren may feel a twinge of what is today called "ethnic pride" when they read that Sholom Aleichem's funeral in the Bronx was attended by one hundred thousand people; the grandparents would simply have accepted this too as an aspect of the culture of poverty. If the poor were both audience and material, then the writer's voice was their voice simply because neither they nor the writer had any recognizable existence outside of the other. Yiddish literature had to be parochial, since its concerns, even in America, were rooted in the history and condition of its audience. Its parochialism was of its audience's world. In his introduction to *A Treasury of Yiddish Stories*, published more than twenty years ago and still the best essay available in English on Yiddish literature, Howe wrote: "Because of its own limitations, the world of the East European Jews made impossible the power hunger, the pretensions to aristocracy, the whole mirage of false values that have blighted Western intellectual life. The virtue of powerlessness, the power of helplessness, the company of the dispossessed, the sanctity of the insulted and injured—these, finally, are the great themes of Yiddish literature."

Such themes are rooted not in the writer but in the culture itself. We have, of course, confronted this kind of thing in others: in the Orwell who stalks the streets of Paris and London trying to expiate in himself the sins of capitalism and the crimes of colonialism; in Silone's understanding that socialism must derive as much from the *cafoni* of the Abruzzi as from the relentless theorizing of its intellectuals; even, perhaps, in the harsh ambivalence of Lawrence's attitudes toward the English working classes or Faulkner's mellowing willingness to let the Snopeses, the "white trash" of his world, speak for themselves and possess their triumph. But none of these writers embodies the attitude of an entire culture toward poverty.

In *World of Our Fathers* Howe has managed that most difficult of historical voices, a mixture of objectivity and compassion. And he never permits himself to fall into the temptation to sentimentalize, to make of the Yiddish Lower East Side world something greater than what it was. He knows that much of the power it exerted and the loyalty it commanded were directly due to its parochialism. He knows that, like other languages, Yiddish was subject to short spasms of growth interrupted by long periods of quiescence. But he also knows that Yiddishkeit as a cultural force was impossible to replace. With its demise whatever cohesiveness there had been to American Jewish life began to disintegrate. At one and the same time Yiddish had turned inward and outward, embracing American life yet retreating from American values, acculturating American parochialism (articles in the *Forward* explaining baseball to bewildered *grine* fathers) yet insisting on its singularity. A culture of contradictions, Yiddishkeit brought its tensions to American shores. It was, in fact, confused by American life. What was bewildering about America was that it could not really be explained in terms of the *shtetl* past; it threatened the Jew in areas in which he had been most secure and did not threaten him in areas in which he had been most vulnerable. "In America," my grandmother used to tell me, "they kill us with candy."

Howe begins his history of the Eastern European Jewish encounter with America with the pogroms that followed the assassination of Alexander II in 1881. This was the signal that set in motion the great migration to America, just as it was the event that gave impetus to the small but growing Zionist movement in Russia. The story of the migration has been well-documented, and Howe draws upon the richness of the Yiddish sources not to repeat what we already know but to create a composite portrait of an experience that, no matter how singular it seemed to the immigrants, was essentially collective. But while "Toward America" is fascinating, the true power of *World of Our Fathers* is not really developed until the long second and third sections, "The East Side" and "The Culture of Yiddish."

In "The East Side" the isolation and astonishment of the new immigrants are portrayed through a composite of recollections. In large part the Jewish immigrants were simply experiencing what other non-English-speaking immigrants had experienced. It was not poverty that plagued them, since they were conditioned to poverty. But the *shtetl* world had broken up, and what took its place was the Lower East Side. The immigrants who came between 1881 and 1905 were the lost souls, the *farloyrene menshn*, of the Yiddish world. Even today, in the rapidly dwindling population of the Yiddish-speaking world, it is a generation that possesses an awesome moral currency. To mention the first wave of immigrants is to evoke images of a world so strange, so hostile, that survival as Jews simply could not be assumed. And yet America was—and Howe takes great pains to show this—generous to the new immigrants. Ultimately the majority managed to find work, to begin the process of acculturation, to lift themselves up economically. And they were treated relatively decently by those who, like the Irish, and the German Jews, had themselves arrived in America only a few decades earlier. It is in Nathaniel Hawthorne's words that Howe summarizes the condition of the first immigrant generation: "In this republican country, amid the fluctuating waves of our social life, somebody is always at the drowning-point."

But the sense of loss overwhelmed them. Russia, the land from which they had fled, became a kind of inverted passion, a cultural barometer by which all else was measured. No matter how raw and cruel and brutalized life had been there, it possessed the stamp of the familiar. "I am overcome with longing," Howe quotes one of the early immigrants, "not only for my Jewish world, which I have lost, but also for Russia." Only one among the multitude of ironies that dot the landscape of Yiddishkeit. But it is an important one. It helps to explain a great deal about the attitude the Jews brought to America and that they were to will their children. And it forces one to recognize the sense of déjà vu that lingers about Jewish life in America. The grandchildren and great-grandchildren are still players of the Yiddish game—even if they are incapable of recognizing it. Compare this description of radical Yiddish intellectuals in the 1880s with their Ivy-educated offspring of the 1960s and '70s: "They knew little about the conditions of the Jewish working class in Eastern Europe, still in its early stages of formation, and knew next to nothing about the conditions of the working class in America, either native or immigrant. Declamatory, impassioned, theoretic, and sectarian to the marrow, these pioneer radicals sometimes called themselves socialists and sometimes anarchists, but they really had little of any tradition to go by. They were a mixture of socialist, anarchist, positivist, village atheist, and enlightened young Jews in love with the heroic style of the Russian populists."

The stereotypes that have been thrust upon the American Jew, from the much-derided "Jewish mother" to the idea that Jewish socialism was cultural rather than political, are a useful index to the dissolution of Yiddish culture in America. Inheriting the culture of contradictions, the Jew's adaptation to the demands of American life was itself contradictory. And yet the compromises that he made were fairly successful. If Jewish trade unionism represented the victory of practical politics over faith in messianic socialism, it was a victory with which the mass of Jewish workers was content to live. Even in the most radical of the Jewish unions the leadership had to face the problem, so common in American life, of sacrificing long-range goals for short-range interests. Jewish workers were probably more class-conscious than their native American counterparts. But their class-consciousness could not survive in isolation. The failure of the Jewish Left, if that is what it is, reflects the wider failure of the Left in America. And the self-educated Jewish worker, so memorably brought back to life in these pages, remains one of the more attractive figures produced by any working class. He serves too as a useful reminder of a time when, for the worker, "liberation" meant both the ability to live without hunger and the time to ponder "the connection between Herbert Spencer and the Vilna Gaon." Like the Jewish mother, the passion for education that was so vital an aspect of the culture of Yiddishkeit has been transformed into a vulgar joke, a transformation accomplished by those who benefited from the passion.

In "The Culture of Yiddish" Howe depicts a culture in the strikingly singular position of moving from parochialism toward complexity as it moves toward its own destruction: "Is there anything comparable in the whole modern period? An uprooted people, a broken culture, a literature releasing the crude immediacies of plebian life, at once provincial in accent and universalist in its claims." The question is not merely rhetorical. The deepest attraction that the Yiddish world can claim today is that it was a true culture of *folkmassn*. If its relationship to modernity remained peripheral, its strength lay in its unusual melding of worker and intellectual. When Shelley labeled poets "the unacknowledged legislators of the universe," he was indulging in rhetoric. But when Peretz wrote, "Art is the soul of the people, the personality of a nation," his audience understood that if it was *his* art, it was *their* soul and personality he was talking about. To a degree perhaps never since matched, worker and artist were united in the Yiddish world. Often they were indistinguishable: "Imagine in any other literature the turn to impressionism or symbolism being undertaken by a shoemaker and a house painter, the dismissal of the social muse by men laboring in factories!" Yiddish was a language used, inevitably, to keep the non-Yiddish world at a distance: "As against the crumbling of history, the Yiddish world remained an unsleeping witness."

World of Our Fathers is an act of piety, but of a remarkably objective piety. Howe writes with a certainty of purpose, a sense of finality, that is one of the sadder gifts his history imposes. Only in the final section, "Dispersion," where he traces the breakup of the fathers' world and deals directly with the contributions of their offspring, does the reader suspect that Howe is not altogether at home with his material. For Howe's argument with the descendents has become part of his argument with our times. It is difficult to see where one can draw the line. *World of Our Fathers* is itself part of the argument—at least I suspect it is. In insisting on our recognition of the achievement of Yiddishkeit, Howe indicts all cultural disaffiliation.

And yet something of the culture lingers. It will not wholly die, nor is it absorbed in quite the way Howe indicates here. There remains, on his part, a kind of impatience with the young, as if they, in some mysterious manner, were responsible for the inability of the culture of Yiddishkeit to get beyond its tragic history. It is a disturbing quality in a historian so compassionate and a critic so catholic. One sees this quality at work in a review Howe wrote of Leonard Michaels's *I Would Have Saved Them If I Could*. What is peculiar about this is that Michaels is one of the very few writers I know of who is trying to bridge the gap between Yiddishkeit and modernism, to cement the parochial complexities of the remnants of Lower East Side life to the freezing away of *menschlichkeit*, both Jewish and American. He does not always succeed in this, but he is one of the few who makes the attempt. And, as Howe himself points out, it is the question of how we are to live that "is the single commanding power of the Yiddish tradition." In our own time the question is still asked, and the attempt to answer it must still be made—even by the grandchildren. Now, here, and in an America that grows daily as distant from us as it must have been from our parents.

But that is a personal argument, the kind *World of Our Fathers* inspires. In a brilliant essay on Eastern European Jewish history as it seemed after the Holocaust, Abraham Heschel wrote, "Solidarity with the past must become an integral part of our existence." *World of Our Fathers* is a remarkable example of such solidarity. To read it is to be in Howe's debt.

18

Alvin H. Rosenfeld

Of Yiddish Culture and Secular Jewishness

Alvin H. Rosenfeld is professor of English and Jewish Studies and director of the Institute for Jewish Culture and the Arts at Indiana University.

> To recognize that we were living after one of the greatest and least explicable catastrophes of human history . . . brought a new rush of feelings, mostly unarticulated. . . . It brought a low-charged but nagging guilt, a quiet remorse. . . . We could no longer escape the conviction that, blessing or curse, Jewishness was an integral part of our life, even if—and perhaps just because—there was nothing we could do or say about it. . . . We could not turn back to the synagogue; we could only express our irritation with "the community" which kept nagging us like disappointed mothers; and sometimes we tried, through imagination and recall, to put together a few bits and pieces of the world of our fathers.

Seven years after Irving Howe first wrote these lines (in "The New York Intellectuals," an essay published in the fall of 1968), the "bits and pieces" have come together as a massive chronicle of Yiddish culture in America, a full-scale social and cultural history of the immigration of the East European Jews to this country and the life they found and made here. *World of Our Fathers* delineates this life from its origins in the cities and towns of Poland, Russia, and Romania, through the difficulties of the Atlantic crossing and the perplexities of early transplantation, to its moments of flowering and fading in the new world. All the once-legendary names—Jacob Schiff and Louis Marshall, Lillian Wald and Emma Goldman, Jacob Adler and Boris Thomashevsky—are recalled, and the spectacle of a life once full to the brim is set before us. Yet it seems clear to Howe that the once-vigorous Yiddish tradition has had its day and is now irreparably in decline, a perception that cannot help but color the tone of this book—its dominant note of attentive, respectful factuality undercut by currents of personal loss. History of this kind often begins with, or functions as an analogue to, family history, and while it need not end there, the sense of an ending is strong today and almost inevitably will influence conclusions. The works and days of the immigrant generation are all but over, in Howe's view of them, and as the author nears the end of his book and focuses on the receding traces of that familiar world, it is apparent that he is writing as the elegist as well as the historian of Yiddishkeit. This personal note—a blend of tribute, affection, and respect tinged by a stoic's salute to a passing glory—far from detracting from the scholarly value of this history, humanizes it and doubtless helps to account for the warm reception *World of Our Fathers* has enjoyed ever since the first moment of its publication.

The book is organized in four broad sections plus an epilogue. It is also copiously illustrated by photographs and reproductions of line drawings by Jacob Epstein; and it is accompanied, as any scholarly book of this kind should be, by ample notes and bibliographical references.

The first section, "Toward America," offers a brief account of Jewish life in Eastern Europe in the last decades of the nineteenth century as well as a somewhat fuller account of the reasons for emigration and the double shocks of the ordeal by steerage across the Atlantic and the babel that seemed everywhere upon arrival at Ellis Island. Some two million Jews, most of them Eastern Europeans, came to America between 1881 and 1914, the largest number of them settling in New York. Working from a variety of sources in Yiddish and English, Howe follows them from *shtetl* to the Lower East Side, describing in moving detail the mixture of heroism and confusion that characterized their lives. Numerous quotations from memoirs, diaries, and letters from this early period of migration and settlement give this section the rich anthological effect that marks much of the narrative of *World of Our Fathers*.

The second section, "The East Side," runs to some 350 pages and could easily stand as a separate book by itself. Chronologically it spans the half century between 1881 and the early years of the Depression, while culturally and sociologically it encompasses everything from the poverty and toil of the sweatshops and tenements, through the strivings of a new generation of English speakers at public school and City College, to the fun of candy stores, comic strips, and the Catskills. Howe writes with equal ease about street life and lecture hall, the weary round of peddling and the buzz and whirl of activity at the theaters and cafés. We are given brief but vivid sketches of major personalities of the East Side—among others not already mentioned, Abraham Cahan and Hayim Zhitlovsky, Morris Hillquit and Morris Raphael Cohen, David Dubinsky and Belle Moskowitz. The true hero of this part of Howe's story, though, bears no such prominent name and played only a background role in public events; nevertheless, in Howe's view he epitomized the immigrant Jewish culture at its highest and best and is accordingly given a place of special esteem in *World of Our Fathers*: "There began to emerge a new social type who would become the carrier, and often the pride, of Yiddish culture: the self-educated worker-intellectual, still bearing the benchmarks of the Talmud Torah, forced to struggle into his maturity for those elements of learning that his grandsons would accept as their birthright, yet fired by a vision of universal humanist culture and eager to absorb the words of Marx, Tolstoy, and the other masters of the nineteenth century."

A product of the Jewish labor and socialist movements, these self-educated workers suffered the fate of the movements' decline and are "all gone now, almost forgotten," yet Howe sees in them a "grandeur of aspiration" and celebrates the type as "the glory of the immigrant world." The author's affection for Jews of this kind is strong, so much so that if there is a felt nostalgia in *World of Our Fathers*, it derives from Howe's feelings of regard for and loss of the values exemplified by "the persuasion of restlessness [that] moved these men . . . in behalf of a freedom they associated with the life of the mind." That is Howe's definition of an intellectual, at one time a seemingly natural product of the Jewish working class but today dispersed from its site of origins and concentration and also greatly diluted. No wonder that Howe, himself a late product of this same immigrant world and an exemplar of one of its highest vocations, becomes a bit mournful in writing this part of his history.

The elegiac strain is even more prominent in the long chapters on Jewish socialism, which are crucial to this section of the book and carry much of its speculative weight. Howe writes perceptively and with a kind of fraternal pride about the origins and accomplishments of the Jewish labor movements; at the same time he is frank about the intense factionalism that weakened the alliances of the Jewish workers and moves knowingly through the maze of "splits and splits within splits" that continually plagued and finally destroyed the politics of the Left. Although he is not a doctrinaire exponent of this politics, it is clear that Howe, like so many others of his generation, invested considerable hope in the movement's success. Its failure, while frankly acknowledged, is nevertheless softened by a romantic attitude toward the legacy of immigrant socialism, a legacy that is easier to embrace as wish than as fact:

> Jewish socialism was primarily a political movement dedicated to building a new society. . . . [But] sharing the program of international social-

ism, the Jewish socialists largely shared its fate. There is a simple, perhaps decisive sense in which Jewish socialism can be said to have failed, quite as American or French socialism failed: it did not lead to the creation of a new society in which all men would live without want, in freedom and fulfillment. But just as international socialism helped to transform the consciousness of humanity, so did Jewish socialism transform the consciousness of the Jews . . . creating a new type of person: combative, worldly, spirited, and intent upon sharing the future of industrial society with the rest of the world.

If that new type of Jew exists today in any abundance, he is far more likely to be found in Israel than in the United States, a product more of Zionism (which, to be sure, shared some of the ideals and motive force of socialism) than of the Jewish labor movement in America, which, as Howe admits, declined "from a politics into a sentiment." The sentiment is a noble one—who would not wish for a society freed from want and oppression?—but it found little chance, in the Jewish immigrant generation or any other, of entering history unbloodied and in a fully transforming and lasting way.

That a similar fate of cultural disappointment and decline has overtaken the language of the immigrant Jewish masses is a premise behind virtually all of the chapters in the third section of *World of Our Fathers.* An informative survey of American Yiddish literature, theater, scholarship, and the press, this part of Howe's book is also long enough and detailed enough to stand by itself as a separate monograph. Over the years Howe has been working with Eliezer Greenberg on a series of anthologies of Yiddish literature, and their combined efforts, partially adapted for the present volume, have given Howe a close familiarity with Yiddish and an obvious affection for it. As a result the four long chapters that make up "The Culture of Yiddish," while still an introduction to the subject, are written with that note of authority that comes when substantial scholarly research is invigorated by a long-standing personal investment in the life of books—and in the life *behind* books.

By Yiddish Howe means not only the language of the immigrant Jewish masses "but the whole era in cultural history, first in Eastern Europe and then, for a few decades, in the United States." The literary expression of that culture seemed at one time to be accumulating the kind of energy and sophistication that indicate the beginnings of a true cultural renascence. Yiddish had begun to produce poets who were intimate with the modernist writers of Europe and America and who could, at their best, rival them. A body of critical prose was also growing alongside the creative work to explain and judge it in exacting terms: "But there was no time: a blink of history and it was all over." A number of the older poets and fiction writers persisted—what else could they do?—but all were conscious that they were the writers of an abandoned culture.

What accounts for the snuffing out of what seemed a bright and promising moment? A variety of causes were at work, no doubt, ranging all the way from the linguicide of Hitler's Holocaust against the Jews of Eastern Europe to the subtler workings of acculturation in America. Howe does not say so at any great length, but it would seem that a major impulse behind the dwindling of Yiddish in America, as of other aspects of Jewish culture, must be attributed to the desires of the immigrant generation itself. To many who wanted to appear less "alien," the language carried with it the embarrassments of separateness and foreign birth and was an unwanted impediment to success in the public schools and universities, in American business and gentile society. Yiddish, the *jargon* of the Jews, must have seemed a guarantee *against* such success, a lingering whiff of the *shtetl* that threatened to keep them—and even worse, their children—out of the promise of the American dream, forever down in the crowded tenements and sweatshops of the Jewish streets. For a time Yiddish was right for the marketplace, where one could haggle with pushcart dealers in it; and for the theater, where one could laugh and cry in it without shame; and for the newspaper, where over the kitchen table it afforded some manageable contact with an increasingly puzzling world. Finally, though, it was to be abandoned, like an old, once-comfortable coat exchanged for brighter, more stylish goods.

A culture needs a language of its own in order to thrive, and the consequences of letting Yiddish slip away are today everywhere apparent. The twenty Yiddish theaters that existed in 1918 have now dwindled to one or two. A similar fate has overtaken the once-thriving Yiddish press. Howe's description of the current state of the *Jewish Daily Forward*—"Writing to the End"—is ominously titled and could serve equally well for this whole long section of his book. The end does not seem far off.

Just what was the historical phase of Yiddish, and what has been its legacy to the present generation of Jews in America? These are the questions that are asked and answered in "Dispersion," the fourth and final section of *World of Our Fathers*. While continuing his work as chronicler, Howe devotes the main thrust of this section to historical analysis and speculation. The culture of Yiddish, as he evaluates it, "represents a major break within—and perhaps from—the [Jewish] tradition," and the lives and works of those artists and intellectuals who descend from the generation of immigrant Jews are "marked by rupture, break, dissociation, by a will to flee, and, once and for all, be done with it."

Yet "tradition seemingly discarded can survive underground for a generation," and, although "broken and crippled," traces of the Yiddish tradition still "display enormous power over those most eager to shake it off." The journeys outward from the center of the immigrant experience—geographically into the suburbs as well as culturally into the American mainstream—were not made altogether without some of the accents of Yiddishkeit traveling along. Although countless numbers of Jews have by now fully entered the American bourgeoisie, "the strains of immigrant Yiddish culture, usually blurred, sometimes buried, [are] still at work" in their lives, and some of "their deepest inclinations of conduct, bias, manner, style, and intonation [bear] heavy signs of immigrant shaping." While greatly weakened and seemingly without the means of self-recovery, then, the Yiddish tradition can still be detected as a lingering cultural force among American Jews.

In a brief epilogue, entitled "Questions upon Questions," Howe pays a final, respectful tribute to this tradition. He also ruefully acknowledges its closing, for with "the crumbling of Yiddish culture" an end point in a generation's history seems to have been reached: "For all its impressive qualities and achievements, the culture of Yiddish necessarily had to drift toward a self-dissolution: it could not, by itself, sustain Jewish life for very long." After all that has preceded in this book, that seems a sad but accurate conclusion, one that the working historian is obliged to make but the feeling man cannot easily bear—hence the subjective and slightly plaintive quality of the epilogue. There is nothing remiss or exhibitionist about this open display of feeling. It is one thing, after all, for a scholar to come generations after the passing of a once-vibrant culture and give an accounting of its rise and fall, but it is another thing altogether—and an infinitely harder thing—for a living son of that culture to chronicle its still-transpiring demise. Howe has taken on that latter task, as his concluding paragraphs freely and movingly admit: "The story of the immigrant Jews is all but done. Like all stories of human striving, it ought to be complete, with its beginning and its end, at rest in fulfillment and at ease with failure. A story is the essential unit of our life, offering the magical imperatives of 'so it began' and 'so it came to an end.' A story encompasses us. Justifies our stay, prepares our leaving. Here, in these pages, is the story of the Jews, bedraggled and inspired, who came from Eastern Europe. Let us now praise obscure men."

And, as most readers would be moved to assent at this point, let us now praise Irving Howe for telling the story so well.

Yet does it properly end with the ending that Howe provides for it? The story of the immigrant Jews that he has given us, while complete in its own terms, surely does not speak the whole truth for all of our fathers, whose world encompassed dimensions of experience and value that are only touched on in this book. The culture of Yiddish that *World of Our Fathers* presents was not all of Yiddishkeit by any means, and some large additions and correctives to Howe's version of immigrant Jewish life need to be made.

One of these involves the religious dimension of that life, which Howe refers to briefly but nowhere attempts to adequately explain. While Judaism was not carried over intact from Eastern Europe (it was far from intact even there in the period preceding that of mass emigration), it is nevertheless still the case that multitudes of men and women among the immigrant generations knew themselves, often in the first place, within the traditional definitions of Judaism. The religious life did not provide them with their sole source of self-definition, to be sure, but it did contribute far more than one would ever imagine from a reading of *World of Our Fathers*. While Howe nowhere seems hostile to Judaism, neither does he seem to know it intimately from within; as a result he has given it far less currency and weight than it should have in a book of this sort.

The implications of this diminution of a major factor in the culture of the immigrant Jews are serious and detract from the story that Howe sets out to tell. A people that is intent on a future for itself, after all, will take pains to ensure the survival of those things that it cares most about and sees as vital for its own ongoing existence. Yiddish, sadly, was not one of these, as the decline of literacy in the language and the lack of a viable network of Yiddish schools today sorrowfully attest. Socialism, which Howe celebrates as being at the ideological and political heart of the immigrant Jewish experience, was obviously another, as the present diminished state of the Jewish labor unions and their fraternal organizations likewise attests. Although these may have once appeared to be in the vanguard, it is pretty clear that they are today without significant force and lack the kinds of mechanisms necessary for continuity and regeneration. One imagines that if the immigrant Jews and their immediate offspring truly valued these dimensions of Yiddish culture and saw them as indispensable, they would have guaranteed the means of their survival. Why they let them weaken and pass into exhaustion is a matter that may be open to question, but that they have so weakened is not.

By contrast, if one looks into American Jewish life today and tries to determine what, if anything, is in the ascendancy, some prominent cultural forces that are all but absent from Howe's accounting present themselves. One cannot be too sanguine about any of these, for all are highly problematic; still, certain currents are now clear enough, and these can be identified and spoken of. The religious life is one of these. Not all seders are simulated ones, after all, and while the raids on Hasidism may be merely literary or faddish on the part of some, they are quite authentic on the part of many others. The grand temples have lost their hold on many, but the smaller *shuls* have attracted many more. And, most significantly, while large numbers of Jewish children grow up knowing all too little about the world of their fathers, some 185,000 others are presently enrolled in Hebrew day schools throughout the country. In sum, whereas the religious life plays a minor role, or no role at all, in the lives of countless numbers of American Jews, there has been an unexpected revival and intensification of Judaism in the lives of countless others, a fact basic to the story that Howe wants to tell but hardly to be found in his pages.

One also misses in *World of Our Fathers* a fuller and more sustained attempt to understand the impact of the Holocaust and Zionism on American Jewish life. Both are mentioned, to be sure, but in nothing like the detail that each requires (a few paragraphs only, in "The Holocaust and After" and "Israel and the American Jews"). Howe acknowledges that "memories of the Holocaust pressed deep into the consciousness of Jews" but then concludes that "there was nothing to do but remember, and that was best done in silence, alone." Yet that is precisely the *antithesis* of Jewish remembering, which is always done communally, even liturgically, not in silence or alone. While it would be folly to minimize here the difficulties of assimilating that immense historical tragedy to understanding or commemoration, it is simply not the case that Jews have lacked all means of response or that they have been suffering in solitude the specter of a terror-ridden fate.

One response—and that it is directly bound up with the Holocaust is becoming ever more clear—is American Zionism, a complex mingling of national feeling, religious obligation, and social and political impulse that has gripped virtually every Jew in the country. A majority of American Jews may have no direct family in Israel and may never have set foot in the land; few perhaps possess a detailed knowledge of Israel's history or topography, and fewer still will leave to take up settlement there. Nevertheless, Israel has become a deep-seated and authentic passion in the lives of American Jews, who devote an inordinate amount of their time and money to help secure its survival and well-being. For many this may be a kind of surrogate Judaism, but there is no doubting its present strength or its promise for the future. The links that American Jews have to Zionism—and they are the same Jews who descend from the European immigrants—are not to be minimized or discounted, and it is odd that Howe does little more than refer to them in passing.

The absence of substantial attention to Judaism and Zionism, the two most encompassing cultural forces in American Jewish life in the post-

Holocaust years, points to a blind spot in Howe's study that is doubtless a result of the author's guiding philosophy of history. "The central premise of Jewish survival," he writes, "is a defiance of history; the cost, beyond measure." The fact is, the cost can be measured, and *World of Our Fathers* sets out to measure it. It does so, however, with a set of cultural and historical indexes that afford clear recognition to certain currents of Jewish life and virtual nonrecognition to others. Howe's is a very localized, pragmatic history, sensitive to the great and small moments of social, political, and cultural activity on the Lower East Side but almost without the means to see beyond its immediate boundaries. The broader national and religious lines of Jewish existence hardly come into this focus, with the result that the two most compelling historical events of the century after the period of mass emigration almost do not register at all.

Yet the fact is, the Holocaust and Israel carry enormous emotional and ideational weight for Jews everywhere and have not failed to make themselves felt—for many in truly transforming ways—in the culture of American Jews. Howe's shaping view of history, however, does not easily accommodate experience of any metaphysical implication or magnitude and consequently misses what may be the deepest stirrings in Jewish life today.

If there is an ideology implicit in *World of Our Fathers* that may help to account for these oversights, it is that of secular Jewishness. The term is imprecise and may even be an oxymoron; still, it points a direction that most readers will be familiar with. As defined by some of Howe's own terminology, secular Jewishness implies a commitment to "liberalism, tolerance, science, progress, . . . cosmopolitanism, a diffused this-worldly messianism." It locates the sources of these values in *menshlichkeit* and in the idea of an enlightened, progressive society, which it will help to bring about. It shuns the synagogue and yeshiva and stresses instead the "cultural" sides of Jewishness and its "ethical" and "universal" importance. It espouses the natural dignity of man, decency of feeling, and the responsibilities of the liberated mind. Its aim—a noble one—is a culture of democratic humanism.

In writing *World of Our Fathers* Irving Howe has given us a comprehensive history of the American phase of secular Jewishness, but that is not one and the same with a history of the culture that the Eastern European Jews brought to this country and the life they and their children have created here. Vigorous in its day, secular Jewishness at one time fired the spirits and embraced the allegiances of large numbers of Jews, but that culture is now badly worn down and lives on mostly in the nostalgic memories of the dispersed children of the Lower East Side. Howe himself is too honest and demanding a writer to persist for long in mere nostalgia, and his book is not one more rehearsal of the Joys of Yiddish, yet it does movingly express the author's esteem for and devotion to his own origins. He has done these a formidable service in this history, which succeeds admirably in clarifying the lines of secular Jewishness. In following these out, though, Howe apparently discovered that they no longer lead anywhere, that the culture that set him on his way almost has no extension beyond the midcentury point. In fact Howe may be its last serious exponent within American Jewish intellectual life and presently the single commanding voice of its vision. We are all in his debt for keeping it alive a little longer, but we need not conclude with him that the story of the immigrant Jews is over. His version of it may compel an ending, but, as always in Jewish life, forces of renewal assert themselves to guarantee continuation beyond any present moment of fading. Among these, devotional Judaism and Zionism are today preeminent and should be recognized as part of the legacy given us by the world of our fathers.

19

Edward Alexander

Standing Guard over Irving Howe's Reputation;

Or, Good Causes Attract Bad Advocates

Edward Alexander has been professor of English at the University of Washington in Seattle since 1960. He has also taught at Tel-Aviv University, Hebrew University, Tufts University, and Memphis State University. His early work centered on Victorian literature and included several books of scholarly criticism: *Matthew Arnold and John Stuart Mill* (1965), *John Morley* (1972), and *Matthew Arnold, John Ruskin, and the Modern Temper* (1973). He has also published three scholarly editions of work by J. S. Mill, the Victorian philosopher and social critic: *John Stuart Mill: Literary Essays* (1967), *On Liberty* (1999), and *The Subjection of Women* (2001).

His other scholarly-critical interests have been Jewish literature and the war of ideas over the Holocaust and Israel. He has published two books on the Yiddish writer Isaac Bashevis Singer: *Isaac Bashevis Singer* in 1980 and *Isaac Bashevis Singer: A Study of the Short Fiction* in 1990. His book *The Resonance of Dust: Essays on Holocaust Literature and Jewish Fate* (1979) was one of the earliest to deal with the challenge posed by the Holocaust to the literary imagination. A second book on the Holocaust, entitled *The Holocaust and the War of Ideas* (1994), interprets representative works from the three main bodies of Holocaust literature—Yiddish, Hebrew, and American—in relation to the controversies that surround the Jewish catastrophe of World War II.

Alexander has published two collections of his essays, both dealing with highly charged and contentious issues. *The Jewish Idea and Its Enemies*, published in 1988, addresses the uneasy relationship between liberalism and Judaism in such figures as Lionel Trilling, Leftist anti-Semitism in writers ranging from Karl Marx to Gore Vidal, and the ideological assault on Zionism. In 1996 Alexander published a collection of polemical essays entitled *The Jewish Wars: Reflections by One of the Belligerents*, which discusses such individuals as Edward Said, Noam Chomsky, Alexander Cockburn, Desmond Tutu, Patrick Buchanan, and Michael Lerner in a style that Cynthia Ozick described as "gloriously intolerant . . . of the shady, the shabby, and the sham."

Alexander's acquaintance with Irving Howe began in 1972 when Howe wrote to compliment him on an article about Chaim Grade that he had published in *Judaism* that year. They met occasionally and continued to correspond until a few days before Howe's death in 1993. Alexander's published work on Howe includes a review of *World of Our Fathers* in the *American Historical Review*; an obituary of him in *Congress Monthly*; a lengthy lecture at the University of Cincinnati (in the Rabbi Louis Feinberg Memorial Lecture Series) in 1995 entitled "Irving Howe and Secular Jewishness: An Elegy"; and the first biography of Howe, *Irving Howe: Socialist, Critic, Jew* (1998). The book is primarily a biography of Howe's mind, a study of his intellectual development as socialist, literary critic, and "secular" or "partial" Jew. It is both reverential and critical, adhering to the principle that a critic need not be an enemy.

Alexander's most recent book, *Classical Liberalism and the Jewish Tradition* (2002), brings together his Victorian and Jewish interests in essays on (among others) Mill, Thomas Arnold, George Eliot, and Benjamin Disraeli.

Although I had published nine books prior to *Irving Howe*, this was the first one that elicited warnings from its prospective publisher (Indiana University Press) about the prejudices of book reviewers in the field. One of Indiana's editors, a scholar in his own right, urged me to drop criticisms of the Israeli Left and of Howe's links with it via Peace Now. If I didn't, he predicted, the book would go unreviewed (as indeed it did) in the *New York Times*, the *New Yorker*, and the *New York Review of Books* or be savaged in most "liberal" journals. I complied, but (as would soon be evident) inadequately: I reduced twelve pages on this topic to eight (in a book of 284 pages).

Early reviews of the book, in librarians' and publishers' journals, by Nathan Glick in the *Washington Times*, and by Sanford Pinsker in the *Philadelphia Inquirer*, were very favorable, and the book became a Jewish Book Club selection. But then came the most prominent review of the book, by a weighty critic in an important journal: namely, Robert Alter in the *New Republic* (July 6, 1998). Alter was the first, but by no means the last, reviewer of liberal persuasion to present himself as a guardian of Howe's reputation and to imply that one of my main aims in writing a book about a man who had been my friend for over two decades was to dance, or perhaps spit, on his grave.

For example: "Alexander needs to mention Howe's change of name [from Horenstein] again and again—perhaps twenty times in the book before I stopped counting." Alter apparently did not drop his abacus before the end of the last chapter, for twenty is indeed the number of times that Howe's original name has by then been mentioned. That name appears fourteen times in the first two chapters for the (not very sinister) reason that they deal with Howe from birth through 1942, when Horenstein was indeed his real name (as it would be until 1946). The subject of name-changing comes up several times because Howe himself discussed it repeatedly, although in his youth he usually neglected to mention his own case. In 1966 he condemned Jewish radicals for choosing "for their 'party names' almost anything that did not sound Jewish"; in 1982 he said that Jewish name-changing had "less to do with Marxist strategy than our own confused and unexamined feelings about Jewish origin." Name-changing is also relevant to Howe's activity as a union organizer and to his quarrels with Philip Roth and Sidney Hook, who once accused him of manipulating pseudonyms to evade responsibility. (Once, when I visited Irving in his CUNY office, he made a point of showing me the entry for one Kalman Trilling in Bialystok community records so that I would know that "Lionel, contrary to what many people thought, never changed his name.") But nowhere do I say or imply that Howe's change of name was, in Alter's grotesque formulation, an "act of turpitude . . . that put him on a footing of lifelong probation."

In order to show his intellectual growth over the decades, I contrast Howe's 1938 "Trotskyist" invocation (as recalled by Daniel Bell) of "historical necessity" to justify his hero's suppression of the Kronstadt sailors' rebellion of 1921 with his explicit rejection of this totalitarian rationale for murder in his 1986 *New York Times* book review of Israeli novelist Aharon Appelfeld's *Badenheim 1939*. Alter blusters furiously over the first item in the contrast—why, he asks, criticize someone for views he held at twenty?—but omits the second. Why? So that two paragraphs later he can (mis)report that "Alexander makes no mention" of Howe's "prominent laudatory reviews of . . . Aharon Appelfeld and other Hebrew novelists." My attempt to show the process of maturation in Howe is thus depicted as meanspirited insistence on recalling the sins of his youth, and Howe's use of Appelfeld's novel to make his point disappears.

About my suggestion that Howe felt some (guilty) responsibility for creating the New Left, Alter sneers: "[Imagine] the Weathermen reading *Politics and the Novel*." But Howe had written much more than *Politics and the Novel* (a book I praise unstintingly) prior to the 1960s. Bernadine

Dohrn, Tom Hayden, and Todd Gitlin may not have read that book, but they certainly had read and taken to heart much that was published in *Dissent*, for example, Norman Mailer's "The White Negro," published in the very same year (1957), which became the bible of New Left nihilism. Does Alter suppose that Howe in later years deeply regretted printing that piece because he didn't like the way Mailer was now growing his hair, or because he felt complicit in the monstrosities that "The White Negro" had engendered and had come to believe that, as he wrote in 1960, "at some point sorcerers must take a bit of responsibility for their strayed apprentices"?

But most of all it was my criticism of Howe's dealings with Israel and of the Israeli Left that enraged Alter. His untidy passions on this topic had been on display in his sledgehammer attack on Ruth Wisse (*New Republic*, November 1992) for her book *If I Am Not for Myself* . . . , which criticizes the liberal betrayal of Israel and also the dramatic and moral bias of leftish Israeli novelists, who tend to charge fellow Jews for incurring the hatred against Israel. In May 1993—it is probably relevant to observe—I defended her book against Alter in the pages of *Commentary*.

The subject of Howe's relationship to Israel and Zionism is a complicated one. Although he once wrote that "in this era of blood and shame, the rise of the Jewish state was one of the few redeeming events," his support of Israel was often conditioned upon the hope that socialism, dead in the United States, could be resuscitated in Israel, "as good a model as we have for the democratic socialist hope of combining radical social change with political freedom." But should support of Israel's "right to exist" (a chilling phrase redolent of Nazi lucubrations on whether Jews had the "right to live") be contingent on its being virtuously Leftist? In early June 1967 Howe signed his name to a *New York Times* ad calling on the United States to reopen the Gulf of Aqaba, blockaded by Egypt, and to "safeguard the integrity, security, and survival of Israel and its people." But in the (post–Six-Day War) August issue of *Dissent* he insisted that he was neither a Zionist nor a Jewish nationalist. Again in 1982, and with characteristic honesty, he stated that "I still don't think of myself as a Zionist—I'm not a Zionist." But Alter would have none of this, and so he excoriated me for intolerantly refusing to grant that Howe represented one (and, as it happens, Alter's very own) part of the "spectrum of Zionist" opinion.

Several subsequent assaults on my book showed the influence of Alter's, especially in their resistance to contrasts between "early" and "late" Howe. These are contrasts that Howe himself made repeatedly in his autobiography, where he says that when he had occasion to look back over his early work, he took a mild pleasure in noticing that, whatever his foolishness and self-importance in those days, at least he could write a passable sentence.

Stephen Whitfield, writing in *American Jewish Archives* (1998), whipped himself into an indignation similar to Alter's over the very same passage about Howe's early Trotskyism. "Trotskyism," writes Whitfield "is [for Alexander] unforgivable. As late as page 194 . . . Alexander still cannot help scorning Howe's rationalization of the Bolshevik suppression of the Kronstadt rebellion of 1921. Howe's remarks, the biographer does not bother to remind the reader, occurred at the age of eighteen." Apparently Whitfield, professor at Brandeis, could not figure out that my reference on this very page to "the Howe of 1938" is a reference to Howe "at the age of eighteen." The discussion in question here runs from page 194 to page 195 of my book, so, far from being "scornful," it is—as a normally attentive sixth-grader could tell—entirely laudatory and devoted to showing "just how far Howe had come with respect to the invocation of 'historical necessity' as justification for murder." Whitfield had read Alter's review much more carefully than he had read my book—which, by the way, describes *Leon Trotsky* as "one of Howe's most impressive achievements."

Whitfield also apes Alter's resentment of my criticism of Howe's youthful extremism in opposition to the war against Hitler. He suggests that the scores of articles Howe wrote (and, as an editor of *Labor Action*, caused to be written) before age twenty-eight should be ignored because they "had no consequences whatsoever." At what age, one wonders, should a biography written according to the Whitfield rules begin? Should one omit mention of George Eliot's life while the great Judeophile novelist was still Mary Ann Evans and insisting—this at age twenty-eight—that Jews are an "inferior race" and that "everything specifically Jewish is of a low grade"?

Following a similar line was Deborah Dash Moore of Vassar, standing guard over Howe's infallibility in the journal *Sh'ma* (April 1999). She found the book "unpleasant" because it "reads like a long, argumentative tirade" against Howe. In a letter to the journal (unpublished, like the one about Whitfield) I recalled that I had not only written favorably of every book Howe ever published but had praised him for "a kind of life-wisdom that went beyond political differences [and] expressed itself in a prose as supple . . . and analytically precise as that of any critic writing in English in this century" and even urged that "if the world of American letters cannot emulate [Howe's] intellectual heroism and tenacious idealism, it should at least remember them." Moore alleged that the book contains nothing except "sniping and criticizing [of Howe's] views." Since she did not bother to say just *which* "views" I had criticized, I took the trouble of specifying: they were his belief (held until 1947) that the Allies should not have gone to war against Hitler and his advocacy of the pro–Palestine Liberation

Organization policies of Peace Now, one of the "smelly little orthodoxies" (Orwell's words) of the academic world that Moore inhabits.

Sometimes a journal's letter refusing to print my rebuttal of a review was as solemnly idiotic as the review itself. Alan Cooper, writing in *Left History* (1999), not only identified me—as did some other reviewers—as a tribune of *Commentary*, a person who felt personally "threatened" by "Howe's godlessness" and a dubious claimant to Howe's friendship (in Cooper's world George Eliot's precept that "opinions are a poor cement between human souls" is unknown). He also complained that I had made no reference to "correspondence carried on outside of periodicals" until the last chapter. When I laboriously documented the falsehood of this allegation with a long list of previously unpublished letters cited in earlier chapters, the editors replied that as a journal of history they were not concerned with "factual criticism," only "intellectual substance."

I venture to think that Howe would have been embarrassed by these febrile defenders of his complete life and works, standing guard over his reputation from age sixteen to seventy-two. Unlike them, he did not hold the jejune notion that liberals should always stick together, praise each other when they speak well and praise each other when they speak ill, support each other when they are right and support each other when they are wrong. He understood that the real measure of a thinker is the ability to enter the minds of people formed in schools opposed to his own, and he was always mindful of the fact that, as he liked to say, good causes often attract bad advocates.

20

Leon Wieseltier

Irving, In Memoriam

Leon Wieseltier has been literary editor of the *New Republic* since 1983. He is also the author of *Kaddish* (1998).

It was a moody September morning in 1991, and we were walking down Madison Avenue, gossiping about books, when Irving Howe changed the subject. "Something happened to me in Paris that you might understand" was how he began the least likely conversation we ever had. "I was in the garden at the Rodin Museum. For a few minutes I was alone, sitting on a stone bench between two long hedges of roses. Pink roses. Suddenly I felt the most powerful feeling of peace, and I had the thought that death, if it means an absorption into a reality like the one that was before me, might be all right."

That was all. I mumbled something about the importance of such an experience and said nothing more; illuminations are not occasions for criticism. But I was filled with gladness for my friend. He had recently recovered from a rattling period of physical infirmity; and during those months, when he fought his fear with the help of Haydn, and Proust, and the first tranquilizers of his otherwise urbane life, I had wondered whether his urbanity, his intellectual strictness, his decades of dialectic, had adequately prepared him for the times that humble the mind. I learned, that morning on Madison, that he was not unprepared.

I was not altogether surprised. Over the years of our friendship I discovered that Irving, who died May 5, 1993, was not just the god of rigor and reason that his admirers, the socialists and the secularists especially, made him out to be. He was, of course, a master controversialist and fierce in his insistence on clarity in thought and in prose; and it did not make your own thinking and writing any easier to know that sooner or later Irving would have a view of it. For many people he was the perfect representative of the

"New York intellectuals"—those brilliant critics of politics and culture who believed in many things in the course of their extraordinary lives but most of all believed in brains.

In truth Irving was rather an imperfect representative of the breed. In politics he was steadier and had no craving for conversions; and in his later life this proved much of an impediment for a man with a romantic view of marginality. (This almost never made him doctrinaire. Irving had a gift for feeling certain that you were wrong without feeling certain that he was right.) More important, it was Irving, in his unforgettable essay "The New York Intellectuals" in 1968, who warned of the limitations of brilliance, of the gladiatorial excesses of the metropolitan style of mind.

There was something unexpectedly concrete about the man and his work. He was intrigued by the utopian imagination, but he had a vivid sense of the facticity of life. He understood the importance of the common touch, even if he lacked it. He suspected things that dazzled. He liked ideas more than theories, reasonableness more than correctness. His tone, when he was interpreting a novel or analyzing a historical figure, was often provisional, gracious, patient with perplexity, collaborative. He was always in the middle of trying to get something right. He enjoyed admiring more than he enjoyed criticizing.

He was a great authority on radicalism, not least on the sources of its appeal, which were, in his case, a childhood in the Depression and a virtually European fascination with the career of ideas in politics. Yet he was, in a way, divided against himself, for his temperament was not at all radical. Irving had no weakness for totality, no innocence about revolution. All his life he proudly called himself a socialist, or more precisely a democratic socialist. He was the terror, so to speak, of the Stalinist Left. About the shabbiness of many of its notions, nobody was more withering. He castigated his own congregation as naturally as he castigated the others. And so his congregation kept shrinking, and the honor of belonging to it kept growing.

I have an allergy to socialism myself, and so I was impressed by the infrequency with which our ideological difference amounted to a political difference. May his comrades at *Dissent* forgive me, but Irving struck me finally as a welfare-state liberal with a fluency in the Marxist tradition. I remember the evening—it was early in the 1980s, at the height of the Reagan dizziness—when he argued against the uncritical praise of the market on the ground that it missed what was valuable about the market, which was its amenability to reform. He despised those who refused to see the suffering that capitalism sometimes caused; but capitalism, he said, is an economic system that may be politically corrected. In recent years, after the collapse of state socialism in the big Soviet Union and all the little Soviet Unions under its sway, Irving interested himself in the possibility, conceptual and practical, of "market socialism." It looked to me like a contortion, but it was proof, if proof was still needed, that he was a man with his eyes open, and his heart.

What kept his eyes and his heart open, however, was not politics. It was literature. He loved nothing more. As a critic Irving came to occupy a peculiar position. He was both anachronistic and urgent. In an era of literary theory he was dead to literary theory; and yet you had to read him, because his humanism was sophisticated rather than sentimental. Irving's approach to poems and novels was part Matthew Arnold, part East Bronx. That is, he turned to literature to learn about life, but the life about which he most wished to learn was the hard and lumpy and common one. He despised proletarian art and the ways in which populism and mass politics tortured the writer; but he had little patience for art's high priests. He preferred beauty to estheticism. Hardy, Sherwood Anderson, Faulkner: the writers about whom he wrote books (how magical still are the opening pages of his study of Hardy!) were masters of form who found in ordinary people difficulty and dignity enough. Irving's greatest thrill was high art that felt democratic. (And so he was devoted to the ballets of Balanchine.)

He had no illusions about the extent to which the world was changing and he was not; but no change struck Irving with greater force, and made him feel more like the end of the line, than the eclipse of Yiddish—the language, the culture, the sensibility. I have never known anyone in whom the paradoxical Yiddish inflection, the cheerful grimness, the sunny decay of hope, survived so purely. For decades Irving threw himself into the task of rescue, editing and introducing and writing about what he made famous as the "world of our fathers." He was without nostalgia, but he was not without grief. I cannot count the number of breakfasts at Leo's on East Eighty-sixth Street that were taken up with the disappearance of that world, with the decline of secular Jewishness.

As a Jew Irving felt almost like a man without contemporaries. All that remained of Jewish identity, he would argue, was religion or nationalism, and he was excluded, by experience and by conviction, from both. I would argue that, as foundations for identity go, religion and nationalism are not bad; and then I would gently suggest to him that he was not as alienated from either Judaism or Israel as he thought. (About the philistinism of the American Jewish community, however, I offered no disagreement.) The Yom Kippur War left him fearing for Israel's safety, and he was passionately drawn into the great Jewish debate about the Palestinian question. His wife, Ilana, an Israeli woman of great cultivation, filled the apartment with

Hebrew writings and sometimes with Hebrew writers. He even started to visit the synagogue on Yom Kippur—not to find God, of course, but not many Jews visit the synagogue to find God.

Irving and God? Not a chance. And yet, when he wrote or lectured or just talked about the deeper and the more difficult themes, Irving was surrounded by the atmosphere of intellectual seriousness and intellectual tolerance that the rabbis describe as "for the sake of Heaven." He was, this skeptic and secularist and socialist, a great-souled man. And he was the man who, more than any American intellectual of his generation, by his work and by his example, conferred greatness upon the homeliest of qualities, the quality that transforms controversy into a search for the true and action into a search for the good, the quality that mattered most to Orwell and Silone, who were, we may now say, Irving's true company: the quality of decency. It is, in his absence, a quality more strained.

Revaluations

21

Gerald Sorin

The Relevance of Irving Howe

Gerald Sorin has taught history at the State University of New York at New Paltz since 1965. He has also taught in the Netherlands at the University of Utrecht's School of Journalism and at the University of Nijmegen, where he held the John Adams Distinguished Chair in American Studies as a Fulbright professor. He is the former chairman of the history department (1986–96) at SUNY, New Paltz, and continues there, since 1983, as director of the Jewish studies program. In 1989 he founded and continues to direct the Louis and Mildred Resnick Institute for the Study of Modern Jewish Life. And in 1994 he was awarded SUNY's highest rank—Distinguished University Professor.

His early work centered on the Civil War era, slavery, and the abolitionists and included several essays and two books: *The New York Abolitionists: A Case Study of Political Radicalism* (1970) and *Abolitionism: A New Perspective* (1972), which was nominated for the Pulitzer Prize in history. Sorin's interest in radicalism carried over into his later work in Jewish studies with essays in scholarly journals and with his book *The Prophetic Minority: American Jewish Immigrant Radicals, 1880–1920* (1985). He went on to write *The Nurturing Neighborhood: The Brownsville Boys Club and Jewish Community in Urban America, 1940–1990* (1990), a work described by critics as "a model account of neighborhood life, adolescent culture, generational change, and American ethnicity." This was followed by *A Time for Building: The Third Migration, 1880–1920*, which is part of the acclaimed five-volume series *The Jewish Experience in America*, edited by Henry Feingold (1992). In 1997 Sorin published his concise interpretative overview of three hundred years of American Jewish experience, *Tradition Transformed*.

His work on Irving Howe began with his article "Irving Howe's 'Margin of Hope': *World of Our Fathers* as Autobiography," published in *American Jewish History* 88, no. 4 (2000), and culminated with *Irving Howe: A Life of Passionate Dissent* (2002), a biography that won the National Jewish

Book Award in history for 2002 and was awarded the Saul Viener Prize by the American Jewish Historical Society for Best Book in American Jewish History 2001–2002.

"It is hard," one critic wrote of Irving Howe in the year 2000, "to imagine another individual who achieved so much success during his lifetime in such disparate fields of endeavor and yet whose contributions are more thoroughly ignored today."[1] The critic errs immediately in seeing Howe's three main professional interests—democratic radicalism, literary criticism, and Jewish culture—as "disparate" but even more profoundly in assuming Howe's contemporary invisibility and even irrelevance.

Howe had to struggle mightily at times to reconcile his desire to live the introspective, reflective life of a critic with his need to contribute actively to progressive social change. But he did manage to combine the contemplative and the active partly through his writing. Howe's many seminal and provocative essays, including "This Age of Conformity" (1954), "The New York Intellectuals" (1968), and "Writing and the Holocaust" (1986), made him an instructive spokesman for culture at the crossroads of literature and politics.

Whether he had successfully synthesized his cultural, literary, and political aspirations, however, was less important a question for Howe than whether his political conscience, partly shaped by his urban secular Jewish experience, led him to support good causes and whether his critical consciousness led him to write pieces up to the standard of George Orwell and Edmund Wilson, the essayists he most admired. But Howe's writing, his public life, and the disputes he entered—disputes about Ezra Pound and T. S. Eliot, Ralph Ellison and Hannah Arendt, race and multiculturalism, Marxism and postmodernism—demonstrate that critical consciousness and political conscience did continue to inform one another in powerful ways. This process of mutual reinforcement moved Howe to a broader, more humane conception of creative writing and helped him produce work—political, literary, and Jewish—that was analytically sharp, lucid, accessible, and ethically meaningful.

Howe himself, late in his life, sometimes used the phrase "lost causes" when referring to his three campaigns: his battles to promote an anti-Stalinist, democratic socialism; his effort to protect literature and criticism from the abstract theory and unrestrained relativism of the deconstructionists; and his attempts to rekindle the golden glow of Yiddish culture in the face of what he thought was its final sunset. But in each case he retained "a margin of hope," a faith in the resilience of the human spirit and imagination, which allowed him to do the "steady work" so inspiring to readers and colleagues.

The socialist idea, Howe knew, had been poisoned, perhaps irreparably, by the way it had been implemented in totalitarian regimes, especially in the Soviet Union and China. But even after it had taken another brutal beating in the late 1960s, when one deluded faction of Students for a Democratic Society turned to Maoism and another, the Weathermen, to terrorism, Howe retained the socialist label. By that time, however, socialism was for him less an ideology, political formula, or economic program and more the name of his "desire," his vision of a more egalitarian and fraternal society, less a blueprint for the future and more a moral yardstick against which to measure changes in American society and culture.

Howe was far from certain that socialism would ever be more than a marginal phenomenon in America. But he believed that some form of democratic radicalism was necessary in order to achieve greater human fulfillment. To give up this kind of utopian vision, Howe thought, would not only leave many social injustices, including economic and racial in-equality, unchallenged; it would be a failure of the imagination. It would turn against the entire experience of humanity, which needs the dream of community and egalitarianism, Howe argued, as much as it needs the reality of bread and shelter.[2] In the twentieth century, the century of Auschwitz, the Gulag, and global interethnic mass murder, it was hard to sustain po-litical certainties and difficult to take pride in one's humanity. Yet Howe continued, throughout, to live a life of conviction and commitment. A rare achievement, but also a model for a new generation seeking to understand the meaning of critical engagement.

In the realm of the study of literature, as in his pursuit of the socialist ideal, Howe also faced disappointments, but again he was not completely defeated. A supremely astute critic, Howe moved in his essays from a daz-zling virtuoso prose, full of polemical thrusts, to what he called the difficult "discipline of the plain style," from the self-conscious brilliance of the New York intellectuals to greater and greater lucidity in his own voice. The spare style of his essays, most of which originated from a passion, a moral striving, and an abiding faith in the common reader, was meant, Howe intimated, "as a political challenge to the obscurantist prose of academic criticism."[3] He continued to believe, unlike the deconstructionists, that life is the most important subject for fiction and that literature is indeed the subject of literary criticism. And he asked, with bitter humor, for a return to English, "a language that for some time served criticism well."[4]

Howe's writings may be out of fashion now at universities caught in the fog created by the convoluted theorizing and impenetrable jargon of the postmodernists. But his struggle, even in the face of seemingly insuperable odds, to make the necessary fight for intelligible and humane criticism will continue to inspire those who oppose literary studies that are inaccessible to anyone but academic specialists. And his example and good works will continue to sustain those teachers and writers who believe in the progressive idea that the common citizen can "rise to articulation and authority."[5]

If Howe's socialist idealism and literary criticism have suffered a decline in serious attention, this is a loss for us all. His Jewish works, however, continue to attract a wide readership. This is especially true for his award-winning *World of Our Fathers* (1976), a richly textured portrayal of the East European Jewish experience in New York and a culmination of Howe's own "reconquest of Jewishness," his personal journey from alienation to identity. In *World of Our Fathers* Howe honored a Jewishness infused with the quest for a better future. Even while warning against the excesses of secular messianism, Howe acclaimed the thirst for, and the deeply felt expectation of, producing a better world on this earth through righteous collective action. He thought that this Jewishness and even its more modest political expression in democratic socialism were at death's door, overcome by social mobility and assimilation. Indeed, *World* was often described by reviewers, and even by Howe himself, as an elegy. But here too, as with both democratic socialism and the intrinsic value of literature, Howe retained an admittedly slim but nonetheless palpable "margin of hope"—his hope for Jewish continuity, a continuity partly based on those dimensions of the Jewish experience that "prompted some of us to a certain kind of politics," the politics of Left-liberalism.[6]

Howe argued that for many American Jews, including himself, social liberalism was a kind of secular religion, "the precious salvage from their immigrant and East European heritage, the embodied value of a major segment of Jewish experience."[7] But to the end Howe maintained a creative tentativeness. He continued to wrestle, even in his last public lecture, with the question of Jewish identity, concluding ultimately that the wrestling itself was "the very mark" of that identity.[8]

Perhaps, finally, Irving Howe's relevance resides in the long list of his ardent loyalties—to the secular Jewish tradition, represented mainly by Yiddish culture and the pursuit of social justice; to socialism, both as a fulfillment of that tradition and as a profound extension of democracy; and to accessible liberal arts education, as both a way forward and a stout link to the past. He was committed to literature as a dynamic force in society, not just in politics but in the heart and conscience. And he never gave up on the imagination as an active element in human affairs. Irving Howe's life and writings still have much to teach us.

Notes

1. D. Mesher, review of Edward Alexander, *Irving Howe: Socialist, Critic, Jew*, in *American Jewish History* 88, no. 1 (2000): 151.

2. Irving Howe, "Questions We Ask Ourselves and Sometimes Answer," *Dissent* (Spring 1992): 143–46; Irving Howe, "Two Cheers for Utopia," *Dissent* (Spring 1993): 132–33. Days after Howe died, Alfred Kazin said, in a handwritten addition to an unpublished typescript, that Irving was "the last Jewish utopian" in a world grown "increasingly crass."

3. Nicholas Howe, introduction to Irving Howe, *A Critic's Notebook* (New York: Harcourt Brace Jovanovich, 1994), 5, 14.

4. Irving Howe, "The Treason of the Critics," *New Republic*, June 12, 1989, 30–31.

5. Irving Howe, "The Value of the Canon," *New Republic*, February 18, 1991, 47.

6. Irving Howe, "American Jews and Israel," *Tikkun* 4 (December 1988): 71–74.

7. Irving Howe et al., "Liberalism and the Jews: A Symposium," *Commentary* (January 1980): 48.

8. Irving Howe, *The End of Jewish Secularism* (New York: Hunter College, City University of New York, 1993), 13.

22

Michael Levenson

A Steady Worker

Michael Levenson attended Harvard College as an undergraduate (1969–73) and received his Ph.D. from Stanford University (1980). He accepted an academic appointment in 1979 at the University of Virginia, where he is now professor of English. He is the author of *A Genealogy of Modernism* (1984) and *Modernism and the Fate of Individuality* (1991). He has edited the *Cambridge Companion to Modernism* (2001), and with Karen Chase he has written *The Spectacle of Intimacy: Family Life on the Public Stage* (2000).

Levenson has published essays in a wide variety of scholarly journals and in the *New Republic* and the *New York Times Book Review* and has given public lectures at, among others, Harvard, Yale, the University of Chicago, the University of Warwick, and Concordia University. In 1995 he led a National Endowment for the Humanities seminar for college teachers. He recently served as chair of the English department at the University of Virginia.

Levenson works in nineteenth- and twentieth-century intellectual and cultural history, pursuing subjects on both sides of the Atlantic. The culture of London, the American '60s, and the theory of fantasy are among his recent intellectual emphases.

Irving Howe often puzzled over the coherence of his thought. Did all that abundance and diversity resolve into an underlying pattern? Or did the separate commitments—the politics, the literary criticism, the Jewish history, the editorial labors, the life of a university professor—fly off into a miscellany? At the opening of the collection of essays gathered in *Steady Work* he lays claim to the "firm unity" of the book, even though it roves over two decades, crosses continents, and moves from Boris Pasternak to Barry Goldwater. Just a few years later, though, invoking what he calls "the famous question of 'unity,'" he shruggingly puts the problem aside, calling it "tiresome." But it wasn't too tiresome for him to return to it again and again, pondering the wholeness of his life.

It's not hard to see why the question kept coming back. In the long course of a brilliant career Howe repeatedly shifted his attention, readjusted his focus, changed his mind. Naturally there were continuities, some of them rich and striking, but there were also gaps and interruptions. In writing of literary modernism he saw it as abandoning traditional aesthetic unity in favor of "*a jagged and fragmented expressiveness.*" This is one way of looking at Howe's own career, as an escape from coherence into sharp-edged, angular, jagged expression. Or, to use other terms with which he described modernism, his life replaced the satisfactions of "composure" with those of "struggle." What makes the issue important is that Howe never saw his life as his own but as a product of the changing history he was trying to understand. Even as he admitted that his divided beliefs invited "the charge of intellectual schizophrenia," he insisted that the real problem wasn't his mixed convictions but the "mixed character of the present reality." The raggedness of his life corresponded to the raggedness of the age.

The very fact that "unity" became a problem for Howe is a sign of triumph, because at first it wasn't a problem at all. He came to politics early and fully. Born in 1920, he arrived at political consciousness in the cauldron of the '30s. He often described the recognition scenes: the dawning awareness that his Jewish immigrant parents didn't comprehend the whole world; the encounter with left-wing politics on the New York streets; the immersion in Trotskyist agitation; the endless discussions at City College with Daniel Bell, Irving Kristol, and others. Until he was nearly thirty Howe remained within the strict "unity" of his political faction. To his great credit he contended with the well-organized and far more numerous Stalinists, but to his shame he opposed American participation in World War II, arguing that it was a class war waged by capitalists and that left-wing revolutionaries shouldn't sully their hands in a sordid cause. Most troublingly, Howe, the Jew who had changed his name from Horenstein, largely ignored the threat of the Holocaust and never saw it as a justification for supporting the Allied struggle against Hitler. The gross neglect disturbed the older Irving Howe; it also opened him to cutting critique.

By 1950 Howe had broken free from his political narrowness, but he never broke free of politics. If we celebrate, as we should, this moment of expansion when the great trajectory of a public intellectual begins to show itself, we should be no quicker to forget the early years of dogmatism than Howe himself was. He later mocked Dwight Macdonald, "who at each point in his life has made a specialty out of mocking his previous beliefs," while it became Howe's rightful pride to hold on to the early socialist vision, even in lonely and unpropitious times. He threw off an orthodoxy while he struggled to maintain the fury of opposition. From this point forward, both for himself and the others he called the "New York intellectuals," "the comforts of system would have to be relinquished." All around him a showy migration took place—left-wing radicals converting to apologists for the status quo—but Howe's less dramatic movement from Trotsky to democratic socialism may have been the more difficult change.

In deep and surprising ways it was literature that pried open the confinement of the first Trotskyist phase. Howe became a contributor to *Partisan Review* just after the war, and that lively, opportune journal gave him a stage on which to perform his self-revision. The challenge of the new *PR* was to offer left-wing politics alongside the culture of modernism and to insist on the pressing claims of both; in Howe's incisive formulation "*Partisan Review* was the first journal in which it was not merely respectable but a matter of pride to print one of Eliot's *Four Quartets* side by side with Marxist criticism." Whether it was because he was witness to this political/cultural collision or because he was one its agents, Howe came to see both the entanglements of literature and politics and also their irreducible difference.

During his early political activism he had been a half-hearted undergraduate English major at City College, but in his postwar career literature—especially literary modernism and particularly the novel—became a fascination in its own right and a register of social health. The disturbing examples of modernist politics, the fascism of Yeats and Pound and the communism of Brecht, led to hard pondering on the relations between "literature" and "commitment." "In retrospect," he writes, "even those of us committed—however uneasily—to the need for 'commitment' will probably have to grant that it would have been much better for both literature and society if the modernist writers had kept themselves aloof from politics." This is not only a point about a modernist fall toward totalitarianism; it's also a question of the endlessly puzzling connection between literary vision and social life. The more Howe reads, teaches, and writes about literature, the more he envisions "a literary history that is autonomous, with its own continuities of decorum, its own dialectic of strife, its own interweaving of traditions." And yet, immediately after writing these words, he insists that "literary history must be affected by the larger history of which it is a part."

Politics and the Novel (1957) was the outcome of his long reflection on the problem. Its preface announces the work as a study of "what happens to the novel when it is subjected to the pressures of politics and political ideology." But the book that follows pays little attention to the politics and ideology outside the literature and instead gives itself to the novels themselves. What happens when fiction attempts to "incorporate" ideology into its "stream of sensuous impression"? To put the question like this is to reverse the relations of container and contained. Now it is not a problem of literature within politics but of politics within literature. Yet Howe never gives up the conviction that literature is molded by the social world around it. The novel contains the politics containing it. Just as the realm of social struggle shapes the literary imagination, so the literary work reshapes that struggle. Autonomy and embeddedness move in a perpetual dance. Within our social commitments we act according to our most profound beliefs, only to discover a "radical sundering" between what we must believe and what we choose to imagine.

All through the decade of the '50s Howe saw this question of independence and engagement as fundamental: American power was entrenched; Soviet Communism had petrified; the forces of opposition languished. He was one of the early prophets of the rise of a "new conformity" in the '50s. Everywhere he looked, he saw the machinery of absorption draining away the force of critique. Modernist literature could no longer rouse enmity. Now even its most savage provocations won applause, because

> the middle class has discovered that the fiercest attacks upon its values can be transposed into pleasing entertainments, and the avant-garde writer or artist must confront the one challenge for which he has not been prepared: the challenge of success. Contemporary society is endlessly assimilative, even if it vulgarizes what it has learned, sometimes foolishly, to praise. The avant-garde is thereby no longer allowed the integrity of opposition or the coziness of sectarianism; it must either watch helplessly its gradual absorption into the surrounding culture or try to preserve its distinctiveness by continually raising the ante of sensation and shock—itself a course leading, perversely, to a growing popularity with the bourgeois audience.

This is an insight that has since become a commonplace, but what gives it strength in Howe is that it reaches so far into the workings of the culture. The problem of conformity, of an endlessly absorptive middle-class culture, is more than a dilemma for modernist artists. It's a condition that threatens a deadly historical impasse. It affects, for instance, the life of the university, which, like modernist literature, risks dissolving into the currents of mere pleasure and efficiency, losing the purchase of opposition. Soon Howe will find himself in the uncomfortable position of defending the disinterestedness of academic life. The unrepentant socialist justifies the "old-fashioned traditional scholar sticking by his narrow specialty no matter who gets bombed or what freedom march occurs" because only such detachment will ensure the independence of the university. He admits to being "caught in a tension between my belief that serious men must be involved in the political struggles of their day and my belief that the university . . . should serve as a center of intellectual detachment, a place devoted to scholarship and disinterested thought."

That tension is not only unavoidable and worrisome for Howe; it's also productive and stimulating. In surrendering his Trotskyist convictions he came to see that neither Nazism nor Stalinism nor American capitalism could be understood in class terms alone. Alongside "class" must stand the concepts of "mass," "mass society," and "mass culture." The twentieth century had shown how in both totalitarian and capitalist countries classes can become pulverized into masses, which can be trained or terrorized, distracted and numbed, manipulated and chastened in ways that cannot be captured by class analysis alone. Marx never foresaw what both Hannah Arendt and Herbert Marcuse now described: the growth of mass culture, the power of manipulation, the rise of totalitarianism, and the palliating conditions of leisure in advanced capitalism.

What this meant for the public intellectual was a vexing, unstable existence that required vigilant refusal of new temptations. Like the once resistant art of the modernists, the American intellectual now met the lure of absorption on all sides. Especially for someone like Howe, who saw the brutality of Soviet Communism, the Cold War was an invitation to join the ranks of policymakers and to abandon opposition. The evidence of prosperity seemed to argue for an end to intellectual challenge. "What is most alarming is that the whole idea of the intellectual vocation—the idea of a life dedicated to values that cannot possibly be realized by a commercial civilization—has gradually lost its allure," Howe says in "The Age of Conformity." To keep up the relentless attack on Stalinism and capitalism was to risk being seen as a crank.

In the face of that risk Howe's essays of the '50s and early '60s may represent the most distinguished phase of his career. On the one hand he recognized the dangers to free thought; he willingly revised his own terms of understanding to include "prosperity" as itself part of the problem; he saw signs of misery within mass-produced happiness. On the other hand he relentlessly opposed authoritarian communism and all those he saw as its sophistic defenders: Isaac Deutscher and Paul Sweezy chief among them. Yet in the face of failures to the right of him and failures to the left Howe resisted the temptations of helplessness. Where Herbert Marcuse developed a theory of mass culture emphasizing the "universal passivity" manufactured in both power blocs, the world of "total administration,"

Howe moved instead to a more flexible vocabulary of commitment. No theory invalidated terms like *freedom, democracy*, and *solidarity*. If he could be grimly skeptical about the drift of history, he refused the language of inevitability. The radical, he always insisted, was both more pessimistic and more optimistic than others. Let the complacent talk about necessity; "in the end we know that 'history' guarantees us nothing: everything is now a question of human will."

Howe understood the difficulty in trying to locate some shifting and unsteady middle, open to critique and contempt from two sides. More-over, there wasn't one middle; there were as many middles as there were extremities. Within his political life the abandonment of Marxism and the revulsion against Stalin pulled the scale one way, and he worked hard not to tip toward the rabid anticommunism of the Cold War Right. His demo-cratic socialism was always understood as a hope *between*, the one chance to avoid "the insufferable choice between capitalism and Communism." In the '50s Howe worked to keep alive an anemic Left, but then in the '60s he suddenly faced the reverse problem, one of the most difficult of his life, the challenge of the New Left. Howe had yearned for a revival of the left-wing movement in the United States, but when it came in the aspect of Tom Hayden and SDS, he found it not only disappointing but frightening. He saw the New Left as infatuated with personal style, with the romance of revolution and the charisma of authoritarian leaders; he bridled at the contempt for the democratic socialism he had labored to perfect. From the distance of more than three decades it's possible to see that his preoccupa-tion with SDS may have foreclosed an active dialogue with the rest of the antiwar movement. Where he might have been an experienced mentor to the nonrevolutionary Left, he was instead a bruising polemicist.

And yet it's exactly such willful, unapologetic insistence that gives this body of work such power. When Howe joined with others to found *Dissent* and when he began to edit it with Lewis Coser in 1954, he established both a forum and a name for his stringent perspective. He saw American socialism as moribund and ineffective, but he roused his will to carry on with a small band of supporters. To dissent from orthodox Stalinism, from complacent capitalism, from sentimental liberalism, and then later from the New Left—this was the brazen program, and while the perspective evolved over the next four decades of Howe's editorship, the journal never subsided into a polite murmur.

The founding of *Dissent* crystallized a form of writing for Howe, a style of intellectual engagement that is part of his signature. In the early years of street-corner politics he had gradually developed a skill in sharp speech, but as long as he remained within the Trotskyist enclosure, the rhetoric

was stiff and inflexible. The very crisis in his convictions honed his gifts
as a controversialist. Now not only did he have opponents on every side,
but his own past beliefs were opponents too, forcing him to engage in "the
grim exercise of intellectual reconsideration and self-scrutiny" and to take
up "the vocabulary of ambivalence and complexity." He knew himself to
be vulnerable to criticism, partly because his enemies and erstwhile allies
never let him forget it. Still, within the confusion of left-wing thought in
the '50s Howe never hesitated to take up a tension-heightening combative
pose. This for him was the condition of intellectual life: "in the political
tradition from which I derive, it has been common to write with polemical
sharpness—hopefully an impersonal sharpness—and then to expect one's
opponent to reply in kind. You argue, you let some heat come through, you
don't pretend that gentility is the ultimate virtue; and then, a little later, it
may even be possible to come to agreement, or work together, or accept the
fact of difference." Polemic was his form of writing, even his form of life.

Part of what gave taut complexity to his work is that he was now moving
between two distinct zones of intellectual life. In 1953 he took up a teaching
position at Brandeis; in the early '60s he moved briefly out to Stanford, and
then in 1963 he came back east to City University of New York. He published
books on Sherwood Anderson and William Faulkner (1951–52) and followed
these with *Politics and the Novel* (1957) and *Thomas Hardy* (1967). All of
these literary studies can fit within a recognizable academic tradition. And
yet they maintain their distance from an emerging professional discourse
that Howe watched with wariness. He noted the rise of New Criticism
and later myth criticism; he saw the vogue for "original sin" as a kind of
universal solvent for literary interpretation. All these movements struck
him as fashions, likely to dissolve as soon as they met the cold air of the
world beyond academic walls. This was the advantage of his journalistic
vocation. It always furnished him with a refuge from a university-enclosed
professionalism, a refuge unconstrained by the decorum of the common
room. He mocked the academic cant that dismissed "mere journalism."

It can be fairly said that for Howe the essay was his natural unit of expression. In the important memoir "The New York Intellectuals" he remarks
offhandedly that, "Were I writing a book rather than an essay, I would
have to describe in some detail the relationship between the intellectuals
who came on the scene in the thirties and those of earlier periods." But
even when he did compose books, and with the partial exception of *World
of Our Fathers* (1976), he still wrote from the perspective of the essayist,
someone who makes no claim to offer a final or definitive or even inclusive
account but who aims to offer clear, pointed, and partial views. With the
urgency of someone who felt there was so much to discuss, Howe avoided

the magisterial academic ambition to be exhaustive: rather than exhaust his subjects, he wanted to renew them for ongoing debate. Looking back at "This Age of Conformity," he notes that "I wrote as a polemicist, not as a historian or a sociologist of knowledge; and if that limited the scope it did not, I think, blunt the point of my attack." "Images of Socialism" was composed in 1954 (with Lewis Coser) as a considered "statement of principles" for the mission of *Dissent*, and still, when Howe reprinted it, he commented: "Necessarily the essay is fragmentary; that is its nature. Necessarily it is argumentative; most often with itself or with the ideas we once held, ideas that hover over it, shadowlike." Nothing is settled in an essay, because so much else remains to be done.

Working as an editor of others' essays, while he prolifically composed work of his own, Howe became a whirring machine that kept finding new subjects of interest. American literature, Yiddish poetry, Stevenson, Kennedy, mass culture, Pirandello, Berkeley, Vietnam—he worked to express views on all these objects and many more. Perhaps before all else, before even his politics, he was a *writer*, someone compelled to formulate his convictions and to publish them, to find words for his beliefs, to devise a tone for his difficulty. Part of the splendor of the career is the invention of a voice, clear, direct, open, that doesn't twist itself in rhetorical virtuosity or theoretical ambition but that carries on a quick conversation, always ready to engage with the next curiosity, the latest emergency. Within each self-contained piece of prose, whether it stands as an essay proper or a chapter of a book, Howe bestows his gift of attention; he is able to look at the particular object in front of him. What he wrote of Victor Serge, we might say of him: "he cared about nuances, textures, and quirks of experience, he refused to dissolve men into historical forces."

Still, the vocation of the intellectual, the calling of the essayist, comes at a cost. Howe quotes Camus's description of the intellectual as "someone whose mind watches itself." That is a significant part of the truth of Howe's writing life, in which he was forced to remember his revisions and recantings. In the preface to *Socialism and America* (1985) he calls for "sustained self-scrutiny, hard self-criticism, and, perhaps in consequence, a partial self-renewal," and in his personal writings, especially in the memoir *A Margin of Hope* (1982), he turns the edge of his polemic on himself. Yet he was never consumed by his failings. As essays within this volume show, Howe has been roundly criticized for not fully confronting his political follies and his religious evasions, and it's surely right that he never cared to excavate all the recesses of the self. Partly this may have been an act of self-protection, but partly it was lack of interest in the mystery of his own personality. He didn't ignore his former self, but he never found it fascinating.

Here is the sense in which Camus's formula is only half true. Howe did watch himself, but only as one object in his field of vision. Whatever his motives, he also had principles. Invoking the words of Philip Rahv, he wrote that "during the greater part of the bourgeois era intellectuals preferred alienation from the community to alienation from themselves." This is what gave them boldness, strength, and "speculative power." But now, he notes in "New Styles in Leftism," a reversal has taken place in the term *alienation*: "For where intellectuals had once used it as a banner of pride and self-assertion, today it tends to become a complaint, a token of self-pity." Howe, in short, does have a mind willing to think about itself, but also a mind that girds itself against the decadence of self-absorption, that keeps calling itself back to a social world and a historical destiny.

In the unsteady dance of engagement and withdrawal, politics and literature, the university and the streets, the self and its society, Howe's Jewishness came to play a decisive part. His entry into politics in adolescence was a fierce repudiation of the immigrant Jewish world. He changed his name, stopped speaking Yiddish, withdrew from his family, and committed himself to a revolution hostile to "archaic" religious belief. It was several years after the end of the war before Howe began to coincide with his origins. An oft-repeated story tells how Philip Rahv invited him to choose a book to review in *Partisan Review*. Browsing among the books on the shelf, Howe reached for a volume of Sholom Aleichem. Who knows what impulse moved his hand? But from that point forward Jewishness joined politics and literature in what John Simon has called the "triple perspective" of the Howe "triumvirate."

The recovery of his Jewishness, as Edward Alexander has well shown, tore through the seamlessness of Howe's Trotskyism. If it never became his faith, it did become a subject and a subjectivity that changed the terms of his thought. This was, first, because it made clear to him that problems of race, ethnicity, and religion, and, still more, the catastrophe of mass slaughter, could not all be understood in terms of a Marxist account of class struggle. But it was also because the history of Jewishness corrected the political "ultraism" that Howe saw as the special fatality of the twentieth century. The re-vision began in the late '40s. But it culminated in *World of Our Fathers*, which was more than a history of the Jewish immigrants in America; it was a rewriting of twentieth-century history from the wide perspective of Jewish history. It showed a long rhythm of endurance marked by as many defeats and successes; it chastened the desire for justice in our time, revolution by our hands.

Jewishness, especially in the form of Yiddish literature, also changed Howe's reading of cultural value and the achievement of modernism.

Among the strongest claims that Howe made for the postwar moment of *Partisan Review* was that its intellectual circle brought about the internationalizing of American culture. It "sanctioned the idea, perhaps the most powerful cultural idea of the last half-century, that there existed an all but incomparable generation of modern masters who in a terrible age represented the highest possibilities of the imagination." Yet Howe, as we've seen, was among the first to understand the deliquescence of modernism, its loss of force within an assimilative culture. Then, as he taught himself to live past the glamour of Eliot and Kafka, Woolf and Pound, he went further. He began to ask whether the modernist revolution had ever been as glorious and as liberating as it once seemed. And here is where the encounter with Yiddish writing became so important. Now he noted, in "The Culture of Modernism," that "in every important literature except the Yiddish, the modernist impulse was accompanied by a revulsion against traditional modes of nineteenth-century liberalism and by a repugnance for the commonplace materials of ordinary life"—Joyce being the splendid exception. What Yiddish literature and Jewish immigrant intellectuals shared was an immersion in "thisworldly" experience, an "earthboundedness," which meant, as he noted in "Strangers," that "our appetites for transcendence had been secularized, and our messianic hungers brought into the noisy streets."

Once, the revolt against liberalism would have seemed part of the modernist glory, and the indifference to daily life would have been a sign of noble experiment. But when Howe begins to see the twentieth century as a relentless series of catastrophically failed revolutions, when he sees a Yiddish alternative to cultural extremity, then modernism changes its aspect. In his essay "Literature and Liberalism" of the 1970s he places an unglamorous, modest, no longer heroic liberalism against a modernism that "has strained toward extreme instances, impatient before compromise and commonplace, and a vision of the agonistic, the ultimate." Howe does not pretend that liberalism will be the basis of literary achievement; indeed, the virtue of liberalism, he now thinks, is that it can inspire artists "to take a measure of its failings, to rail against its deficiencies of vision, to cry out that a merely tolerable world is not enough." But at the same time he warns a future culture not to "repeat the terrible mistake of a good many writers sixty and seventy years ago, which was to help create an intolerable world."

No one should underestimate the extent of the reversal. From a conviction that Trotsky and T. S. Eliot could make revolutions side by side, Howe came to believe that experimental literature shares blame with revolutionary politics for the creation of a barbarous century. But it's much too easy and too sour to see Howe as the chastened visionary, scurrying back to a safe, incremental reformism. From the moment he abandoned Marxism after the war, he understood his difficulty. Free of the mystique of absolutism, he committed himself to political and cultural struggle in the real world that stretched before him. But he also held to the claims of the Not-yet and the Not-here, the world still to come. When Daniel Bell criticized American socialism for its failure to "relate itself to the specific problems of the here-and-now, give-and-take political world," Howe accepted this as a half-truth, rejoining in words drawn from Max Weber: "Certainly all historical experience confirms the truth—that man would not have attained the possible unless time and again he had reached out for the impossible." Even in bad times socialists need to keep up "the idea of historical transcendence, the vision of *another* society." "In an age of curdled realism," he wrote in "Images of Socialism," "it is necessary to assert the utopian image."

To work in the here-and-now world and also to sustain the utopian vision—this is the burden Howe accepted for more than four decades. It made stability impossible. Every significant turn in politics and culture required a response; no theory could settle opinions in advance. This meant that he was often "battered by history" and subject to challenge. It meant that his writing was agitated, restless, often overheated, always looking for its next subject. He once described the intellectual as "*a noise-maker*," the one "who keeps talking even after the room has been emptied and the shades drawn." Howe was the radical as essayist, the intellectual as noisemaker, and even now that it's over, and the shades have indeed been drawn, we can still hear his voice. It was proudly indefatigable. We can do no better than end with the epigraph he chose for *Steady Work*: "Once in Chelm, the mythical village of the East European Jews, a man was appointed to sit at the village gate and wait for the coming of the Messiah. He complained to the village elders that his pay was too low. 'You are right,' they said to him, 'the pay is low. But consider: the work is steady.' "

Afterword

Irving Howe:

Finding the Right Words

Morris Dickstein

In any discussion of the reader, the political critic, or the public intellectual in the second half of the twentieth century it would be hard to find a figure more exemplary or more controversial than Irving Howe. Since Howe's death in 1993, at the age of seventy-two, his work and even his personal aura have had a strong afterlife. Literary criticism, like most political writing, usually fades with time. Once off the scene the writer can no longer bring old ideas up to date or lend them coherence by sheer force of personality. Irving Howe, on the other hand, remains a vivid figure, and not simply among his acolytes. His work is quoted at least as frequently as that of any other critic of the period. His death was followed by many memorial tributes, along with attacks by prominent neoconservatives who saw him still as a thorn in their side—too smart a writer, too biting a critic, to be easily set aside. More comment followed when his son, Nicholas Howe, brought out his last and most literary work, *A Critic's Notebook*. With his sharp-tongued humor and debater's edge Howe played a central role in an excellent documentary about four New York intellectuals, Joseph Dorman's *Arguing the World*. A leading professional journal, *American Jewish History*, devoted a whole issue to a not altogether friendly reconsideration of Howe's masterpiece, *World of Our Fathers*, which lies like a lion across the path of historians of Jewish immigrant life. There have already been two well-researched intellectual biographies, one by a militant conservative, Edward Alexander (1998), who is critical of Howe's politics, early and late, the other by a sympathetic liberal, Gerald Sorin (2002).

More than a decade after his death Howe continues to attract fierce censure and grateful praise. I'm not the only writer who still hears his voice echoing in my head, wondering at times what he might have thought of this book or that political twist or turn. *Dissent*, the social democratic journal he founded with Lewis Coser in 1954, remains intellectually robust—an ecumenical magazine of the beleaguered Left, as flexible in its social criticism as he became in his lifelong commitment to socialism. As in the 1950s it finds itself trying to carve out a "decent" Left in a period when conservatives are dominant, liberals often feel demoralized, and radicals blame the United States for all the world's ills. Moreover, *Dissent* now embraces many cultural issues Howe tended to exclude from what he conceived as a forum for discussing politics and social policy. By making his peace with the aging radicals of the '60s generation in his last decade, though he didn't always approve of where they stood, he insured that the magazine would not only survive but flourish, even as the world's political agenda dramatically changed.

Howe saw himself as a perpetual dissenter, but there were always others ready to follow where he led. His socialism seemed an anomaly in the 1950s, as American power grew and American intellectuals grew more complacent and self-satisfied. Yet he also felt shunted aside by the young Leftists of the 1960s and responded with a steady barrage of criticism so intemperate that it might have permanently alienated him from those who shared his deepest aims. (He certainly earned the enduring enmity of Tom Hayden.) But three decades later there is no writer more revered by intellectuals who combine hopes for greater economic equality with a stubborn faith in democracy, who criticize their country for falling short of its ideals but refuse to see it as the root of evil in the world. For political writers like Richard Rorty, Michael Walzer, Todd Gittlin, and Paul Berman he remains a model of the activist thinker who somehow escaped the clutches of what Orwell called the "smelly little orthodoxies" of the twentieth century, very much as his old antagonist, the protean Ralph Ellison, became the unlikely model for a generation of black intellectuals who had outgrown the ideologies on which they cut their teeth, including black nationalism and Marxism.

The changing fortunes of Howe as a literary critic tell a similar story. The rise of theory, including deconstruction, academic feminism, ideological critique, and postmodernism, isolated him even more dramatically than the waves of conservatism and radical leftism. His style as a critic was marked by the vehement clarity of someone schooled in political argument, who had also learned his craft in the late 1940s as a rebellious protégé of Dwight Macdonald and as an anonymous book reviewer for *Time* magazine. Even in his longest literary essays Howe remained a working journalist who made certain to give a clear, vigorous account of a writer's career, a book's texture and style, a character's human density, and a work's compelling claim on the reader—an approach that went out of fashion in academic criticism after 1970.

Howe saw this happening even earlier. In a stinging attack on Leslie Fiedler's *Love and Death in the American Novel* he anticipated what would later be called "the hermeneutics of suspicion," the critic's search for a buried subtext that could reveal the writer's unconscious motives or be used to arraign the work itself: "Like a mass-culture imitation of a psychoanalyst, Fiedler refuses on principle to honor the 'surface' events, characters, statements and meanings of a novel. . . . He engages not in formal description or historical placement or critical evaluation, but in a relentless and joyless exposure. The work of literature comes before him as if it were a defendant without defense, or an enemy intent on deceiving him so that he will not see through its moral claims and coverings." Writing in 1960, Howe had little inkling of how fashionable such an adversarial posture would later become for many academic critics.

Beginning with his first major work, *Politics and the Novel* (1957), Howe had made his reputation as a social and political critic of literature, not a strictly aesthetic one. But in trying to connect intimately with the literary text and make sense of it to a broader public, he cast his lot, surprisingly, with the formal critics, both New and old, whose approach was already going out of style. After a period of "painful soul-searching" around 1948 he reacted sharply against his own sectarian background and the Marxist criticism it had fostered. He felt a growing delight in literature itself, apart from any ideological tendency. Fiedler's imperious psychoanalytic method, he says, "disregards the work of literature as something 'made,' a construct of mind and imagination through the medium of language, requiring attention on its own terms and according to its own structure." We rightly think of Howe as a historical critic, yet he always grounds his commentary in a writer's language and style, the emotional patterns revealed in the work, and the unique or familiar ways the writer remakes the world.

For many years the clarity of Howe's prose, along with this focus on the individual author, the individual work, made him seem like an old-fashioned figure on the critical scene, more the journalist and omnivorous reviewer than the full-fledged critic. Yet on writer after writer as different as T. E. Lawrence, Sholom Aleichem, Louis-Ferdinand Céline, Ignazio Silone, George Orwell, Isaac Bashevis Singer, Edith Wharton, Isaac Babel, and Theodore Dreiser, his essays were almost the first place the general reader might turn for critical illumination. As a sometime radical with a deep, abiding sense of privacy, Howe did not reveal much of himself in these essays. Yet his grasp of these writers was so immediate, so personal, so determined to find the living pulse of their work—and to articulate something almost unsayable in his own response—that we feel we know him intimately. His sharp, relentless, often scathingly funny voice is no doubt indebted to his political writing but also reenacts his probing, invasive way of reading. Even his longtime antagonist Philip Roth acknowledged that Howe was a real *reader*, one of the chosen, whose criticism could cut to the quick.

Like Lionel Trilling, Howe took every literary work, as he took many political issues, as a moral challenge, a set of embodied convictions on how to live. This led him into sweeping polemics in which he would play the provocateur, evoke passionate controversy, but at times go badly astray. It was the outraged moralist in him that led him to attack James Baldwin and Ralph Ellison for betraying the legacy of rage in the work of their mentor, Richard Wright, and to revile Roth in *Portnoy's Complaint* for putting his talent "to the service of a creative vision deeply marred by vulgarity." The same puritanical streak led him to travesty the "new sensibility" of the 1960s as a toxic dose of primitive innocence, a form of moral anarchy, and to wonder "whether this outlook is compatible with a high order of culture or a complex civilization." Despite a lifetime's work fighting for social justice, Howe, like other Jewish writers (including Freud and Trilling), was caught up in a tragic vision marked by almost insoluble moral tension and irreconcilable conflict. In a brief essay on Isaac Babel he picks up Trilling's cue that Babel, riding with the Red Cossacks through territory dotted with his fellow Jews, "was captivated by the vision of two ways of being, the way of violence and the way of peace, and he was torn between them." But typically Howe, speaking out of his own sense of the conflicts between politics and art, gives a historical coloring to Trilling's timeless observation, seeing the soldiers' brutality in political terms: "Babel understood with absolute sureness the problem that has obsessed all modern novelists who deal with politics: the problem of action in both its heroic necessity and its ugly self-contamination." In other words, though radical goals may be admirable, the means at hand to realize them could easily prove offensive, unpalatable. In one story Babel's protagonist, part journalist, part combatant, is bitterly berated by a Russian soldier for riding through battle without cartridges in his revolver. "Crouching beneath the crown of death," the writer ends up "begging fate for the simplest ability—the ability to kill a man." In another story he meets an old Jew who feels as abused by the Revolution as by the feudal Polish landowners who are fighting against it, who longs for something "unattainable," a "sweet Revolution," the "International of good people." Characteristically Howe shows how this tension is enacted in Babel's famously laconic style, where it becomes a tremendous source of energy. Taking up John Berryman's comparison of Babel with Stephen

Crane, he writes that "in both writers there is an obsessive concern with compression and explosion, a kinesthetic ferocity of control, a readiness to wrench language in order to gain nervous immediacy. Both use language to inflict a wound."

This is no casual insight, no imposed melodrama, but a remark dredged up from deep within the critic's own psyche. Trilling and Howe, both conflicted Jews, respond strongly to the ambivalence about Jews, about violence, about revolution that makes Babel's *Red Cavalry* so piercingly effective but would one day make the author one of Stalin's victims. This personal identification gives power to Howe's essays, which are often obliquely autobiographical. In a memoir of one of his mentors, *Partisan Review* editor Philip Rahv, with whom he later quarreled, Howe describes how Rahv turned cautious in the conservative climate of the 1950s, provoking others (including Howe) to write the provocative critical essays Rahv himself might have done. By holding back, Rahv lost his "élan, his nervousness": "He could still turn out a lively piece full of the old fire and scorn, but he had made an estimate—politically mistaken, morally unheroic—that this wasn't the time to take chances. And by not taking chances (they didn't turn out to be such big chances either), he allowed his energy to dribble away, his voice to lose its forcefulness." Howe himself, at Rahv's urging, wrote the famous 1954 polemic "This Age of Conformity," one of the key dissenting texts of the decade, which Rahv then published in his magazine. In Howe's account Rahv's cunning and timidity did him in; as Howe sees it, personal authenticity, keeping faith with one's convictions, is inseparable from political and moral daring. Rahv's flaw, his failure of nerve, gives Howe's portrait of him its tragic cast at the same time that it justifies Howe's own zeal for controversy, his take-no-prisoners approach to public argument, his lifelong persistence as a political campaigner, and the peculiar nervous intensity of his own style.

Howe's personal voice, his refusal to rest or desist, brought him back into fashion as a critic in the same way that he became the political conscience for many in the younger generation. Just as he lived to see the end of the Reagan revolution and the fall of the Soviet Union, he saw the beginning of a tectonic shift in the world of literature and criticism. Thanks mainly to the humiliation of the Left in the culture wars of the late '80s and early '90s, a new fascination with the public intellectual challenged the long dominance of theory, with its arcane professional languages. In an obituary tribute to Lionel Trilling many years earlier, Howe recalled asking Trilling whether he wasn't terrified of the new methodologists who were taking over the field. (Trilling responded puckishly that he was terrified of everything.) By the time Howe died, the theorists had more or less had their day, and

Howe himself became an important model for young literary scholars like David Bromwich and Ilan Stavans who were as interested in politics as in culture and were eager to write for larger audiences without intellectual compromise. For me he had always been such a model, ever since I began reading him as an undergraduate around 1960. When I published my first piece in *Partisan Review* in 1962, I got a complimentary note from Howe, ever on the lookout for young talent. He invited me to write for *Dissent*, something I didn't actually get to do until twenty-five years later. I didn't meet him until the early '70s and disliked much of what he wrote in the interim about politics and the arts in the 1960s. It amazed me that he could write a sympathetic essay on Berkeley's free-speech movement one year, then publish a furious onslaught against the New Left barely a year later. When Philip Rahv criticized him for setting up "anti-Communism as the supreme test of political rectitude on the Left," when Raymond Williams attacked the "rancor" of his tone, its sense of "unjustified superiority," I completely agreed, though Rahv had scarcely earned the right to attack him from the Left and Williams's position boiled down to the hoary dictum, "No enemies on the Left."

Howe escaped from politics, as he had done since the '50s, through his invaluable work on Yiddish literature, editing a series of anthologies, with superb introductions, that brought this largely invisible body of work into the mainstream. Toward the end of the decade he also wrote two landmark essays summing up the culture of modernism and the world and style of the New York intellectuals, essays that showed not only his wide purview and bold synthesizing powers but his rueful sense, perhaps premature, that these chapters of cultural history were more or less over. Just as Howe saw himself as a latecomer to Yiddish literature, which paradoxically made him a pioneer in its dissemination to an English-speaking audience, he felt a sense of belatedness in both modernist culture and the fractious circle of the New York writers. Caught between vigorous participation and an elegiac sense of farewell, he became the boldly assertive chronicler who brought the whole subject into focus, as he had done with the work of a good many individual writers. Yet he also believed that cultures could flourish brilliantly in their moment of decline, as Isaac Bashevis Singer, Chaim Grade, and Jacob Glatstein had shown in the waning days of Yiddish literature, as Southern writers and Jewish American writers had done when their cultural roots were (in his view) already disintegrating.

Not long after I met Howe I joined his department, the doctoral program in English at the City University of New York, and very soon the wariness between us dissolved. In the face of the rising neoconservative tide he had turned left again in the early 1970s, bringing *Dissent* along with him. But

I was twenty years younger, with a certain awe of him, and he tended to be abrupt and impatient with everyone, which often made me feel I was keeping him from more important business, indeed, from getting his work done. The publication of *World of Our Fathers* in 1976 made him a household name in a way he never expected to become, and it also increased demands on his time. He had little small talk, and our conversations were swift, amusing, and often practical—a student to be examined, a wrinkle in a writer's work to be ironed out. (I remember one phone call in which he questioned me about the shifting names of the protagonists in Delmore Schwartz's elusive but mesmerizing stories.) I admired him for his political probity, literary intelligence, and scorching wit and felt he was someone I would never really know well but was glad to have on my side. I got to know him better through his writing, which never failed to engage me, and through his public appearances, where he was always a master of argument, than through our snatches of conversation, which often seemed a little truncated. I find today that I annotated almost every page of his 1982 memoir, *A Margin of Hope*, agreeing and disagreeing more vigorously than I ever did when he was in the room. Yet when he died, I felt a gap in my life that has never really been filled.

On an impulse Howe retired from active teaching in 1986 but continued writing, editing, and lecturing until his death. In his reviews he often praised his subjects for staying the course, getting the work done even in the face of defeat, discouragement, aging, and illness. He says of Edmund Wilson that "his career took on a heroic shape, the curve of the writer who attains magisterial lucidity in middle age and then, in the years of decline, struggles ferociously to keep his powers." In describing his flawed heroes Howe often enriched the portrait by projecting his own fears. The illnesses of his last years often left him depressed, and more than once I heard him wonder whether the world really needed another book from him. But he enormously admired Norman Thomas, the perennial Socialist candidate, for sticking to his political mission and even for his eloquent style in debate ("he knew more, he talked faster, and—miracle of American miracles!—he came out with comely sentences and coherent paragraphs"). He described him as "the only truly great man I have ever met." Howe reserved his contempt for the former radicals of his City College days who had grown up poor but turned comfortable and conservative, losing their feeling for the world they had left behind. Another hero of his, a figure of genuine moral authority, was the Italian novelist Ignazio Silone, "the least bitter of ex-Communists, the most reflective of radical democrats," whose later books were nonetheless weakened by "his exhausting struggle with his own beliefs, the struggle of a socialist who has abandoned his dogmas yet wishes to preserve his animating values," something Howe himself understood very well.

It's hard not to see the touches of self-reflection in Howe's portraits of Wilson and Silone. Howe had begun redefining his socialism as early as the 1950s, transforming it from historical dogma to moral critique—"the name of our desire," as he called it, using Tolstoy's phrase. Eventually it became a more forceful extension of liberalism, an unwavering commitment to the labor movement and the welfare state, and a branch of the left wing of the Democratic party. The very word *socialism* became a mantra for persistence and determination; it was his link to the radical past even as he was adapting it to the needs of the present. In the introduction to his 1966 collection of political essays, *Steady Work*, he describes himself as "a man of the left, in dialogue with himself, asking which of his earlier ideas should be preserved, which modified, which discarded." This tentativeness is borne out not by the essays themselves, which are never less than emphatic, but by the unresolved conflicts between them. This is especially true of his essays on the New Left, which are marred by his impatience with a generation he clearly hoped would follow his political lead. Howe could be polemical, at times even infuriating, without losing his grasp of the complexity of the subject. Echoing Trilling's well-known critique of liberalism in *The Liberal Imagination*, he describes a commitment to socialism in the mid–twentieth century as "a capacity for living with doubt, revaluation and crisis" yet also calls it "an abiding ideal." Socialism for him became a politics of conscience rather than a specific program or a set of goals; he came to admire figures who put their conscience, as well as their powers of observation, before their theories and ideas.

Howe saw Orwell, like Silone, as a writer trying to live by a consistent set of values after they had lost their ideological underpinnings. Aside from *A Margin of Hope*, Howe's 1968 essay on Orwell is perhaps the closest thing he ever wrote to a self-portrait. He sees Orwell as someone who kept his head, "wrote with his bones," through the worst political episodes of the twentieth century: "the Depression, Hitlerism, Franco's victory in Spain, Stalinism, the collapse of bourgeois England in the thirties." Howe writes that "for a whole generation—mine—Orwell was an intellectual hero." He saw in Orwell many of the qualities he aspired to or regretted in himself. Like his other heroes, including Wilson, Orwell was an irascible, even "pugnacious" man, whose essays are rightly admired for their "blunt clarity of speech and ruthless determination to see what looms in front of one's nose." He notes, without really complaining, that Orwell "is reckless, he is ferociously polemical," even when arguing for a moderate position. In the face of those who see Orwell as some kind of secular saint, he doubts that Orwell "was particularly virtuous or good." Although Orwell "could be mean in polemics," he sometimes befriended those he had criticized, for he was driven not by personal animus but "by a passion to clarify ideas, correct errors, persuade readers, straighten things out in the world and in his mind." He admires Orwell's "peculiar sandpapery humor" and the "charged lucidity" of his prose, which nicely describes some of his own. Like Howe, Orwell "rejected the rituals of Good Form" and "turned away from the pretentiousness of the 'literary.'" He notes that Orwell "had a horror of exposing his private life," a theme that surfaces repeatedly in Howe's pieces (on Joyce, for example, and on Salinger) but also informs his own memoir. Finally Howe examines the formal features of Orwell's essays, especially their superb endings. Beginning with Orwell as a moral exemplar who is himself less than a perfect man, who is in fact a difficult man, he ends by scanning Orwell's great essays for lessons on how to write. In Howe's final work, *A Critic's Notebook*, he is still searching and still learning.

The best responses to Howe's work were as attentive to his style as he was of those he reviewed. A few reviewers took due note of his remarkable growth as a writer. Early on, in 1964, Ted Solotaroff observed how the critic and the socialist intellectual converged in him, not only in his sense of cultural crisis but in "his crisp, meticulous prose, his skill at literary description, his grasp of the relevant issue quite equal to any serious book or audience. He is almost always telling you something sound and worthwhile and he is almost always as clear as glass." In Howe's earlier work this could be a defect. His literary essays sometimes read like position papers, and one could almost discern a shadowy list of points, the skeleton of the argument, behind the merely efficient surface of the writing. But as Howe's politics and even his temperament lost their sharp edges, his feeling for the aesthetic, his exhilaration with the language, took a leap forward. Rereading the large body of Orwell's essays, Howe was surprised to find that "the sheer *pleasure* of it cannot be overstated. . . . Orwell was an even better writer than I had supposed." In his review of Howe's 1973 collection, *The Critical Point*, Roger Sale made a similar discovery about Howe himself—that "he seems to have grown over the years, and his prose is sharper, the insights more precise and flexible." He concluded that Howe "seems to be trusting his human and literary instincts more than he once did."

By attending to the touch and feel of a text, Howe became more of a genuine essayist. As he mellowed, the nuances, reservations, and exceptions that complicated his case became as important as the argument. He came to love the New York City Ballet, where he learned to appreciate Balanchine's dancers for their eloquence of the body, an eloquence beyond language. The felicity of his own prose, once merely workmanlike, increased along with its complex powers of description. Struck by phrases like Howe's description of the "high radiance" of Frost's greatest poetry, Roger Sale remarked that "only the best critics are generous enough to find the right words for their authors." This laconic verbal precision, itself very literary, is the opposite of the tedious elaboration that often mars academic writing, in which every point must be spelled out, every remark illustrated by five examples. Howe later paid tribute to the deeply troubled Delmore Schwartz as "a wondrous talker, a first-rate literary intelligence—the sort who can light up the work of a poet or novelist with a single quick phrase." For a true critic this is a gift as basic as breathing.

Howe never became as fluent a writer as Trilling or Alfred Kazin, or as direct and uncluttered as Orwell and Wilson, those masters of the plain style. Working rapidly, he developed a better ear for his subjects' prose than for his own. He had one gift absolutely essential to a critic—the power of discrimination, the gift for striking the right note and for getting under the writer's (and the reader's) skin. His literary judgment, his intuition, could create a benchmark, a point of reference, for serious readers, even those who disagreed with him. It could reach the writers themselves, as his well-known attacks touched a nerve in Ellison and Roth and galvanized them toward an eloquent defense, in Ellison's case, or even a subtle change in direction, for Roth, whose later work, with its historical scope and moral urgency, reveals a debt to Howe's critique.

As a writer himself Howe acknowledged that his talent for metaphor was limited. I've always been struck by a certain clumsiness in his account of his "reconquest of Jewishness" in *A Margin of Hope*. But "Jewish Quandaries," the chapter in which this odd soldierly phrase appears, is a penetrating essay (with illustrations from his own life) on the struggle of Jewish intellectuals with their ethnic background; it is also a frank analysis of how his own feelings changed over the years. Speaking for many cosmopolitan radicals who once disdained merely tribal loyalties, he writes that "we had tried to 'make' our lives through acts of decision, 'programs' that thwarted the deeper, more intuitive parts of our own being." Embarrassed by the immigrant poverty and parochialism of his early years, indoctrinated by the universalism of his later Marxist faith, with its trust in collective movements and contempt for bourgeois individualism, Howe never found it easy to talk about himself. It went against the grain. Yet his memoir, if rarely intimate, shows how well he could *think* about himself, trusting his human and literary instincts as he had begun to do in his criticism.

Like all the best critics, he gave his work a strong personal stamp. He himself comes through on every page—awkward, funny, impatient, at moments ruthless, yet with an uncanny ability to get to the heart of the matter, to highlight what really counts. More than a decade younger than Trilling, Rahv, and their generation, he always felt like a latecomer, a brash young man among the grownups, but as a critic and cultural historian he was distinctly an original, a writer with sweeping powers of synthesis whose political savvy, humane moral outlook, and keen feeling for art enabled him to find his own voice and deploy it with unusual power.

Appendix

Wanted by the FBI:

No. 727437B a.k.a. Irving Horenstein

"An Immature Outlook on Life"

John Rodden

I

The FBI file on Irving Howe discloses that the Bureau followed his activities closely for more than eight years. It searched his records extensively; interviewed numerous neighbors and colleagues to uncover information about his activities; and pursued him as a national security risk even long after he had resigned from the Independent Socialist League (ISL), a tiny, New York–based, Trotskyist sect.[1] The file contains 148 pages—15 of them partially or wholly blacked out. It runs from February 27, 1951, to April 14, 1959, and covers reports from regional FBI bureaus in New York City, Albany, Newark, St. Louis, Miami, Boston, and Detroit.[2]

Most of these reports address Howe's activities in the ISL and his membership in Trotskyist organizations in the 1940s and '50s. Much of the file also covers Howe's statements in public lectures and presentations on the Soviet Union and on the changing nature of Stalinism during the 1950s. A revealing (though perhaps unsurprising) feature of the file—which speaks volumes about the standard data-collection methods of secret intelligence agencies—is that no agent ever seems to have read any of Howe's work in order to ascertain his political positions, except for the joint resignation letter that he and Stanley Plastrik submitted to the ISL in 1952, a copy of which was surreptitiously obtained by an informant to the Bureau.

The highlight of the FBI file on Howe (a name that the Bureau persisted in treating as his "alias") is the hour-long interview that two agents sprung on him in August 1954.[3] When they approached him as he entered his car on a street in Cambridge, Massachusetts, the agents were impressed by his "friendly and cordial manner," though they urged that a security index file be opened on him for long-term surveillance. Although Howe was never confronted directly again by any agents or interviewed by them, the FBI kept watch on him for five more years. Reports continued to be placed in his file on his lectures to university audiences and to political clubs and even on his lost luggage in France during a trip to Europe in 1957.[4]

Howe's FBI file also furnishes valuable biographical background for his repeated castigation of McCarthyism in the 1950s: it shows that Howe himself was being "tailed." Such information both contextualizes his radical critique of U.S. policies and undermines part of the *ad hominem* neoconservative attack on his writings during the McCarthy period. Many contemporary critics of Irving Howe have written that his 1954 essay "This Age of Conformity" reflects his hypersensitivity about American complacency in the 1950s regarding First Amendment freedoms. These critics imply that Howe harbored excessive and even irrational fears about government infringement on American civil liberties and encroachments on personal privacy. His first biographer, Edward Alexander, refers to Howe's indictment of liberals who fail to take seriously the threat to civil liberties as "compulsive." But the FBI file makes clear that the so-called compulsiveness was an appropriate vigilance in his own case.[5]

Indeed, Howe's FBI file proves that his concerns voiced in *Dissent* about the sorry state of American civic life were well-founded.[6] His wife was subject to investigation during her years as a teacher at Miss Fine's Day School in Princeton. His own lectures and seminars were attended by Bureau agents or by informants to the FBI, his mail was checked repeatedly, and his personal information (physical characteristics, children, residence, phone numbers, car model) was monitored as it changed—and this eavesdropping continued for almost seven years after his formal resignation from the ISL.[7]

Despite this extensive and intrusive surveillance of his private life, Howe never engaged in McCarthy-baiting. He did not equate the Soviet gulag with McCarthyism. In *A Margin of Hope* Howe grants that the McCarthy years were no "reign of terror." He writes: "In a reign of terror people turn silent, fear a knock on the door at 4 in the morning, flee in all directions; but they do not, because they cannot, talk endlessly in public about the outrage of terror." He adds: "When we printed violent denunciations of McCarthy in *Dissent* during these years, nothing happened to us . . . we had no sense we were taking any great risks in attacking McCarthy."[8]

So Howe's treatment by the Bureau is not a case study in political repression, and he never claimed to be a victim of McCarthyism. But Americans today must expect and remain vigilant about political stupidities like this one. Howe was right not to equate McCarthyism with the gulag or the Holocaust, but his pursuit by the FBI was intolerable and unnecessary, and it demonstrates a skewed understanding of the balance among national security, social order, and personal liberty.

Does the treatment of Irving Howe during the McCarthy era hold any lessons for us today? It may serve as a cautionary reminder that we can make ourselves less free—and the consequence is that we'll become less free, not safer. "Less free" does not equal "more secure"—and interference with our civil liberties is also an assault on the Constitution and the Bill of Rights. Let us transcend the patriotic either/or din and question the crude dichotomies common to both the Red decade and the September 11 decade—that you are either with the United States or with the commies and terrorists, respectively.

But charting such a "third way" is never easy. Indeed, the wasteful, pointless surveillance undergone by Irving Howe is the risk anyone who "dissents" can expect—yesterday or today.

II

An active file was maintained on Howe from 1951 to 1959, including a security index on him in the Boston division. Howe's ethnic background may have been a factor—the Bureau pointedly noted that "his father, David [Horenstein], was born in Russia and was naturalized as a U.S. citizen in 1922, according to the records furnished by CCNY." The Russian birth might have indicated to the FBI a possible sympathy with communism.[9] But the specific occasion for an FBI file to be opened on Howe was the passage of the Smith Act in 1948, which justified scrutiny for national security reasons of all members of "basic revolutionary groups" committed to "the violent overthrow" of the U.S. government.[10] In a letter to the Loyalty Review Board (September 29, 1949)—which appears in Howe's file—Attorney General J. Howard McGrath described the ISL as a "basic revolutionary group," the successor to the revolutionary Workers Party (WP). Howe had belonged to the Workers Party since 1940 (he was a member of the outgoing national steering committee of the Workers Party in 1946), and he had also served as editor of the weekly newspaper *Labor Action*, the official organ of both the Workers Party and the ISL. (*Labor Action* was also specifically cited in the letter by McGrath.)

Despite several background checks on Howe's agitprop activities in the 1940s, the FBI remained unaware that, not long after entering the army, Howe resurfaced in both *Labor Action* and *New International* under the pseudonym "R. Fahan," writing antiwar polemics. His last wartime article appeared in October 1943. He did not return to the pages of *Labor Action* until February 11, 1946, usually thereafter under the name Irving Howe.[11] (Nor did the FBI apparently know that Howe wrote under the name "Theodore Dryden" in 1947–48 for Dwight Macdonald's radical magazine, *Politics*. Nor, indeed, that "subject Horenstein" was not "the father of two boys.")[12]

Typical of the FBI's partial success and misleading emphasis in its intelligence gathering on Howe is its close coverage of the circumstances of his departure from the ISL in October 1952. Although the FBI file contains two copies in full of Howe's three-page resignation letter, Bureau informants in 1954 seem to have been uninformed about the founding of *Dissent* in January 1954—or, indeed, about how total the rupture between Howe and the ISL became. No mention is made in Howe's file that the ISL passed a motion prohibiting its members from contributing articles to *Dissent* unless they received special dispensation. Howe was treated by the FBI as if he were still a member of a "basic revolutionary organization" throughout the 1950s.

Nor was this the Bureau's only important oversight concerning Howe's political activities at this time. Apparently the Bureau missed Howe's published exchange with the ISL two years later—his last contribution to *Labor Action*. In a scathing attack on the inaugural issue of *Dissent*, Hal Draper wrote in *Labor Action* (February 22, 1954) that Howe's break with the ISL and his founding of *Dissent* signified that "those who sympathize with his 'ethos' must likewise abandon any *organized* socialist movement, which is to be replaced by such a center for thinkers as his magazine seeks to make itself." Howe replied to Draper in the March 15 issue of *Labor Action*: "I know this way of thinking, having suffered from it myself for a good many years." Howe maintained that Draper and the ISL were living in grandiose denial about the nonexistence of a socialist "movement," as well as about their influence beyond the suffocating "we" of sectarian circles. Although some individuals in America could still be called "socialists," Howe said, " 'we' have no political significance, whatsoever."[13] Nonetheless, the regular tabs that the Bureau kept on Howe in the early 1950s make clear that the FBI worried that socialists such as Howe might build a movement or gain political significance.

III

Howe's university activities in the 1950s—at Princeton, Brandeis, and the University of Michigan at Ann Arbor—were also monitored periodically by regional FBI offices. When the FBI began its file on him in February 1951, Howe was living in Princeton, residing in a small house financed by a

GI loan. His second wife, Thalia (Phillies), taught Greek and Latin at Miss Fine's, a private day school in Princeton.[14] A colleague of hers, who described herself as "casually acquainted with Irving Howe," provided Newark agents of the Bureau with some information in October 1953 about Howe's status as a full-time independent writer.

Another informant in Princeton was Carlos Baker, the distinguished Hemingway scholar, who taught at Princeton University. Baker was in the university audience when Howe gave a lecture entitled "Politics and the Novel" at the Christian Gauss seminar in the fall of 1952.[15] Baker was forty-three years old and had just published *Hemingway: The Writer as Artist* (1952). A specialist in British and American literature who had been teaching since 1937 at Princeton, where he also attained his doctorate in 1940, Baker was a rising academic star and soon to be appointed a chaired professor and department chairman. Baker was also well-acquainted with Howe's new world of *Partisan Review* intellectuals.

Baker reportedly told the FBI that he knew "so little about the subject [that] he was in no position to provide any recommendations." The agent adds: "But he did notice the subject has a very bright mind, a nervous disposition, and an immature outlook on life."[16]

Although Baker evidently told FBI agents nothing of importance, their conversation with him indicates, at minimum, that he was willing to provide the Bureau with negative impressions of a young man whose background would certainly have been officially suspect. It also shows that the FBI gained access to prominent scholars familiar with Howe's intellectual life and reference groups. (Baker's name evidently appears in Howe's file because he died in 1987; the names of other informants or agents are blacked out.)

In the fall of 1953 Howe joined the faculty at Brandeis University in Waltham, Massachusetts, founded in 1948. (He would officially remain at Brandeis throughout the period of his FBI file, until he left for Stanford in 1961.) Within a few weeks the Boston FBI office was following his activities. One report from spring 1954 reported on surveillance of his home in nearby Wellesley: "From January 16 to February 13, 1954, a mail cover was maintained on the residence of the subject at 87 Parker Road. The following are individuals or organizations from whom the subject received correspondence during this period: *Dissent, Perspectives*, [Stanley] Plastrik, *Partisan Review*."

On June 2 Boston agents wrote: "Asked New York office to identify and check the references of some 15 correspondents of the subject. Because considerable agent time would be necessary to cover these leads, the New York office will not cover the leads as set out."

Surveillance of Howe intensified in 1954, perhaps because Brandeis was known as a home for numerous intellectual radicals and Marxists (and ex-Marxists). Doubtless word was also spreading of Howe's growing stature and controversial positions as a New York intellectual. (Brandeis president Abram Sachar apparently regarded Howe's appointment in 1953—at least in hindsight—as "a major coup.")[17] Moreover, Howe was soon to become a well-known campus presence at Brandeis because of his frequent participation in public debates, including face-offs with such figures as Herbert Marcuse, the novelist Howard Fast, and Oscar Handlin (who debated Howe on Israel's capture and planned trial of Adolf Eichmann).

It was the Boston FBI that took the step of tracking "subject Horenstein" for an interview in August 1954, near the Harvard campus.[18] The report of the FBI interview with "Horenstein" opens as follows:

> The Boston office interviewed subject Horenstein without prior notice at 2:00 p.m., August 6, 1954 by two Special Agents, on Boylston Street, Cambridge, Massachusetts. Subject was affable. He stated he would be happy to sit in his own car and discuss ideologies. He continued that this was as far as he would go with the interviewing agents and that he had no intention of identifying or "involving" others in view of what he described as the "misuse" of the Smith Act by the Department of Justice and the use of Executive Order 10450 to "blackball radicals and prevent them from earning a livelihood." It is to be noted that at no time during the course of the interview was the subject hostile, and throughout the interview he displayed a friendly and cordial manner.[19]

The Boston agents continue: "Subject described himself as a 'Socialist' and a lifelong 'anti-Stalinist.' Subject denied membership at any time in the Socialist Workers Party or any other group or organization which advocates the overthrow of the United States government by force or violence."[20]

The report concludes: "In view of the subject's past activities and attitude at the time of interview and his denial of membership in the Socialist Workers Party, it is believed that he should be included in the security index." The report is dated August 26, 1954, and the security index card was prepared that day.[21]

This interview forms the centerpiece of the comprehensive file on Howe compiled by the Boston office on April 8, 1955. That file comprised twenty-six pages, including birth records; educational background; marital status; military service record; employment record; residences; political activities, speeches, and writings; and even speeding tickets in Princeton and nearby Cranbury, New Jersey ("ten dollars paid on February 8, 1953, seven dollars paid on 3/23/53"). The April 1955 file also includes Howe's resignation letter to the ISL (October 12, 1952); a log of his contributions to *New International* between 1946 and 1952; and a summary of three of his fall 1949 public lectures, which reflected the labor policy themes of *The* UAW *and Walter Reuther* and coincided with its publication. [22]

Howe's wife, Thalia, taught at the University of Michigan at Ann Arbor during his leave of absence from Brandeis in 1958–59. The Detroit FBI checked on him in Ann Arbor and also noted that he was "employed at Wayne State University in the English department on a part-time basis." [23]

Detroit agents attended at least three of Howe's *Dissent* lectures during 1956–58. (Much of Howe's energy in the late 1950s went into organizing *Dissent* forums around the country on various political topics, an effort that did not go unnoticed by the FBI.) [24] One informant at a Detroit talk reported that the "principal subject of Howe's talk was how sorry he was to have ever considered himself as a 'socialist' and that if he had to do it over again, he would not associate himself with such a movement because he felt that it would never amount to much more than just a movement. Howe further stated that, in spite of its ideals and some of the fanatics [who] are members of various socialists' organizations, there is no real socialist movement. Howe, during his talk, referred to *Dissent* magazine and its program and stated that the magazine staff had considered dropping the word 'social' or 'socialist' from its program, but had finally decided not to make any change."

This informant was doubtless confusing "socialist" and "Trotskyist," obviously misunderstanding that Howe was referring to his years of membership in the ISL. Even if internal discussions on the *Dissent* editorial board addressed abandoning a formal commitment to "socialism," Howe proudly and publicly referred to himself as a "socialist" throughout the 1950s—and well after.

IV

Several regional bureaus intermittently followed Howe's activities during the late 1950s, as we have already seen. But he was no longer considered a security risk after mid-1955, and little new information appeared in his file as the decade wound down.

On May 19, 1955, the Boston office decided to cancel the security index. But it sought to justify its expenditure of resources, noting yet again that "the subject registered with the Workers Party in June/July, 1946 at which time he indicated he had been a member of the Workers Party since 1940." The four-page report closes: "While the subject has been a member of a basic revolutionary group within the past five years, it is noted that on

October 12, 1952, subject directed a letter to the ISL in which he stated he was formally resigning from the ISL, further it is noted that subject has stated that in the event of hostilities with the Soviet Union, the ISL should support the United States. It is, therefore, recommended that he be removed from the Security Index. The security flash note is also to be removed." This report was filed on June 10, 1955.

Nonetheless, the Boston office still conducted occasional spot checks of Howe. For instance, his file reports a "pretext telephone call to Brandeis University on 10/30/58, in the guise of an associate attempting to locate subject."[25] As we have observed, Boston agents also tipped off other regional bureaus about Howe's whereabouts and coordinated surveillance with them. The Detroit file for March 31, 1959, notes that, on October 18, 1958, Howe "directed a postcard to *Labor Action*" requesting a change of address for his subscription. Indeed, the March 1959 file by the Detroit bureau is a twenty-two-page report, including a nine-page appendix on Howe's memberships in various socialist organizations.

Like the Detroit agents, the Boston bureau was apparently concerned that *Dissent*'s public forums might lead to a socialist mass movement.[26] (A 1959 forum that featured Erich Fromm, a *Dissent* editorial board member, drew seven hundred people.)[27] For instance, the Boston office reported on "Irving Horenstein" at a *Dissent* forum entitled "The Revolt in East Europe" (December 1, 1956) at Adelphi Hall in New York and at a forum in Boston (January 30, 1957) that a lieutenant of the Massachusetts State Police attended. According to the report of the New York talk, which dealt with the Soviet invasion of Hungary in October 1956, Howe "definitely was anti-Communist in his analysis and repeatedly criticized the ruthless attacks by the Russian troops."[28]

In another *Dissent* forum covered by the Boston office (filed on April 4, 1958), Howe reportedly "evidenced considerable dejection over the low level of activity that now characterized U.S. socialism." The file continues: "Howe claims that socialism could meet all the problems that besetted in [*sic*] our country if trends were to continue unchanged. As he saw them, there would probably result in our country a low-charged autocracy, somewhere between freedom and totalitarianism. Howe stated that in central planning even of the socialist variety, there was a danger that the concentration of powerful planning purposes would destroy freedom and to be successful and accepted, U.S. socialism must be democratic and welcome some degree of small independent business. Howe concluded with a plea for studied regroupment of socialist elements." By this time the FBI had in effect acknowledged the obvious fact that Howe was no "security risk." But the reduced scope permitted to the FBI—caused by judicial decisions following the discrediting of Senator Joseph McCarthy's communist witch hunts—also limited the Bureau's pursuit of young ex-Trotskyists like Howe. Indeed, an important reason for the Bureau's dwindling interest in Howe, along with many other former "revolutionaries," was that the U.S. Supreme Court had recently redefined the Smith Act more narrowly. In 1956 the Supreme Court ruled on a Smith Act case in California, saying that, in order to convict, "clear and present danger" must be shown. In 1957 the Supreme Court sharply curbed the application of the Smith Act, allowing it to pertain only to people who engaged in specific insurrectionist activities or incited others to do so.

These developments rendered a third-rank former "revolutionary" from a negligible sect of little interest. On April 14, 1959, the Detroit office closed Howe's file, and other regional offices did likewise. At this time Howe was lecturing at Wayne State University. His file was first declassified in August 1985, with additional material also declassified in September 1997.

Notes

1. The sectarian politics of the 1940s within the Trotskyist movement, which led to the formation of the ISL, were complex. A faction led by Max Shachtman split off from the Socialist Workers Party (SWP) in 1940 to create the Workers Party (WP). They were the minority and claimed they were expelled; the majority, led by James Cannon, claimed that Shachtman had split. All this occurred in the wake of the Hitler-Stalin Pact of 1939, which caused a crisis in the SWP when the Soviet Union attacked Poland and the Baltic States. Some intellectuals associated with Shachtman, such as James Burnham, announced that the U.S.S.R. was a new form of class society, but Shachtman's view of "the Russian Question" was still in formation. The rupture came to a head over organizational issues, and in subsequent months (after the split) Shachtman's new views of the U.S.S.R. evolved: at first the U.S.S.R was superior to the Western imperialist countries, then both were equally bad, and finally Shachtman advocated critical support for the West. The name switch from WP to ISL mainly came from the WP's recognition that it couldn't regard itself as a party when it was basically a political agitprop group. (Shachtman's SWP members followed him and joined the ISL, whose members became known as the Shachtmanites and whose membership in 1943 was approximately five hundred.)

2. Several FBI regional bureaus received copies of Howe's birth records, marriage records, army records from the Veterans Administration in Boston, fingerprinting records, and even photographs from CCNY.

3. One FBI entry begins: "Irving Horenstein was the true name of one Irving Howe." The file repeatedly notes that "Horenstein is his true surname" and refers to the subject's "alias" as "Irving Howe." It observes that "the middle name Arthur is added as shown in the birth records of the subject's children."

4. The American embassy wrote on November 19, 1957, to the director of the FBI that the Paris police had discovered a suitcase containing male and female clothing and that the owner of the suitcase was Howe. (Howe had lectured at the Salzburg Seminar in Austria that summer.) It is interesting that the American embassy chose to contact the FBI in order to get in touch with Howe. His FBI file for December 13, 1957, records the following: "On December 4, Howe advised that he is the owner of a grey leather suitcase, initialed IH, which was stolen from him at Chartres, France last summer."

5. See Alexander, *Irving Howe*, chap. 5, "The Fifties: Age of Conformity, Age of Dissent."

6. Howe's statement of purpose for *Dissent* in its opening issue (January 1954) is entitled, "Does It Hurt When You Laugh?" Its stress is on the condition of civil liberties in America. Since anticommunist liberals at *Commentary* refused to castigate reactionaries supporting McCarthyism, Howe maintained, *Dissent* radicals must "raise the traditional banner of personal freedom that is now slipping from the hands of so many accredited spokesmen of liberalism."

7. Indeed, Howe's marriage records, his birth certificate, and his military records were all recorded. One report states: "Information was circulated among the Albany bureau for the marriage records of the state of New York (June 15, 1941, and April 12, 1947), the Newark bureau for marriage records and for activities in Princeton, including divorce records, and the New York and Boston bureaus."

8. Howe, *A Margin of Hope*, 223. Quoted in Alexander, *Irving* Howe, 90.

9. A 1955 file notes: "New York office reports on May 11, 1955, [based] on records of the Bureau of Vital Statistics from the Bronx: Irving Howe's marriage at the age of 20, his parents both listed as having been born in Russia."

10. Formally known as the Alien Registration Act, the Smith Act made it illegal to conspire against the government. The Smith Act accused members of "revolutionary organizations" of conspiring to teach or advocate the overthrow of the government by force or violence. Adopted in 1940, it was first used against American Leftists in 1943, when leaders in the Socialist Workers Party and their supporters in the Minneapolis Teamsters Union were convicted in Minneapolis for "un-American" activities and sentenced to up to sixteen months in jail.

11. Alexander, *Irving Howe*, 19. As late as 1949, as Alexander notes, Howe was still writing under the name R. Fahan in *Labor Action*. For instance, in one article entitled "Washington Case Raises Civil Liberties Issue: Should Stalinists Be Permitted to Teach?" he opposed all measures that would prevent Stalinists from teaching, disagreeing with Sidney Hook. (While Hook opposed legislation that barred Communists from the classroom, he advocated that universities take action, arguing that Communists had to accept Party discipline and were therefore

not free minds.) Howe wrote a similar piece under his own name, published as "Intellectual Freedom and Stalinists" in *New International* (December 1949).

12. See the Boston FBI report of September 15, 1954, for the latter error. Another report notes: "Birth records were also searched in New York for the subject's two male children [*sic*]. The New York bureau checked under the name Horenstein for the boys' names." An Albany bureau report (March 31, 1955) notes that "a check of birth records, from 1941 to date, under the name Horenstein reflected only one male born during that period with this name. A check of this record reflected that this was not one of the subject's children." (Howe's children are Nicholas and Nina.)

13. The Draper-Howe exchange is discussed in Alexander, *Irving Howe*, 95–96. Howe was already at odds with the ISL because of its failure to support the Marshall Plan and to align itself with the democratic West against Stalinism. In 1951 Howe and Plastrik tried to persuade the ISL, which sponsored *Labor Action*, to also sponsor a quarterly journal that would be similar in style and substance to the defunct *Politics*. The ISL refused.

14. Alexander, *Irving Howe*, 74.

15. The Newark Bureau report is dated September 22, 1952. Following John Hollander, Alexander notes that *Politics and the Novel* (1957) was based on Howe's summer course at the Indiana School of Letters in Bloomington in 1953. (Hollander was a student of Howe that summer and recalled the class with affection in his lecture of April 15, 1994, at the memorial conference, "Irving Howe and His World," held at the Graduate Center of the City University of New York.) But *Politics and the Novel* actually had its origins in Howe's series of six Gauss lectures at Princeton, as the title of his series makes clear.

16. See the Newark report for February 2, 1954.

17. See Alexander, *Irving Howe*, chap. 5. The comment is quoted from Sachar's memoirs.

18. Several FBI memos repeat the caution voiced by one Bureau official: "This investigation must be conducted in accordance with the provisions set forth in the manual of instructions relating to security-type investigations at institutions of learning." Another Boston memo adds: "Interview with Irving Horenstein ok'd, so long as it must be conducted in a particularly circumspect manner, so that no embarrassment to the Bureau will result."

19. Critics of the Smith Act argued that it was an attack on the First Amendment right to free speech, but in June 1951 the act was upheld by a vote of six to two in the Supreme Court. In a dissenting opinion Justice Hugo Black wrote: "These petitioners were not charged with an attempt to overthrow the government. . . . They were not even charged with saying or writing anything designed to overthrow

the government. The charge was that they agreed to assemble and to talk and publish certain ideas at a later date."

But Black's dissenting opinion did little to slow the federal government's dragnet. Federal prosecutors used the Smith Act to put on trial native-born political radicals suspected of seeking to subvert American institutions and professions.

20. Today most historians agree that the Smith Act had little to do with a legitimate fear that "revolutionary organizations" were going to overthrow the United States. The purpose was to curtail opposition to the Cold War, whether that opposition came from organized labor, the civil rights movement, or the peace movement. The main victims were left-wing trade unionists.

Other legislative tools used to crush leftist dissent were the Taft-Hartley Act, which required all heads of union locals to take oaths swearing that they were not Communists, and the McCarran Act, which forced party members of "revolutionary organizations" to register with the government.

21. Howe discussed his swp membership during 1938–40 in *A Margin of Hope*. The issue of Howe's swp involvement is significant, because it was the chief motive and basis for the fbi's surveillance of him. The swp was indicted under the Smith Act in the 1940s and went on the attorney general's list, and that is obviously the main reason why Howe denied his swp membership during the fbi's 1954 interview with him. But he probably also had another, "Trotskyist" reason for denying his old swp connection. The wp claimed in its polemics that the swp was "objectively pro-Stalinist" (in the tradition of Trotskyist polemical rhetoric that the young editor of *Labor Action* mastered so well). So Howe's denial would have been personally important to him, because it deflected any perception of a political taint from a onetime Stalinist affiliation. As Howe probably saw it in the 1950s, and perhaps later, he had only joined the swp in 1938–40 as part of the faction fight that led to the wp.

22. The three lectures were delivered to the University of Chicago Politics Club ("The Need for a Worker's Party," October 14, 1949), to the Socialist Youth League ("Bureaucracy in Trade Unions," August 13, 1949), and to the isl ("Bureaucracy and Democracy in the Labor Movement," September 23, 1949). The Politics Club at the University of Chicago was a Trotskyist group and had been reactivated by the Chicago branch of the Young People's Socialist League in the fall of 1957.

23. This information is in the March 31, 1959, dossier compiled by the Boston office, which also includes the editorial statement of purpose from the opening issue of *Dissent*.

24. *Dissent* launched its first forum in November 1954 in New York. By 1958 a half dozen *Dissent* groups in various cities (among them New York, Boston, San Francisco, and Los Angeles) were meeting regularly to discuss public issues. Often members of the groups invited speakers to address special topics. On the *Dissent* forums, see Lou Anne Bulik, *Mass Culture Criticism and* Dissent, *an American Socialist Magazine* (New York: Peter Lang, 1993), 74.

25. Another FBI memo hilariously refers to "suitable telephonic pretext, Brandeis University," a good example of the jargon that the FBI used to make a phone-call check.

26. These concerns were surely heightened by the unrest in Eastern Europe after the failed Hungarian revolution in October 1956.

27. See Bulik, *Mass Culture*, 74.

28. Howe's lecture, "A Crisis in the Communist World" (delivered November 16, 1957, at the YWCA in Detroit), was also monitored.

Source Acknowledgments

Nicholas Howe, "Reading Irving Howe" (foreword), is a previously unpublished essay, printed with permission of the author.

John Rodden, "Irving Howe, Triple Thinker," is a previously unpublished essay, printed with permission of the author.

Mark Levinson and Brian Morton, "A Man of the Left," first appeared in *New Left Review* (Summer 1993): 111–14, and is reprinted with permission of the authors.

Ronald Radosh, "Journey of a Social Democrat," was first published as "On Irving Howe" in *Partisan Review* 60, no. 3 (1993): 343, and is reprinted with permission of the author.

Ian Williams, "An Ex-Maoist Looks at an Ex-Trotskyist: On Howe's *Leon Trotsky*," is a previously unpublished essay, printed with permission of the author.

Samuel Hux, "Our 'Uncle Irving': Howe's Conservative Strain," first appeared in *Modern Age* (Summer 1995): 330–36, and is reprinted with permission of the author.

Marshall Berman, "Irving and the New Left: From Fighter to Leader," originally appeared in *Dissent* (Fall 1993): 519–20, and is reprinted with permission of the author.

Alexander Cockburn, "Irving Howe, R.I.P.: A Few Tasteless Words," first appeared in the *Nation*, June 14, 1993, 822, and is reprinted with permission of the author.

Joseph Epstein, "The Old People's Socialist League," was originally published in *Commentary* (August 1998): 41–46, and is reprinted with permission of the author.

Robert Boyers, "Politics and the Critic," is a previously unpublished essay (originally entitled "Remembering Irving Howe"), printed with permission of the author.

Nathan Glick, "The Socialist Who Loved Keats," was originally published in *Atlantic Monthly* (January 1998): 99–105, and is reprinted with permission of the author.

Nicholas Howe, "A Lover of Stories," first appeared in *Dissent* (Fall 1993): 532–33, and is reprinted with permission of the author.

Brian Morton, "The Literary Craftsman," first appeared in *Dissent* (Fall 1993): 543–44, and is reprinted with permission of the author.

Paul Roazen, "How Irving Howe Shaped My Thinking Life," is a previously unpublished essay, printed with permission of the author.

John Rodden, " 'My Intellectual Hero': Irving Howe's 'Partisan' Orwell," is adapted, in part, from chapter 6 of *The Politics of Literary Reputation: The Making and Claiming of "St. George" Orwell* (New York: Oxford University Press, 1989) and is printed with permission of the author.

William E. Cain, "Howe on Emerson: The Politics of Literary Criticism," is a previously unpublished essay, printed with permission of the author.

George Scialabba, "Howe Inside My Head," first appeared in *Harvard Review* (Fall 1993) as "A Tired Hero, at Rest" and is reprinted with permission of the author.

Morris Dickstein, "World of Our Grandparents," was first published in a shorter version in the *New York Times Book Review*, April 6, 1997, and is reprinted with permission of the author.

Leonard Kriegel, "Father Figures," first appeared in *Partisan Review* 43, no. 4 (1976): 619–21, as "Irving Howe's *World of Our Fathers*" and is reprinted with permission of the author.

Alvin H. Rosenfeld, "Of Yiddish Culture and Secular Jewishness," first appeared in *Midstream* (October 1976): 80–86, and is reprinted with permission of the author.

Edward Alexander, "Standing Guard over Irving Howe's Reputation; Or, Good Causes Attract Bad Advocates," is a previously unpublished essay, printed with permission of the author.

Leon Wieseltier, "Irving, *In Memoriam*," first appeared in the *New York Times Book Review*, May 20, 1993, and is reprinted with permission of the author.

Gerald Sorin, "The Relevance of Irving Howe," is a previously unpublished essay, printed with permission of the author.

Michael Levenson, "A Steady Worker," is a previously unpublished essay, printed with permission of the author.

Morris Dickstein, "Irving Howe: Finding the Right Words" (afterword), is a previously unpublished essay, printed with permission of the author. Copyright © 2004 by Morris Dickstein.

John Rodden, "Wanted by the FBI: No. 727437B a.k.a. Irving Horenstein, 'An Immature Outlook on Life,' " previously appeared in *Dissent* (Fall 2002): 79–85, and is reprinted with permission of the author.

Index

Adler, Jacob, 163

Agnew, Spiro, 127

Aleichem, Sholom, 14, 15, 23n71, 105, 158, 198, 203; and "The Old Country," 157

Alexander, Edward, 3, 4, 5, 62, 66, 68, 69, 142, 159, 173–78, 198, 201, 214

Allen, Woody, xxi

Alter, Robert, 107, 174–77

American Communist Party, xi, xx, 50, 80

American Scholar, 64, 77, 119

Anderson, Sherwood, xii, xiii, xix, xviii, 51, 70, 108, 119, 181, 196; and *Winesburg, Ohio*, xiv, xviin3

Annie Hall, xxi

Anti-Intellectualism in American Life (Hofstadter), 18

anti-Semitism, 173

antiwar movement: anti-intellectualism of the, 195

Appelfeld, Aharon, 175

Arab-Israeli War, 16n2, 18n15

Arendt, Hannah, xix, 115, 116, 119, 120, 186, 194; and *Eichmann in Jerusalem*, 16, 218; and *Origins of Totalitarianism*, 119

Arguing the World (1998 film), 16n2, 65

Arnold, Matthew, 97

Babel, Issac, 203–5

Baker, Carlos, 217

Baldwin, James, 100, 204

ballet, 11, 14, 49, 93, 181, 209

Baruch, Elaine Hoffman, 48, 49

Bell, Daniel, 11, 57, 65, 149, 191, 200; at City College, 67, 103, 191; and Trotskyism, 118, 175

Bellow, Saul, 2, 70, 87, 98, 99, 105, 106, 125, 127; and *Herzog*, 98

Berlin, Isaiah, 57, 115

Berman, Marshall, 57–61

Berman, Paul, 54, 63, 202

Bernstein, Eduard, 118

Berryman, John, 204

Blumenthal, Sidney, 62

Bolshevik Party, 38

Bolshevik Revolution, 67

Bolshevism, 43, 44

Boyers, Robert, 2, 77–94

Brandeis University, i, 103, 217, 220

Brecht, Bertolt, 144, 145, 192

Bronx (NY), i, xiii, 27, 57, 102, 109, 150, 156, 158, 181

Brzezinski, Z. K., 120

Burnham, James, 28

Buttinger, Joseph, 35

Cahan, Abraham, 164

Cain, William, xxii, 132–42

Cannon, James P., 221

Carmichael, Joel, 45

Carver, Raymond, 108

Castro, Fidel, 60, 103

Céline, Louis-Ferdinand, 32, 203
Chambers, Whittaker, 52
Chekhov, Anton, 14
Chesterton, G. K., 55
China, 187
Chomsky, Noam, 5, 174
CIA: funding of Congress for Cultural
  Freedom by, 21n45
City College of New York (CCNY), xv,
  xx, 67, 68, 96, 98, 221n1
City University of New York (Hunter
  College), 11, 32, 69, 99, 149, 156,
  206
civil rights movement, 33, 81
Cockburn, Alexander, 2, 5, 62–63,
  174
Cohen, Elliot, 33
Cohen, Mitchell, 4
Cohen, Morris Raphael, 164
Columbia University, 80, 157
Commentary, 33, 35, 65, 98, 99, 138,
  139, 176, 178, 222n6; Howe's writ-
  ing for, 70, 149; neoconservative
  emergence and, xxi
communism, 30, 35, 42, 43, 192, 206,
  215; Howe on, 80, 95, 194, 195; fall
  of, 30, 193
Communist Party, xi, xx, 40, 50, 67,
  68, 80
Congress for Cultural Freedom (CCF),
  21n45
Conrad, Joseph, xii, 28, 71, 72, 85,
  86, 91, 100, 115, 120; and *The Secret
  Agent*, 71, 72, 91, 115; and *Under
  Western Eyes*, 71, 72, 91, 100
Cooper, Alan, 178
Coser, Lewis, xx, 20, 29, 50, 64, 80,
  121, 195, 197, 202
Cowley, Malcolm, xii–xiv, 48
Crane, Stephen, 204, 205

Debs, Eugene V., 97
Decter, Midge, 2, 88, 89, 90
Dellinger, Dave, 63

democracy, 28, 36, 42, 44, 46, 89, 95,
  104, 118, 188, 195, 202; and social
  democracy, xxi, 4, 5, 29, 33, 39, 40,
  43, 53, 58
Democratic Party, 32, 107, 208
democratic socialism, xix, xxi, 5, 38,
  39, 44, 103, 104, 118, 121, 186, 188,
  192, 195
Democratic Socialist Organizing
  Committee (DSOC), 33
Democratic Socialists of America
  (DSA), 33, 63
Deutscher, Isaac, 194
Dewey, John, 38
Dickens, Charles, 119
Dickstein, Morris, viii, 10, 14, 149–55,
  201–11
Dionne, E. J., 62
Dissent, xxii, 1–14 passim, 35, 36, 43,
  49, 50, 52, 53, 57–61 passim, 63,
  70, 73, 77–80 passim, 84, 94, 110,
  115, 116, 122, 124, 128, 139, 143, 151,
  176, 180, 185, 202, 205, 206, 214–
  20 passim; and civil liberties, 33;
  Howe as editor of, xi, xix–xxi, 13,
  22n63, 29, 65; origins and goals of,
  29, 30, 103, 104, 121, 195, 197, 216,
  222n6; and Vietnam War, 35, 58–59
Djilas, Milovan, 20
Dohrn, Bernadine, 176
Donoghue, Dennis, 135, 142
Dorman, Joseph, 4, 201
Dostoevsky, Fyodor, xi, 28, 58, 61,
  99, 100, 114, 115, 120; and *The Pos-
  sessed*, 84, 91, 100, 114
Draper, Hal, 216
Dreiser, Theodore, 100, 108, 203; and
  An American Tragedy, 100
Dubinsky, David, 164
Dupee, F. W., 149

Eliot, George, 49, 100, 108, 174, 177,
  178, 199

Eliot, T. S., 51, 70, 82, 98, 144, 186, 192, 199
Ellison, Ralph, 2, 70, 100, 101, 186, 202, 204, 210; and *The Invisible Man*, 100
Emerson, Ralph Waldo, 32, 82, 100, 132–42
Encounter, 96, 103
Epstein, Joseph, 4, 64–73, 88, 164

Fast, Howard, 218
Faulkner, William, xii–xiv, xix, 51, 69, 70, 97, 98, 108, 114, 158, 181, 196
FBI, 10; Boston bureau, 213, 215, 217–20; Detroit bureau, 213, 219–21; interview, 213, 214, 218; New York bureau, 215, 217, 222n7, 227n9, 223n12
feminism, 88, 202
Fiedler, Leslie, 60, 203
Fischer, Louis, 68
Flaubert, Gustave, 9, 10; and "triple thinking," 10, 21n52, 21n53
Fortas, Abe, 116
Freud, Sigmund, 60, 204
Friedrich, Carl J., 120
Fromm, Erich, 220
Frost, Robert, 210
Fuentes, Carlos, 106

Genovese, Eugene D., 35, 55, 56
Gershman, Carl, 63
"Gimpel the Fool" (Singer), 106
Gingrich, Newt, 55
Gitlin, Todd, 2, 176
Glatstein, Jacob, 57, 106, 206
Glazer, Nathan, 65; at CCNY, 103
Glick, Nathan, 96–107, 174
Gold, Michael, 151
Goldwater, Barry, 190
Goodman, Paul, 121
Gorky, Maxim, 14
Grade, Chaim, 174, 206
Grass, Günter, xx, 96

Great Depression, xv, 67, 208
Greeley, Andrew, 3
Greenberg, Clement, 119
Greenberg, Eliezer, xx, 28, 70, 105, 166

Hardwick, Elizabeth, 98
Hardy, Thomas, xii–xiv, xix, 51, 70, 97, 100, 108, 181, 196
Harrington, Michael, 33, 103, 121; and *The Other America*, 103
Hasidism, 170
Hawthorne, Nathaniel, 99, 100, 160
Hayden, Tom, 29, 34, 128, 176, 195, 202
Heilbroner, Robert, 35
Hemingway, Ernest, 98, 101, 144, 145, 217
Hillquit, Morris, 164
Hitchens, Christopher, 44
Hitler, Adolf, 41, 68, 127, 157, 167, 177, 191, 208
Ho Chi Minh, 62, 103
Hollander, John, 223n15
Holmes, Oliver Wendell, 135
Holocaust, 105, 112, 151, 153, 154, 162, 167, 170, 171, 173, 191, 215
Hook, Sidney, xix, 2, 68, 69, 175
Horenstein, David, 215
Howe, Irving: as the "American Orwell," 4, 5; and American Transcendentalism, 100; and biographers, xi, xiii, 3, 17n7, 18n7, 19n32, 32, 66, 173–78, 201, 214; character of, 48–50, 58, 96, 113, 116; childhood of, xx, 67, 180; at City College of New York, 67, 68, 102, 103; and civil liberties, 214, 215, 222n11; and counterculture, xx, 2, 16n3, 59, 152, 154; and cultural conservatism, 52–56; and *Dissent*, 29–30, 33, 65, 103, 121, 195, 202; and Edmund Wilson, xxi, 5, 8–11, 21n48, 21n52, 21n53, 23n71, 64, 67,

Howe, Irving (*continued*)
  70, 99, 107, 122, 186, 207, 208,
  210; and Establishment, xx, 82,
  127; and FBI records, 213–25; and
  Freud, 60, 204; and Ignazio Silone,
  5, 7–9, 20n45, 109, 144, 145, 182,
  207, 208; and individualism, 138,
  139, 210; and Irving Horenstein,
  viii, 67, 175, 191, 213, 215, 216, 218,
  220, 221n3; and Jewish culture,
  10, 28, 41, 163–72, 186; and legacy,
  xix, 1–16, 17n6, 48–52, 55, 62, 64,
  97, 100, 128; and Leon Trotsky,
  xi, xxi, 5–8, 28, 30, 35, 37–47, 67,
  72, 192; and Lionel Trilling, xix,
  xx, 2, 7, 17n7, 18n10, 78, 79, 99,
  107, 116, 118, 123, 124–26, 128, 204,
  205, 208, 210, 211; and literary enthusiasms, 87, 97–111; and literary
  excellence, 16n4, 77–95, 99, 100,
  124; and literary-intellectual influence, 17n7, 70, 97, 100, 128; and
  literary models, 1–16, 101, 122–29;
  and modernism, 7, 54, 58, 70, 97,
  144, 151, 152, 157, 162, 191, 192, 198,
  199, 206; and neoconservatism, xv,
  xxi, 1, 3–6, 12, 18n14, 30, 34, 35, 39,
  41, 43–46, 53, 54, 65, 88–90, 103,
  128, 201, 214; and the New Left,
  xx, 1, 2, 7, 17n5, 22n63, 29, 30,
  34–36, 40, 52, 57–68, 80, 82, 83,
  85, 125, 152, 175, 176, 195, 206, 208;
  and New York intellectuals, xix,
  2, 7, 28, 65, 97, 98, 112, 121, 146,
  151, 152, 180, 196, 201, 206; and the
  Old Left, 1, 3, 18n13, 66, 80, 84,
  127; and Orwell, xxi, 4–11, 21n46,
  42, 64, 72, 73, 99, 107, 112, 113,
  117–29, 145, 158, 182, 186, 203, 208;
  and posthumous controversies, 73;
  and reactionary politics, 66, 100;
  and the Right, xvi, xxi, 1, 2, 5, 52,
  195; and secular Jewishness, xix, 28,
  66, 104, 151–54, 163–72, 174, 181,

  182, 186, 188, 199; and socialism,
  xv, xx, 8, 10, 12, 13, 22n63, 27,
  29–31, 64–73, 88, 104, 118, 124,
  187, 195, 202, 208, 219; and social
  realism, 4, 89, 99, 200; and traditionalist curriculum, 18n14, 20n38,
  54; and Trotskyism, xx, 3, 6, 8,
  10, 16n2, 17n5, 24n72, 28, 33, 35,
  37–47, 55, 67, 68, 117–19, 175, 177,
  191, 192, 194, 195, 198, 213, 219, 221,
  22n1, 224n21; writing style of, xiii,
  1, 14, 17n5, 23n69, 65, 70–72, 78,
  98, 99, 112, 122, 129, 146, 154, 187,
  195, 202, 203, 205, 209, 210; and
  Yiddish, xi, xv, xix, xx, 2, 3, 10,
  12, 14, 17n6, 28, 32, 54, 64, 67, 68,
  70, 105, 106, 150–54, 157–162, 181,
  186, 188, 197–99, 206; and Young
  People's Socialist League (YPSL), 6,
  67, 102, 224n22
—Works: *The American Communist
  Party*, xx, 20n42, 50; *The American Newness*, 11, 132, 138; *A Critic's
  Notebook*, 15, 51, 102, 139, 201, 209;
  "Culture of Modernism," 144; *How
  We Lived: A Documentary History
  of Immigrant Jews in America,
  1880–1930*, 17n7; *Leon Trotsky*, 6,
  37–47; *A Margin of Hope*, 9, 51, 53,
  66, 67, 102, 207, 210; "A Moderate
  Hero," 122; *1984 Revisited: Totalitarianism in Our Century*, 120;
  "The New York Intellectuals," 146,
  196; "Orwell: History as Nightmare," 114–22, 124; *Politics and
  the Novel*, xxi, 22, 70, 71, 77, 84,
  88, 90, 94, 99, 100, 114, 115, 116,
  144, 192, 203; *Sherwood Anderson*,
  xii, 70, 119; *Socialism and America*,
  132, 197; *Steady Work*, 104, 152;
  "T. E. Lawrence: The Problem of
  Heroism," 106; "This Age of Conformity," 16, 21n45, 197, 205, 214;
  Thomas Hardy, xx, 12, 70, 196; *A*

Treasury of Yiddish Stories, 70, 158; "Two Cheers for Utopia," 24n73; *The UAW and Walter Reuther*, 119; *William Faulkner*, 70; *World of our Fathers*, xv, xxi, 3, 4, 18n17, 71, 96, 104, 152, 201, 207; "Writing and the Holocaust," 16n3, 186

Howe, Nicholas, xi–xvii, 37, 108–11

Howe, Nina, xvi

Howe, Thalia Phillies, 217

Hungarian revolution, 225

Hunter College, 3, 153, 156

Hux, Samuel, 48–56

immigrants, xv, xx, 154, 157, 160, 170, 198; and American environment, 105, 156, 159; and language, 105

Independent Socialist League (ISL), 28, 215, 218, 219; Howe resigns from, 213

Indiana School of Letters, 223n15

Israeli Labor Party, 3

Jackson, Jesse, 63

Jacoby, Russell, 29; and *The Last Intellectuals*, 29

James, Henry, xii, 9, 71, 99, 143; and *Princess Casamassima*, 71

Jewish community, 185

Jewish Daily Forward, 167

Jews, 151, 174, 176, 177, 181, 182, 198, 205, 210; and the Holocaust, 68, 153, 154, 167; and intellectuals, 28, 97; and socialism, 27, 166, 188; and success in America, 105, 159, 168; and *World of Our Fathers*, xv, 3, 23n73, 65, 153, 156, 157, 163, 165, 168–72

Johnson, Lyndon Baines, 116

Jones, Le Roi (Amiri Baraka), 82

Joyce, James, 70, 199, 209

Judaism, 105, 151, 169, 170–74 passim, 181

Jumonville, Neil, 142

Kafka, Franz, 70, 199

Kazin, Alfred, 73, 96, 107, 118, 210

Keats, John, 97

Kempton, Murray, 126

Kennedy, John Fitzgerald, 197

King, Martin Luther, 83

Kirk, Russell, 53–55

Klein, Joe, 62

Koestler, Arthur, 42, 96, 120

Konrad, Gyorgy, xx

Kornbluth, Cyril, 41

Kostelanetz, Richard, 2

Kramer, Hilton, 2, 4, 34, 35, 62, 72, 88

Kramer, Michael, 62

Krauthammer, Charles, 62

Kriegel, Leonard, 156–62

Kristol, Irving, 65; at City College of New York, 68, 103, 191

Kundera, Milan, 87

Kuttner, Robert, 4

Labor Action, 68, 118, 177, 215, 216, 220

Larner, Jeremy, 19

Lasky, Melvin J., 96, 103

Lawrence, T. E., 21, 52, 70, 106, 108, 158, 203; and *Seven Pillars of Wisdom*, 106

Leavis, F. R., 149

Left, The, 22n63, 27–31, 68–71, 186–88, 202; and the liberal-Left, 32–36, 37, 47, 117–19, 213–26; and the Marxist Left, 32–36, 199–200

Lenin, Vladimir Ilych, 33, 34, 39, 40, 42, 43, 46, 81, 118

Leskov, Nikolai, 70, 108

Levi, Primo, 113

Levinson, Mark, 27–31, 190–200

liberalism, 35, 86, 87, 103, 115, 116, 122, 126, 171, 173, 174, 188, 195, 199, 208; in America, 35, 116, 125; and intellectuals, 103; Lionel

liberalism (*continued*)
  Trilling on, 208; and literature, 199; socialism and, 208
Libo, Kenneth, 3, 4, 154
Lipset, Seymour Martin, 103
Lowell, Robert, 2, 3, 48, 135
Lowenthal, Richard, 120
Lukacs, John, 55
Lynd, Staughton, 34

Macdonald, Dwight, 68, 97, 118, 119, 191, 202, 216
Magic Mountain, The (Mann), 97
Mailer, Norman, 70, 98, 176; and "The White Negro," 70, 176
Malamud, Bernard, 98
Malraux, Andre, 99, 120
Mann, Thomas, 97
Marat/Sade (Weiss), 78
Marcuse, Herbert, 60, 194, 218
Marshall, Louis, 163
Marx, 58, 82, 143, 165, 173, 294
McCarthy, Eugene, 3
McCarthy, Joseph, 214, 221
McCarthy, Mary, 97
McCarthyism, 29, 32, 33, 214, 215
McGrath, J. Howard, 215
McLuhan, Marshall, 60
menschlichkeit, 162
Mill, John Stuart, 173, 174
Millett, Kate, 70, 88, 91, 152; and *Sexual Politics*, 3, 17, 91
Mills, C. Wright, 121
Milosz, Czeslaw: and *The Captive Mind*, 83
Modern Age, 48, 52, 72
modernism, 54, 58, 70, 97, 151, 152, 157, 162, 191, 192, 198, 199, 206
Moore, Deborah Dash, 177–78
Morton, Brian, 27–31, 112–13
Moskowitz, Belle, 152, 164
Muravchik, Joshua, 63

Naipaul, V. S., 87

Nation, 5, 27, 37, 62
National Book Award, xxi, 96, 100
National Review, 32, 54
Nazism, 68, 194
Nazi-Soviet Pact (Hitler-Stalin Pact), 221n1
neoconservatives, xv, 4, 5, 34, 53, 54, 88, 103, 201
New American Movement (NAM), 22n63
New Conservatives, The, 64
New Criterion, xxi, 34, 90
New Deal, 35
Newfield, Jack, 2
New International, 117, 129, 215, 219, 223
New Leader, 96
New Left, The, vii, xx, 1, 2, 7, 23n69, 29, 30, 32, 34, 35, 36, 40, 52, 57–63, 68, 80, 81, 82, 83, 85, 91, 103, 125, 126–28, 152, 175, 176, 195, 202, 206, 208
New Republic, 4, 32, 62, 64, 66, 77, 94, 112, 128, 142, 149, 174, 176, 179, 189
New York City (NY), xiv, xx, 156, 209, 213
New Yorker, 62, 63
New York intellectuals, 2, 7, 32, 65, 97, 98, 119, 121, 138, 146, 150, 151, 152, 163, 180, 186, 187, 192, 196, 201; Jewishness of, xix, 28; style of, 112, 206
New York Review of Books, 66, 103, 142
New York University, 27, 80, 156
Nixon, Richard, 60, 116
Nobile, Philip, 3
Nove, Alec, 55

O'Connor, Flannery, 109
Oglesby, Carl, 2
Old Man, 39, 41, 43, 113, 125
Orwell, George, xix, xxi, 4–10, 42,

44, 64, 66, 68, 72, 73, 94, 96, 107, 112, 113, 117–29, 145, 178, 182, 186, 202, 203, 208, 209, 210; and *Homage to Catalonia*, 72, 122; and *Nineteen Eighty-Four*, 117–21, 125, 128; and *The Road to Wigan Pier*, 72, 125, 127
Ozick, Cynthia, 174

Pachter, Henry, 80, 84
Page, Clarence, 62
Partisan Review, xi, xx, 7, 8, 65, 67, 97, 103, 105, 117, 138, 149, 151, 192, 199, 205, 206, 217; Howe writes for, 28, 33, 198; and Jewishness, xix; origins of, 68
Pasternak, Boris, 190
Paz, Octavio, 35
Pentagon Papers, 7
Peretz, I. L., 105, 161
Phillips, William, 67, 68, 119
Pinsker, Sanford, 128, 174
Pirandello, 108, 197
Plastrik, Stanley, 213, 217
Podhoretz, Norman, xxii, 2, 128
Pohl, Frederik, 41
Politics (magazine), 216
Popular Front (United Front Against Fascism), 33
Port Huron Statement, 34, 61
Princeton University, 73, 214, 216–18
Proust, Marcel, 70, 179
Pushkin, Aleksandr, 9

Radosh, Ronald, 4, 32–36
Rahv, Phillip, 2, 17n7, 18n10, 67–69 passim, 118, 119, 198, 205–6, 211
Rainbow Coalition, 155
Rees, Richard, 123, 124
Reich, Charles, 60
Reuther, Walter, xx, 24n72, 50, 97, 119, 219
Riis, Jacob, 151
Roazen, Paul, 114–16

Robinson, Edwin Arlington, 54, 100
Rodden, John, 1–16, 117–31, 213–26
Rosenberg, Bernard, 22
Rosenberg, Harold, xix
Rosenfeld, Alvin H., 163–72
Rosenfeld, Isaac, 96, 118
Rossiter, Clinton, 53, 54
Roth, Philip, 2, 4, 70, 98, 100, 101, 107, 152, 175, 204, 210; and *The Anatomy Lesson*, 4, 70, 101; and *Goodbye, Columbus*, 101; and *Portnoy's Complaint*, 107, 204
Rovere, Richard, 124

Saba, Umberto, 108
Sachar, Abram, 218, 223
Sale, Roger, 209, 210
Sarah Lawrence College, 27
Schapiro, Meyer: and birth of *Dissent*, xvi, 121
Schlesinger, Arthur, Jr., 118
Schneiderman, Rose, 152
Schwartz, Delmore, 108, 207, 210
Scialabba, George, vii, 143–46
Serge, Victor, 197
Shachtman, Max, 6, 28, 33, 43, 117
Shakespeare, William, 60, 132
Shaw, George Bernard, 9
Shields, Mark, 62
shtiklakh, 13, 51
Silone, Ignazio, xx, 4, 5, 7–10, 27, 29, 96, 109, 113, 120, 124, 144, 145, 158, 182, 203, 207, 208
Simon, John, 198
Skvorecky, Joseph, 87
Smith, Alfred E., 152
Smith Act, 215, 218, 222n10, 223n19, 224n20
social democrats, 39, 46
socialism, xi, xv, xix, xx, xxi, 5, 7, 8, 10, 12, 13, 28–30 passim, 35, 38, 39, 43–46 passim, 51–55 passim, 68, 69, 72, 73, 80, 87, 88, 97, 103, 105, 106, 118, 121, 123, 124, 128, 132, 133,

socialism (*continued*)
139, 151–53 passim, 158, 176, 180,
181, 186–88 passim, 192, 195, 200,
202, 208, 219, 220; idealism and,
71, 104; and Jewishness, 27, 67,
154, 160, 165, 166, 169
Socialist Party, 28, 39
Socialist Workers Party (swp), 218
Solotaroff, Theodore, 62, 143, 209
Solzhenitsyn, Aleksandr, 14, 87
Sombart, Werner, 133
Sontag, Susan, 57, 60
Sorin, Gerald, 185–89, 201
Soviet Union, 28, 33, 38, 40, 44, 73,
81, 181, 187; collapse of the, 35, 46,
205; under Stalin, 118, 213
Spanish Civil War, 32
Spender, Stephen, 62
Stalin, Joseph, 33, 39–43 passim, 118,
127, 144, 195, 205; Lenin and, 40,
42, 43
Stalin-Hitler Pact, 221
Stalinism, 34, 40, 42, 43, 118, 208,
213; Howe on, 67, 73, 80, 194,
195; and intellectuals, 28, 29; and
Leninism, 40, 42, 43; Popular
Front and, 33
Stanford University: Howe at, xix,
232
Stendhal, xi, xii, 70, 86, 87, 120; and
The Charterhouse of Parma, 86
Stevens, Wallace, 22
Sweezy, Paul, 194

Thomas, Norman, 6, 28, 97, 207
Thomashevsky, Boris, 163
Thoreau, Henry David, 132, 134, 135,
140
Tikkun, 189
Time: Howe at, 20n45, 202
Tolstoy, Leo, xi, 7, 14, 15, 27, 102,
108, 112, 165, 208
totalitarianism: Howe on, 29, 42, 44,

192, 194, 220; and Howe's reading
of *1984*, 119–20, 128, 130
Trilling, Diana, 118, 129
Trilling, Lionel, xix, xx, 2, 17n7, 57,
78, 79, 107, 116, 118, 119, 122, 124,
125, 128, 173, 204, 205, 210, 211;
and *The Liberal Imagination*, 7,
208
"triple thinker," 1–16
Trollope, Anthony, 100, 115, 131
Trotsky, Leon, vii, xi, xxi, 5, 6, 8, 28,
30, 35, 38–47, 51, 67, 72, 114, 118,
192; as "Old Man," 39, 41, 43, 113,
125; and *Terrorism and Communism*, 42
Trotskyism, 33, 35, 38–40, 43–46, 67,
177, 198
Turgenev, Ivan, xi, 86, 99, 120; and
Fathers and Sons, 85, 86, 99
Twain, Mark: Howe on, 23n7

University of California at Berkeley,
85, 108, 197, 206
University of Michigan at Ann Arbor,
216, 219
University of Washington, 66
utopia, 8, 14, 15, 30, 32, 61, 71, 88–90,
95, 104, 123, 180, 187, 200

Viereck, Peter, 53, 54
Vietnam War, xx, 2, 57, 83, 140

Wald, Alan M., xxii
Wald, Lillian, 152, 163
Wallace, Henry, 33
Walzer, Michael, 57, 104, 139, 202
Warsaw Ghetto: Howe on, 112
Wayne State University, 219, 221
Weathermen, 175, 187
Weber, Max, 200
Weinstein, Michael, 62
Weiss, Peter, 78
West, Anthony, 120

Wharton, Edith: Howe on, xii, 70, 108, 203
Whitfield, Stephen, 177
Whitman, Walt, 100, 110, 135
Widick, B. J., xx, 15, 50, 119
Wiener, Ilana (Howe), 108, 154, 181
Wieseltier, Leon, vii, 4, 12, 62, 179–82
Williams, Ian, 37–47
Williams, Raymond, 206
Wilson, Edmund, xxi, 5, 8, 64, 67, 70, 94, 99, 107, 122, 156, 186; Howe on, 9, 207; and *The Triple Thinkers*, 9–11
Wilson, Harold, 127
Wisse, Ruth, 176
Wordsworth, William, 97

Workers Party (wp), 28, 215, 218, 219
Wright, Richard, 100, 101, 204; and *Native Son*, 100
Wrong, Dennis, xxii

Yeats, 85, 192
Yiddish, xi, xv, xix, xx, 2, 3, 10, 12, 14, 17n6, 28, 32, 54, 57, 64, 67, 68, 70, 105, 106, 150–54, 157–69, 171–73, 181, 186, 197–99, 206
Yiddishkeit, 10, 157–64 passim, 169
Yom Kippur, 154, 182
Young People's Socialist League (ypsl), 6, 67, 102

Zedong, Mao, 40, 103
Zola, Emile, xv